THE HANDBOOK
OF EXECUTIVE
BENEFITS

THE HANDBOOK OF EXECUTIVE BENEFITS

Towers Perrin

IRWIN
Professional Publishing
Burr Ridge, Illinois
New York, New York

Senior sponsoring editor: Amy Hollands Gaber
Project editor: Beth Yates
Production supervisor: Pat Frederickson
Designer: Jeanne Rivera
Manager, graphics, and desktop services: Kim Meriwether
Compositor: PC&F, Inc.
Typeface: 10/12 Times Roman
Printer: Quebecor Kingsport

Library of Congress Cataloging-in-Publication Data

The handbook of executive benefits / Towers Perrin.
   p. cm.
  ISBN 0-7863-0185-6
  1. Employee fringe benefits—United States. 2. Executives—Salaries, etc.—United States. 3. Executives—Pensions—United States. I. Title.
HD4928.N62U662   1995
658.4'0725—dc20   94–32794

Printed in the United States of America

3 4 5 6 7 8 9 0 QK 1 0 9 8 7 6 5

Preface

Employers have traditionally used broad-based employee benefit programs to provide tax-sheltered compensation to their executives. Today, however, the value of executive participation in these programs, particularly tax-qualified pension and capital accumulation plans, has diminished. Changes in federal tax policy have resulted in increasingly strict limits on the benefits payable from these plans. Congress has also eliminated some of the tax advantages associated with plan distributions and has imposed an excise tax on distributions that exceed a specified amount.

As a result, many employers have created special supplemental benefit programs for their executives. Many of these programs are intended to restore benefits lost as a result of tax law constraints. But executive benefit plans serve other purposes as well.

This book is intended to aid practitioners in designing and implementing benefit programs that meet corporate objectives as well as the needs of individual executives. The text begins with a description of the legislative considerations that have shaped the development and design of both retirement and health and welfare benefit programs. Subsequent chapters identify various employer objectives served by supplemental executive benefit arrangements and review current practice in executive benefit plan design, including techniques to secure the long-term promises made to executives outside the scope of broad-based benefit plans.

While our focus is on executive benefit programs, these programs cannot be viewed in isolation. To provide the necessary context, we have included a brief overview of more visible elements of an executive's total compensation package, including stock options, in Chapter 2. Other chapters cover relevant accounting and securities law considerations, perquisites, golden parachutes, international issues, the special problems of tax-exempt employers, and issues executives face in retirement.

Despite various legislation restrictions, executives can still receive substantial benefits from broad-based retirement and capital accumulation plans. Readers who seek further information on the operation of these plans may wish to consult two other texts: Everett T. Allen, Jr., Joseph J. Melone, Jerry S. Rosenbloom, and Jack L. VanDerhei, *Pension Planning,* 7th ed. (Homewood, IL: Irwin, 1992), and Towers Perrin, *The Handbook of 401(k) Plan Management* (Homewood, IL: Irwin, 1992).

Many individuals at Towers Perrin have contributed to *The Handbook of Executive Benefits.* We would particularly like to acknowledge Everett T. Allen, Jr., Michael Dickerman, James Durfee, Russell E. Hall, Maureen Huggard, James P. Klein, Herbert I. Kosloff, Christian Lindgren, Leon Poigieter, Diana Scott, Sharon Sherman, Paul T. Shultz III, Frances G. Sieller, and John F. Woyke. We would also like to acknowledge the contributions of Mary T. Steele, First Vice President, SunTrust Banks, Inc.

Marvin H. Greene
Managing Director, Retirement
Towers Perrin
Valhalla, New York

Contents

Chapter Five
GENERAL DESIGN CONSIDERATIONS 55

General Design Considerations, 55
    Internal Equity, 56
    Cost and Accounting Considerations, 56
    Tax Considerations, 57
    Disclosure, 57
General Plan Features, 58
    Eligibility Requirements, 58
    Compensation, 60
    Service, 63

Chapter Six
PLAN DESIGN: RETIREMENT
AND CAPITAL ACCUMULATION 66

Key Factors, 66
    Tax and Legal Environment, 67
    Defined Contribution versus Defined Benefit, 68
    Coordination with Broad-Based Plans, 70
Plan Features, 70
    Retirement Ages, 71
    Benefit Structure—Capital Accumulation Plans, 73
    Benefit Structure—Defined Benefit Plans, 76
    Vesting, 79
    Disability, 80
    Death, 80
OBRA '93, 81
    Impact on Executives, 82
    Shifting Liabilities, 83
    Eligibility Issues, 83
    Implementing the New Cap, 84
    Medicare Tax Issues, 87
Communication, 88
The Performance Link, 89

Chapter One

History and Development

Before Congress enacted the Employee Retirement Income Security Act (ERISA) in 1974, few employers maintained special benefit plans for their executives. According to the then-prevailing view, benefit programs were largely egalitarian mechanisms to maintain all or part of an employee's income in the event of retirement, death, disability, or sickness. Because direct compensation (wages and salaries) presumably reflected the relative value and responsibilities of different positions, uniform application of a benefit program or formula was thought to produce appropriate levels of income replacement throughout the organization.

Today the picture has changed significantly. For one thing, bonuses and other forms of variable compensation now represent a substantial portion of executive income; thus, benefit programs that are tied to base pay—as is often the case with broad-based plans—may prove inadequate. Further, executive turnover is a now a fact of life, and special benefit programs have come to play an important role in helping employers recruit and retain talent and deal with such issues as executive burnout.

Congress has been the single most important force for change in executive benefits, however. To encourage employers to provide benefits for their employees, federal law grants significant tax advantages to qualified employer-sponsored retirement and capital accumulation plans; employers get a current tax deduction for contributions, benefits are not taxable to employees until paid, and investment earnings on plan assets accumulate on a tax-deferred basis. To ensure that these tax advantages do not inure primarily to the benefit of the highly paid, Congress has imposed progressively tighter restrictions on executive participation in tax-qualified plans. As a result, most employers now supplement their broad-based benefit programs with special nonqualified plans designed to meet the needs of their executives.[1]

This introductory chapter summarizes the legislative considerations that have shaped the development and design of executive benefit programs

1

and concludes with an overview of the objectives employers hope to meet in offering these programs.

RETIREMENT BENEFITS

Prior to ERISA, the tax law did not limit retirement benefits for highly paid employees.[2] Tax-qualified retirement and profit-sharing plans could not discriminate in favor of the highly paid, but they could provide pay-related benefits without dollar limitations. Further, qualified plan benefits enjoyed very favorable tax treatment. Lump sum distributions were eligible for long-term capital gain and/or special income-averaging treatment, and employer-provided benefits qualified for estate and gift tax exclusions. With the advent of ERISA, all this began to change.

Section 415

ERISA marked the beginning of a series of legislative changes that have progressively reduced the value of executive participation in broad-based retirement programs by adding Section 415 to the Internal Revenue Code (IRC). Section 415 limits benefits payable to and contributions made on behalf of employees under tax-qualified plans.

The original statutory limit on annual payouts from a defined benefit plan was $75,000 (or 100 percent of pay, if less); annual additions to a defined contribution plan were limited to $25,000 (or 25 percent of pay, if less). Both dollar limits were indexed to rise with changes in the Consumer Price Index (CPI). A combined or overall limit—in effect, 140 percent of the limits considered individually—was applicable to employees covered by both defined benefit and defined contribution plans.

Over the years, Congress has rolled back, frozen, and otherwise reduced Section 415's dollar limits, most recently in the Tax Reform Act of 1986 (TRA '86).[3] The current defined benefit limit is $90,000 (indexed; $118,800 for 1994). The defined contribution limit is $30,000. While this limit is also indexed, it will not begin to rise until the defined benefit limit reaches $120,000—probably in 1995. Congress also reduced the combined plan dollar limit to 125 percent of the dollar limits considered individually.

Other Tax Law Changes

The TRA '86 changes were particularly significant because they also reduced the Section 415 limit for benefits payable at early retirement and for individuals born after 1937. Further, tax legislation has:

- Imposed a limit on pay that can be taken into account in determining contributions and benefits under a qualified plan.[4]
- Limited elective deferrals under Section 401(k) plans to $7,000 (indexed).
- Limited qualified plan benefits and contributions for the highly paid through more restrictive integration rules as well as tighter contribution (ADP and ACP) tests for defined contribution plans.[5]
- Replaced 10-year with 5-year averaging for lump sum distributions, allowing 5-year averaging only once and only after age 59½.[6]
- Imposed an additional 15 percent tax on annual or lump sum distributions that exceed a threshold amount.
- Eliminated the estate and gift tax exclusions for employer-provided benefits.

Collectively, these changes have dramatically reduced the value of qualified plan benefits for the highly paid.

Indexing

Most of the tax law's dollar limits are indexed to increase with upward movement in the CPI. While indexing would seem to offer some relief from these limits, it can actually operate to make the limits relatively more restrictive if executive pay increases faster than the CPI, which is a likely scenario.

Assume, for example, that an executive was earning $200,000 at the time the TRA '86 limits became operative. The $90,000 Section 415 limit then in effect permitted a qualified pension of 45 percent of pay; the $30,000 defined contribution limit permitted an annual addition of 15 percent of pay. Assume further that the executive's pay increases at 8 percent a year, while the CPI increases at 5 percent. After 10 years, the defined benefit limit would be $150,000—only 35 percent of the executive's then current pay of $431,784. The defined contribution limit, which would not begin to increase until the defined benefit limit reached $120,000, would have grown to $36,000—only 8 percent of the executive's then current pay.[7]

These indexing provisions may have another important effect. Pay levels are used to determine who is a highly paid employee for purposes of qualified plan nondiscrimination tests (as well as some of the nondiscrimination tests for welfare plans).[8] This threshold will increase with changes in the CPI, but if pay for middle-management employees increases at a faster rate, more and more employees will ultimately become part of the highly paid group—which could, in turn, create potential problems in maintaining plan qualification.

OBRA '93

Seven years after TRA '86, Congress made another dramatic change in the tax law. In the Omnibus Budget Reconciliation Act of 1993 (OBRA '93), it reduced the Section 401(a)(17) limit on pay that can be taken into account for qualified plan purposes—which had grown to $235,840 for 1993 through indexing—to $150,000 beginning in 1994. While the new pay cap is also indexed, it will only increase in $10,000 increments—that is, only when accumulated changes in the CPI amount to at least $10,000.[9]

Exhibit 1–1 illustrates the impact of this change on two hypothetical executives at XYZ Company, both earning $170,000 in base salary and a $30,000 bonus in 1993. The first executive is 50 and plans to retire in 10 years; the second is 40 and plans to retire in 20 years.

Under pre-OBRA law, the 50-year-old executive could expect to receive 78 percent of his retirement benefit from his employer's tax-qualified pension plan; with the new $150,000 limit, that percentage will drop to 64 percent. Assuming his employer sponsors a supplemental plan to restore benefits lost as a result of the limit, more than one-third of the executive's pension benefit will probably be backed by nothing more than the employer's promise to pay; while qualified plan benefit obligations are backed by assets held in trust, most nonqualified plans are unfunded. As a result, this executive is likely to have growing concerns about the security of a substantial portion of his retirement benefit.

The second executive has even more reason to be concerned, since only about half of her benefit will come from the qualified plan.

Employers have reason to be concerned as well. A company must book a minimum liability on its balance sheet equal to the unfunded accumulated benefit obligation of *each* unfunded retirement plan.[10] As a result of the lower pay cap, a larger portion of an employer's overall benefit

EXHIBIT 1–1
401(a)(17): Impact on Executive Retirement Benefits

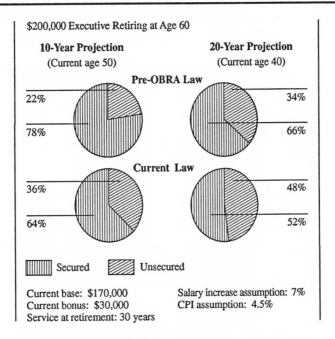

$200,000 Executive Retiring at Age 60

| **10-Year Projection** | **20-Year Projection** |
| (Current age 50) | (Current age 40) |

Pre-OBRA Law

22%   34%

78%   66%

Current Law

36%   48%

64%   52%

▦ Secured   ▨ Unsecured

Current base: $170,000   Salary increase assumption: 7%
Current bonus: $30,000   CPI assumption: 4.5%
Service at retirement: 30 years

obligation will shift to the nonqualified arena, increasing unfunded liabilities. Further, the limit means that a larger group of employees will be looking for supplemental benefits—something that could complicate the status of the nonqualified plan under ERISA.

The impact of OBRA '93 will be covered in more detail in Chapter 6. Suffice it to say for now that the new limit has focused renewed attention on the retirement income needs of executives and on ways to meet these needs efficiently and effectively.

HEALTH AND WELFARE BENEFITS

Employers face far fewer restrictions in providing health and welfare benefits to their executives. There are no adverse tax consequences for special disability income benefits for executives, for example. Employers can also offer discriminatory health care benefits under a fully insured plan.[11]

If employers provide discriminatory group life insurance benefits, key employees lose the tax exemption for the first $50,000 of life insurance that would otherwise apply, and the amount reported as taxable income is determined on the basis of actual cost if that cost is higher than government-published rates. As a practical matter, however, these penalties are not very severe.

Health and welfare benefits for executives are covered in more detail in Chapter 7. Note, for now, that employers have begun to look to these benefits to provide additional compensation to their key employees, particularly in view of the restrictions imposed on qualified plan benefits. Interest in executive medical plans will undoubtedly increase if Congress enacts comprehensive health care reform legislation.

PROGRAM DESIGN: AN OVERVIEW

In broad terms, two factors influence an individual employer's approach to executive benefits: the environment in which it operates, and its specific business and human relations objectives.

Environmental Considerations

Business organizations have individual characteristics and operate in environments that influence what they can and want to accomplish in providing executive benefits. The tax and legal constraints summarized above are major environmental influences. Other factors that can affect executive benefit plan design include:

- Legal status: The employer's legal status—sole proprietorship, partnership, public or private corporation, tax-exempt organization, Subchapter S corporation—determines, for example, whether employer stock can or should be a part of the executive benefit program. In partnerships or Subchapter S corporations, the relative ages of the partners or owner-employees can have a major impact on the choice between the defined benefit and defined contribution approaches to providing benefits. And there are significant limits on the approaches tax-exempt organizations can use to provide retirement benefits.[12]

- Other employer characteristics: Other influential attributes include the maturity of the organization, its profitability, the diversity of its operations (and, as a result, the diversity of benefit structures within the organization), expected growth patterns, short- and long-term capital needs and executive staff needs both now and in the future.

- Industry practices: To remain competitive in recruiting and retaining executive talent, employers usually need to conform to (or exceed) industry benefit practices.

- Executive demographics: The composition of the executive group— by age, service, sex, and compensation level—can influence plan design, plan costs, and the type and level of benefits provided. A younger group of executives may find some type of capital accumulation program to be more attractive than the conventional income-replacement pension plan, for example.

- *ERISA*. Nonqualified plans come within the purview of Title I of ERISA, and absent an exemption, they must comply with Title I's minimum participation, funding, vesting, joint and survivor, and other provisions. In deciding whether to comply with Title I or to proceed under one of the exemptions, an employer must, broadly speaking, weigh tax implications and the degree of benefit security that compliance represents against the design flexibility the exemptions afford. Each option has its pros and cons for both employer and executive. These important issues are discussed in detail in Chapter 4.

- Disclosure: Employers must disclose information on executive benefit plans in their proxy statements. They must also comply with other securities law requirements, as interpreted and administered by the Securities and Exchange Commission (SEC), when benefit programs involve employer stock. These requirements are the subject of Chapter 13.

Employer Attitudes

An executive benefit program should reflect an employer's philosophy on compensation and benefits in general, and executive compensation and benefits in particular. Pertinent issues include the following:

- Are benefits considered part of the organization's total compensation program for executives, or should they be viewed and valued separately?

- To what extent should an executive's total compensation, including benefits, be tied to performance, including the performance of company stock?

- Should executive benefit plans simply restore benefits lost as a result of tax law limits, or should they address such special issues as midcareer recruiting, burnout, estate tax planning and the like?
- What cost and funding limits govern plan design?
- What is the appropriate financial measure for determining the cost of the program and/or benefits to be provided—for example, the employer's cost of borrowing, return on shareholder equity, or an external measure (such as an adjusted prime rate)?
- How important is it to maximize tax advantages?
- Should the total executive benefit program encourage executives to retire on or before a certain age?
- Should the retirement portion of the program focus on capital accumulation or income replacement?
- Who should absorb the cost and/or benefit risks associated with inflation—the employer, the executive, or both?
- How much choice should executives have as to the type and level of benefits they receive?
- How important is benefit security?
- Are there any concerns about disclosing executive benefit programs to shareholders and the public?

Answers to these questions will be extremely important in establishing specific objectives and developing a plan design that supports those objectives.

Objectives

Most employers have certain objectives in mind for all of their benefit plans, whether they cover the entire employee population or just executives: these objectives typically include attracting and retaining employees, achieving tax efficiencies, controlling costs, and simplifying administration.[13] Executive plans are usually intended to meet one or more of the additional objectives summarized in the following paragraphs.

Restoring base plan benefits.   Most major employers have adopted what are known as *excess benefit plans* to replace retirement benefits that would have been payable under broad-based qualified plans were it not for the Section 415 limits. Out of a sample of 300 companies in the

Towers Perrin Employee Benefit Information Center (EBIC) Data Base, 59 percent of the companies that sponsor defined benefit plans maintain defined benefit excess plans as well. At present, only 34 percent of the employers that maintain broad-based defined contribution plans have also adopted defined contribution excess plans, though this percentage is likely to increase in the future.

Many employers have also acted to restore qualified plan benefits lost by reason of other tax law provisions, such as the limit on pay that can be taken into account for qualified plan purposes. Plans designed with this objective in mind are likely to become more prevalent now that the limit has dropped to $150,000. In such cases, the term *executive benefit plan* will be something of a misnomer, since employees who would not be considered executives in organizational terms may be affected by the limit and thus given the opportunity to participate.

Providing more benefits.   Perhaps the simplest and most direct objective of an executive benefit program is to provide a *higher* level of benefits than that generated by the company's broad-based plans. The relationship between Social Security and employer-sponsored plans is a case in point. Social Security will replace a relatively high percentage of pay— as much as 35 to 40 percent—for lower-paid employees, but will replace only 5 to 10 percent of pay, and sometimes even less, for the highly paid. Because of tax law provisions governing the integration of Social Security benefits with broad-based retirement plans, a qualified plan designed to provide reasonable total benefits for the rank-and-file will probably provide inadequate benefits for the highly paid. If the broad-based plan is structured to provide what the employer believes to be an adequate pension for the highly paid, combined pension and Social Security benefits for the lower paid could be excessive. One solution to this problem is to design the broad-based plan to meet the needs of a majority of employees and to provide the highly paid with a supplemental plan.

Group life insurance is another case where broad-based programs may not meet the special needs of executives. While all employees need a certain amount of coverage to protect their survivors, the highly paid may need additional life insurance to pay estate taxes and/or to create estate liquidity.

Midcareer recruiting.   An executive who changes employers in mid- to late-career could suffer a significant loss in expected pension benefits because the pension from his former employer, although vested, will be frozen at his pay level at the time of change. Even though pension benefits from his new employer will accrue at future pay levels, the total benefit payable from the two sources could fall substantially short of the benefit that might have been payable had he been employed by only one employer for his entire career.

Consider an executive who changes jobs at age 50. Assume that both his former and new employers' plans provide for a pension of 1½ percent of final average pay multiplied by years of service. The executive has completed 20 years of service with his first employer with final average pay of $100,000; his vested pension is $30,000 (1.5 × 20 × $100,000). If he goes to work for the second employer and retires at age 65 with final average pay of $150,000, his pension from that employer will be $33,750 (1.5 × 15 × $150,000). His total pension from both employers will be $63,750. Had he stayed with his first employer and retired at the same pay level of $150,000, he would have had a pension of $78,750 (1.5 × 35 × $150,000).

While many factors influence an executive's decision to change jobs, the prospect of losing pension benefits can be a major concern. One way for employers to address this problem is to establish a supplemental retirement plan that provides additional benefits to an executive hired in mid-career—by recognizing service with the former employer as though it were service with the current employer, for example, or by granting relatively generous accruals for the first few years of new employment.

Recognizing incentive pay.   Many broad-based retirement plans provide benefits related to base salary only; other forms of compensation, such as overtime, shift differentials, and bonuses, are not included in the plan's definition of earnings.

Incentive pay normally constitutes a significant part of total compensation for executives, however, and many employers believe that at least some incentive pay should be treated as an element of pay for benefit purposes—in part because an executive's standard of living is based on total compensation, and in part because they believe an executive whose pay is at risk should also reap commensurate rewards.

While employers can base benefits for all employees on total compensation, this approach generates a high level of benefits and high costs. Many companies are more comfortable establishing supplemental plans for executives for the express purpose of providing benefits related to incentive pay.

Note that death and disability income plans can define compensation to include only base salary and incentive pay—that is, to exclude overtime and shift differentials. Such a definition would generally be considered discriminatory in a tax-qualified defined benefit or defined contribution plan.

Executive transfers.   If an organization's benefit programs are not uniform from one operation or location to the next—differing to reflect such factors as industry practice, profit margins, local competitive practice, and the like—executives could gain or lose benefits every time they transfer jobs within the organization. A disruption in benefits could present significant problems in individual situations. One solution is a supplemental *umbrella* program that makes up any difference between the specified umbrella level of benefits and the benefits provided at the location where the executive is employed.

Other objectives.   Other executive benefit program objectives include the following:

- *Recognizing deferred compensation.* It is relatively common for employers to permit executives to defer some part of their base salary and/or incentive pay.[14] Some employers may even require that some part of compensation be deferred. Because deferred compensation cannot be considered as pay for determining qualified plan benefits or contributions, employers often establish supplemental arrangements to provide benefits related to deferred amounts.

- *Golden handcuffs.* Unfunded executive retirement plans need not comply with the vesting requirements that apply to broad-based plans.[15] Thus, they can be written so that a terminating executive will forfeit accrued benefits unless termination occurs under circumstances where the employer is willing to provide these amounts— for example, termination after age 62. Pension benefits accrued under one of these arrangements can be substantial, and the prospect of losing them may deter an executive who is otherwise thinking of leaving the organization. Thus, a supplemental plan with rigorous vesting standards can help retain key executives.

- *Noncompete provisions.* Broad-based retirement plan benefits cannot be forfeited once they are vested; such is not the case for unfunded supplemental executive retirement benefits, which can be forfeited even after they are in payment status. Making benefits subject to forfeit if an executive goes to work for a competitor after retirement could be a way of providing some protection against this event.

- *Golden handshakes.* A number of factors, including human resource needs and deteriorating performance, may make it desirable to encourage certain executives to retire before their normal retirement ages. If benefits available under broad-based plans are not sufficient to meet the financial needs of these executives, supplemental benefits can be used to provide incentives to retire early.

- *Uniform treatment.* Organizations often enter into different deferred compensation and supplemental benefit arrangements with individual executives, usually as a result of negotiated employment agreements or corporate acquisitions.[16] Supplemental executive benefit plans can be used to standardize these arrangements, thus establishing a uniform policy and avoiding the need for special contracts and disclosure.

Plan design issues are covered in detail in Chapters 5, 6, and 7 of this book. To provide the additional background necessary for an understanding of these issues, Chapters 2 and 3 discuss the elements of executive compensation and benefit programs and the tax rules that govern deferred compensation arrangements, respectively, while Chapter 4 summarizes the ERISA rules that apply to executive benefit plans.

NOTES

1. The tax law requirements governing qualified plans do not apply to executive plans, which by definition discriminate in favor of the highly paid and thus cannot achieve tax-qualified status.

2. The term *retirement benefits* obviously encompasses any benefits available after retirement, including medical coverage and life insurance as well as benefits payable under pension and capital accumulation programs. To avoid confusion, however, we will use retirement benefits to refer to pension and capital accumulation programs, and will refer to other benefits as, for example, postretirement medical or retiree life insurance.

3 The percentage-of-pay limits have not changed.

4. IRC Section 401(a)(17). The original limit was $200,000 (indexed), but has since been reduced to $150,000 (indexed). The impact of the new limit is discussed later in this chapter and in Chapter 6.

5. The actual deferral percentage (ADP) and the actual contribution percentage (ACP) tests are designed to limit the contributions made by or on behalf of highly compensated employees relative to the contributions made by or on behalf of all other eligible employees.

6. Proposed legislation (which has received House approval as of this writing) would eliminate five-year averaging tax treatment except for certain grandfathered individuals.

7. This example ignores the effect of the 401(a)(17) pay cap. Although the IRS has not formally ruled on the issue, it appears that the 401(a)(17) pay cap does not apply in calculating the Section 415 limits. See Chapter 6.

8. See Chapter 10, footnote 14.

9. OBRA '93 also uncapped the amount of compensation subject to the 1.45 percent Medicare tax (paid by both employer and employee). See Chapters 7 and 18.

10. The accumulated benefit obligation (ABO) is the present value of benefits earned by participants prior to the measurement date.

11. Uninsured health care benefits can be taxable to executives if the plan is discriminatory.

12. See Chapter 14.

13. For a more comprehensive discussion of overall employer objectives in designing employee benefit plans, see Everett T. Allen, Jr., Joseph J. Melone, Jerry S. Rosenbloom, and Jack L. VanDerhei, *Pension Planning,* 7th ed. (Homewood, IL.: Irwin, 1992).

14. Deferred compensation arrangements are discussed in more detail in Chapter 3.

15. See Chapter 4 for a discussion of exemptions from ERISA requirements.

16. See Chapter 3.

Chapter Two

Total Executive Compensation

Taken together, retirement programs, health and welfare benefits, and perquisites—the focus of this book—generally constitute the smallest segment of an executive's overall compensation package. Thus, these benefits cannot be examined in a vacuum. In fact, no single element of executive compensation can be weighed properly without taking the other elements of the total compensation package into account. To determine whether salary is set at an appropriate level, for example, it is important to factor in payouts from bonus programs. Similarly, pension benefits cannot be considered in isolation if they are part of a retirement income stream that includes payouts from long-term incentive plans, which are often substantial.

This chapter begins with a brief description of the key elements of total executive compensation: salaries, bonuses, long-term incentives, and retirement benefits.[1] The next section summarizes current trends and practices in total compensation, providing a context for the information presented later in the text. The chapter concludes with a discussion of employment contracts—the legal documents often used to specify, among other things, the compensation an executive will receive from his or her employer.

SALARY AND BONUSES

The *salary* for a given position generally reflects competitive market considerations. Competitive pay levels for top executives tend to be set on a national, rather than regional or local basis. Factors influencing executive pay include the nature and scope of the job, the company's size and industry, and the experience, credentials, and reputation of the incumbent.

Industry and company size are particularly important—the former because industry and service sectors have distinct job requirements, and the latter because the magnitude and complexity of the job often increase as the size of the business increases.

Annual *bonus* plans often specify target bonus amounts payable when an executive meets predetermined performance goals. The target bonus is usually stated as a percentage of salary; the target for the lowest level executives in the bonus plan may be 10 percent to 15 percent of pay, for example, while the top executive's target may be 50 percent to 100 percent. Actual awards will vary above and below target levels, depending on the executive's success in achieving his or her goals and the company's commitment to paying for performance. The executive may have the opportunity to defer payment of all or part of a bonus until a future date.[2]

LONG-TERM INCENTIVES

In addition to base salary and annual bonus, an executive may realize gains from long-term incentive awards cashed out during the year. In most companies, fewer employees are eligible for long-term incentives than for annual bonuses. For those employees who are eligible, long-term incentives can represent a significant element of pay. Towers Perrin's 1994 Executive Compensation Study, which examines pay levels in close to half of the S&P 500 companies, reveals these incentives represent an average of 41 percent of total CEO pay, for example, while salary and annual bonus represent 36 percent and 23 percent, respectively.

A long-term incentive plan may give the executive an opportunity to defer an award until termination of employment, with interest or some other measure of gain added to the original amount.[3] Long-term incentive plans can take several forms, including the following:

- *Stock options* permit executives to purchase company stock at a stated price (e.g., current market value at grant date) during a given time period (e.g., 10 years). The two types—incentive and nonqualified—differ primarily in tax treatment.
- *Stock appreciation rights* (SARs) are typically granted in tandem with options and allow executives to capture any gain in stock price between grant and exercise dates without actually having to purchase shares.
- *Restricted stock/stock grants* give executives shares or share equivalents at no or nominal cost. Grants are generally subject to a

specified restriction period (e.g., three to five years) and may have to be forfeited if the executive leaves before the end of the period.

- *Performance plans* provide contingent awards earned partly or wholly according to the degree of achievement of predetermined performance goals over a specified multiyear period (e.g., three to five years). Awards can be expressed as shares or share equivalents (with ultimate award value also depending on stock price), performance units (usually having a fixed dollar value), or cash.

- *Phantom stock* involves units analogous to shares of company stock. Payments are made after a specified period of time and typically equal appreciation in the value of the underlying stock (plus, frequently, an amount reflecting dividends paid during the period).

As is the case with annual bonuses, the amount of a long-term award is usually expressed as a percent of salary, with the percentage increasing for the highest paid executives. While measurement of expected grant date value is often speculative, it is not unusual to see annual grants of 100 percent to 200 percent of salary for performance over three to five years.

Table 2–1 shows the prevalence of various long-term incentive plans among the companies in the Towers Perrin survey cited above. Among large publicly traded corporations, stock option plans are by far the most common form of long-term incentive. (They are virtually unknown among nonpublic companies.) These plans are often responsible for the size of the executive pay packages that appear on the "highest paid" lists in the popular and business press each year.

Two features have made the stock option plan very attractive to employers:

1. There has been no charge to earnings for the grant of the option.[4]
2. There is no cash cost to the employer even when the option is exercised; in fact, there can be a significant positive cash flow from the option price payment and, in the case of nonqualified stock options, the tax deduction on the exercise gain.

Executives find these plans attractive because any rise in the stock price over the duration of the option (typically 10 years) will eventually wind up in their pockets, without the downside risk involved in actually owning stock. Strong interest in equity-based compensation has given rise to alternatives besides options. One is the restricted stock plan referred to above, whereby shares of stock are transferred to the executive but must be returned to the employer unless the executive performs substantial

TABLE 2–1
Prevalence of Long-Term Incentive Plans

Type	Percent of Respondents Using
Options*	85%
Restricted stock	33
Performance shares	18
Performance units/cash	23
Stock grants	6
*including plans with tandem SARs	

services. Most such plans simply provide that restrictions will lapse after a specified amount of time has passed.

Criticism of traditional, time-lapse plans as giveaways has given rise to new restricted stock plan designs. In some plans, shares are granted only after executives meet annual or longer-term performance goals. In others, restrictions lapse (or lapse sooner) when performance standards are met. Some companies are also paying out other forms of earned compensation (e.g., annual bonuses) with restricted stock, or allowing executives to exchange salary for restricted shares. The link between pay and performance is discussed in more detail later in this chapter.

EXECUTIVE BENEFITS

Executives usually participate in the broad-based plans their employers make available to all employees, including pension and capital accumulation, medical, life insurance, and disability plans. In addition, they may participate in plans that supplement the benefits available under these broad-based plans. Finally, they may be eligible for certain benefits—including, for example, perquisites and golden parachutes—available only to the executive group.

Each of these benefits will be covered in detail in subsequent chapters. Because executive retirement plans constitute a particularly significant element of total compensation, however, we will include a brief overview of these plans in this introductory chapter.

Supplemental Executive Retirement Plans

Special retirement plans known as SERPs—Supplemental Executive Retirement Plans—are generally the most valued (and expensive) of the benefits employers make available to their executives.

The term *SERP* is used broadly to include all types of executive retirement arrangements. Thus, for example, it includes what are sometimes called restoration plans—those that restore benefits lost under qualified plans due to IRC restrictions—as well as plans that provide distinctly supplemental benefits for the executive group.

Restoration plans may include benefits that are not payable under a qualified plan because of any number of IRC limitations, including Section 415, the $150,000 (indexed) pay limit, and the $7,000 (indexed) elective deferral limit.[5] A restoration plan that provides *only* those benefits lost by reason of Section 415 is known, and referred to in ERISA as, an excess-benefit plan.[6]

Of 209 companies in the Towers Perrin Executive Benefit Data Base, 189 maintain a total of 283 SERPs—205 restoration plans and 78 SERPs designed to meet other employer objectives.

SERPs are not tax-qualified plans. As a result, SERP design is not restricted by the qualification and nondiscrimination requirements that apply to broad-based plans.[7] But certain of the tax advantages of qualified plans are not available to SERPs. Any investment income on plan assets will generally be taxable, for example, and lump sum distributions will not be accorded special tax treatment. Further, the doctrine of constructive receipt will apply.[8] The tax treatment of SERPs is covered in detail in Chapter 10.

SERPs can be funded or unfunded. A plan is funded when assets are irrevocably committed to provide benefits. Some plans may earmark assets for the payment of benefits (as is often the case with corporate-owned life insurance), or may conditionally transfer assets to a trust (as with a so-called rabbi trust), but these plans are not considered to be funded.[9] Most SERPs are unfunded.

The impact of ERISA and the tax law can differ depending upon whether a plan is an excess benefit plan or a more all-encompassing SERP, and whether it is funded. ERISA requirements are discussed in detail in Chapter 4. The tax treatment of executives and employers is discussed in Chapter 10.

TABLE 2–2
Example: SERP Benefit

Assumptions: Executive, age 51
Current pay of $400,000
Retirement age, 62
Pension of 60% of final pay
No survivor benefit

Annual % Pay Increase*	Pay At Retirement	Annual Pension
0	$ 400,000	$ 240,000
5	680,000	408,000
8	930,000	558,000
10	1,140,000	684,000
15	1,860,000	1,116,000

*Annual pay increases each year until retirement.

Plan Design

SERPs are typically designed to replace about 60 percent of an executive's final income (averaged over a one- to three-year period). The benefit may accrue over a short period or a full career (e.g., anywhere from 10 to 30 years). The SERP benefit is usually offset by benefits from Social Security, qualified plans, and in the case of some very rapid accrual formulas, by pension benefits from prior employers. It is unusual to offset capital accumulation plan benefits against a SERP, however.[10]

SERPS can provide substantial benefits. As an example, consider an executive, age 51, earning $400,000. Assume that he has just become eligible for a SERP that will pay him 60 percent of final pay at age 62 less the qualified plan benefit. (We will ignore this offset for purposes of this example; the employer pays for the qualified plan benefit as well.) Table 2–2 illustrates the annual pension benefit for this individual under several final pay scenarios.

As noted, most SERPs are unfunded and represent unsecured contractual obligations to employees for future payments. Thus, executives may
be concerned about the security of their benefits in the event of changes in
future management or ownership, deterioration of the business, insolvency, competing creditor claims, and other contingencies. Employer
efforts to deal with the security issue are addressed in detail in Chapter 10.

TRENDS IN TOTAL EXECUTIVE COMPENSATION

Executive compensation has been the subject of increasing scrutiny in
recent years—from shareholders, employees, the media, legislators and
regulators, and the public at large. Critics contend that expenditures on
senior management are often excessive, noting that many executives continue to reap large rewards even when corporate performance is lackluster.

Interest in the executive compensation issue has prompted the
Securities and Exchange Commission to revise its proxy disclosure rules
to require broadened disclosure of pay practices for top management.[11]
Further, OBRA '93 imposed a $1 million limit, effective in 1994, on the
deductions a company can claim for compensation it pays to each of the
five executives named in the proxy statement.[12] Performance-based incentives that meet certain criteria are exempt from the cap. To qualify for the
exemption, incentive awards must be made under shareholder-approved
performance pay plans that are administered by compensation committees
made up of at least two outside directors who are allowed only limited
discretion.

These activities have prompted many organizations to take another look
at their compensation practices and, if necessary, to take steps to ensure
that they link pay more closely to performance.

Pay for performance has long been cited as a first principle in compensation planning, but stock option grants to executives have not, in and of
themselves, fully linked executive and shareholder interests. Stock option
programs have traditionally included upside potential, permitting executives to gain from a rise in the stock price, but have included little in the
way of downside risk—that is, exposure to loss when the price of the
stock drops.

Newer incentive programs are designed to hold executives accountable
for the results of their actions, producing meaningful rewards when those
actions build value, and withholding rewards when those actions fail to

build value. As a first step, many organizations are emphasizing the variable and long-term elements of compensation and opting for moderation in annual increases. In Towers Perrin's 1994 study, for example, 27 percent of CEOs got no salary increase from the previous year or saw their base salaries decline, while 41 percent got no bonus or a smaller bonus. Other trends include the following:

- Exchanging cash for stock—for example, taking a bonus in the form of restricted stock, or taking such stock in lieu of a portion of base salary.
- Adding or raising performance requirements for option and restricted stock payouts—for example, granting premium options with an exercise price above the current market value at the time of the grant. Unless the price of the company's stock rises, the executive will have no gain.
- Tying compensation to measures of value creation—for example, making payouts from a long-term incentive plan only if the company's total shareholder return over a three-year period exceeds that of 60 percent of S&P 500 companies.
- Requiring—or strongly suggesting—that executives own specified amounts of company stock.

Another possible approach, the executive investment option, would require an executive to pay cash or exchange part of his or her salary or bonus as a down payment on an option. The executive might pay $20,000 to receive an option grant worth $100,000, for example, later paying $80,000 to complete the option exercise. When the option is structured this way, the executive would have downside risk—a real possibility of losing real dollars—as well as upside potential.

In the past, retirement plans have been largely unaffected by corporate or individual performance. Today, however, continuing shareholder scrutiny of executive compensation has increased interest in retirement plan designs that include a link to performance. This issue is discussed in more detail in Chapters 6 and 11.

OUTSIDE DIRECTORS

Though a lengthy discussion of the subject is outside the scope of this text, it is worth noting that trends in outside directors' pay are mirroring the evolution of executive pay practices. Boards are under increasing pressure to guard the interests of shareholders, and as a result directors' roles and responsibilities have expanded greatly.

Cash retainers and meeting fees are the mainstay of directors' pay. The median annual retainer reported by participants in Towers Perrin's 1994 Executive Compensation Study was $30,000, while the median board and committee meeting fee was $1,000. But variable devices that directly link directors' pay to company performance are becoming more common. Stock options for board members are used by 30 percent of the companies in the survey group, while 19 percent use restricted stock. Some companies have also established stock ownership requirements for outside directors. Some 70 percent of respondents offer retirement benefits for directors, but a few companies report that they have replaced these benefits with stock.

EMPLOYMENT CONTRACTS

The use of employment contracts for executives varies from company to company and industry to industry. Such contracts are increasingly common for CEOs and, though to a lesser extent, for other senior officers. This top-heaviness is largely due to the fact that the contracts generally benefit the executive more than the company with respect to the terms and conditions of employment. Absent a contract, U.S. legal principles generally favor the rights of an employer over those of an employee. Thus, contracts typically cover only those employees who have sufficient negotiating power.

It is interesting to note that employment contracts are somewhat more common among senior executives in Europe. Although impossible to confirm, this may be due to the fact that employers there are not giving up as much by memorializing the terms of an employment relationship in a contract, because employees in Europe tend to have greater noncontractual employment rights than those in the United States.

An employment contract can provide certainty for both executive and employer on many critical issues. For example, the contract will specify a term of employment, providing a covered executive with assurance that his or her job and income will continue for at least the minimum period specified. The contract will also typically specify duties and responsibilities, protecting the executive against a constructive termination through a diminution in duties, and will spell out the payments to which the executive is entitled if employment terminates under a variety of circumstances.

The typical contract will also specify compensation (at least initial salary) and the plans and programs in which an executive will be entitled to participate, such as the annual bonus program and stock option plans. It may also protect the employer by including a covenant from the executive not to compete and imposing an affirmative duty not to disclose trade secrets or other confidential information.

Deferred Compensation

An employment contract may make some provision for the deferral of compensation for the covered executive. This may take the form of an elective arrangement under which the executive may decide, within limits, on the amount of compensation to be paid currently and the amount to be deferred. Alternatively, it may take the form of an automatic and explicit deferral. For example, the contract may specify that the portion of a bonus exceeding 50 percent of an executive's salary will be deferred for payment on termination of employment. Finally, the contract may provide for an implicit deferral of current pay. In such cases, there is no explicit reduction in the executive's current pay in exchange for deferred compensation also provided under the employment contract. However, it is likely that both current and deferred compensation as well as other elements of pay would be considered together in deciding on the appropriate level for each such item.[13]

Retention Arrangements

Deferred compensation may be used as a retention device by conditioning an executive's right to receive payments on continued employment—until a stated age and/or number of years of service. An executive's right to receive a supplemental pension benefit from the employer might be conditioned on the executive's continued employment until at least age 55 with at least 20 years of service, for example.

If an executive covered by such a contractual provision is involuntarily terminated by the employer, the circumstances surrounding the termination will often govern whether the executive will be entitled to receive the deferred compensation. For example, such benefits will normally vest if termination occurs in connection with a change in control of the employer or if the executive is terminated without cause (as defined in the employment contract). A termination for cause will sometimes mean that benefits are forfeited. Some contracts provide that an executive will forfeit all rights to deferred compensation for certain breaches of the terms of the contract even if those breaches occur after the executive has otherwise become vested in the deferral by fulfilling the minimum age or service conditions.

The retentive aspects of deferred compensation may be particularly helpful when a midcareer executive joins a company. The executive may seek additional supplemental deferred compensation from his new employer to make up for lost pension benefits as a result of his job switch. While the new employer may be willing to provide such a makeup, it may want to ensure that the executive will remain in its employ for a specified period. By conditioning the executive's right to receive makeup benefits on fulfilling a stated service/age condition, the employer will help ensure its objective is satisfied.

Involuntary Discharge

A key part of most employment contracts is a provision for payments to the executive in the event of involuntary discharge. Such payments typically take one of several forms. One approach is to provide for a continuation of salary and sometimes bonus (at target levels) for the remaining term of the contract. A more common approach is to provide separately for an amount payable in the event of such termination. For example, the contract might provide that the executive will be entitled to a payment equal to a stated sum or an amount determined as a multiple of salary and average bonuses. Such severance pay is usually paid in a lump sum, but is sometimes paid in installments.

The events that constitute an involuntary discharge for purposes of triggering severance pay should be defined carefully. The usual definition excepts discharges for dishonesty or gross negligence on the part of the executive. Most contracts that deal with this subject also define involuntary termination as including a constructive discharge—a material reduction in the duties or responsibilities of the executive or in the principal location in which the executive is required to work.

Postemployment Consulting Contracts

Postemployment consulting contracts are another way to provide deferred compensation to executives. In form, such arrangements do not really involve deferred compensation; consulting fees are paid to the terminated executive for making himself or herself available to the company and/or for actual consultation. In substance, such arrangements may be viewed by the parties as an additional source of posttermination income for the executive, particularly when the terms of the consulting arrangement are incorporated into a pretermination employment contract.

Some consulting arrangements provide that payments will be made to the executive for several years after termination and do not condition such payments on the actual performance of work. They do stipulate that the executive will make himself or herself available at reasonable times and places to advise the company.

NOTES

1. Health and welfare benefits are covered in Chapter 7; perquisites are the subject of Chapter 16.
2. See Chapter 3 for a discussion of these deferred compensation arrangements.
3. See Chapter 3.
4. The Financial Accounting Standards Board has now proposed significant changes in accounting for stock options, however; see Chapter 8.
5. See Chapter 1.
6. ERISA Section 3(36).
7. In addition, Title IV of ERISA (requiring sponsors of qualified defined benefit plans to pay premiums to the Pension Benefit Guaranty Corporation for plan termination insurance) does not apply to SERPs.
8. See Chapter 3.
9. The use of permanent life insurance in conjunction with executive benefits is discussed in Chapter 12. Rabbi trusts are covered in Chapter 10.
10. For a more detailed discussion of plan design issues, see Chapter 6.
11. The proxy disclosure rules are covered in detail in Chapter 13.
12. For a discussion of other OBRA '93 provisions, see Chapters 1 and 6.
13. Deferred compensation arrangements are the subject of Chapter 3.

Chapter Three

Deferred Compensation

Executives have long been given the opportunity to elect to defer receipt of their year-end bonuses and salary. These traditional deferred compensation arrangements can be distinguished from supplemental executive-retirement plans insofar as SERPs generally do not involve any direct reduction in an executive's current pay. With the growth of, and limits on, executive participation in, 401(k) plans, however, these distinctions have blurred. It is now common for companies to allow executives who cannot fully participate in their company's 401(k) plan to elect to reduce their current pay by the amount that could have been contributed to the 401(k) plan but for the these statutory limits and to receive corresponding credit under a nonqualified deferred compensation plan.

This chapter covers the tax and design issues raised by traditional voluntary deferred compensation arrangements.

STRUCTURE

In form, a voluntary nonqualified deferred compensation arrangement resembles a 401(k) plan for executives. Each participating executive is permitted to decide whether to receive current salary or bonus at a normal level or to receive a reduced amount and defer receipt of the remainder to a future date.

There are also some basic differences between a 401(k) plan and a non-qualified deferral arrangement, however. Most significantly, amounts deferred by an executive are not typically set aside in a separate trust. Instead, the employer simply credits deferred amounts on its books. Thus, these arrangements represent the employer's unfunded and unsecured promise to pay deferred amounts at the future specified payment date.

Further, the rigid restrictions on pretermination distributions from a 401(k) plan do not apply to a traditional deferred compensation arrangement. Such plans can therefore provide for any payment date that suits the objectives of the employer and the executive making the deferral (subject to restrictions imposed due to the IRS doctrine of constructive receipt, described below).

OBJECTIVES

As of 1993, a 36 percent tax rate applies to taxable income above $140,000 (for married individuals filing joint returns) and a 10 percent surtax applies to taxable income above $250,000 (for an effective tax rate of 39.6 percent on income in this bracket). Properly designed, an elective deferral arrangement can help executives avoid current income taxes on deferred amounts. The executive will be subject to income tax on those amounts—both the principal amount deferred and any credited earnings—only when they are actually paid out.

Assume, for example, that an executive elects to defer receipt of a $50,000 bonus for five years. The employer agrees to credit the deferred amount with interest compounded annually at 6 percent. The executive is not subject to income tax on either the $50,000 or the $16,911 in credited interest until he receives payment in the fifth year. If he is in the 39.6 percent tax bracket, he will have a tax bill of $26,764, and will net $40,147.

The executive would find it difficult to replicate this savings opportunity on his own by taking the bonus as current cash in the year earned, paying taxes, and investing the balance. After taxes he would have only $30,000 to invest. Assuming he could earn 6 percent per year on a tax-deferred investment, he would have a total of $40,147 after five years. After paying taxes on his investment earnings in year five (at 39.6 percent), he would net $36,088, which is $4,059 (10 percent) less than he had under the nonqualified deferral arrangement.[1]

An executive who voluntarily defers current pay may also hope to be in a lower tax bracket when he eventually receives payment—during retirement, for example. Whether this happens will depend on two things: his total postemployment income and Congress. Income from qualified plans and IRA distributions, supplemental executive pension benefits (and even a portion of Social Security benefits for higher-income individuals) may actually boost some executives into a higher marginal tax bracket after retirement.

Congress is a factor in the deferral decision because it has the power to raise and lower tax rates. Thus, an executive will want to give some thought to possible future tax rate scenarios in weighing the options.

TABLE 3–1
Projection of Maximum Break-Even Tax Rates

	Break-Even Tax Rate If Executive's After-Tax Rate of Return Is:	
Deferral Period	7%	5%
5 years	47.8%	52.5%
10 years	54.5%	62.3%
20 years	65.5%	76.3%
30 years	73.8%	85.1%

Table 3–1 projects the maximum future tax rate that would have to prevail before deferral would adversely affect the executive. The table assumes the current tax rate is 39.6 percent and the employer credits a 10 percent rate of return. One projection assumes that the executive could earn 7 percent after taxes; the other assumes a 5 percent after-tax return.

As the projections illustrate, the longer the deferral period, the higher the break-even tax rate. Further, the greater the spread between the employer crediting rate and the executive's after-tax rate of return, the more favorable the deferral results for the executive.

Leaving aside tax rate considerations, an executive may want to defer current income to increase postemployment income, using the deferral arrangement as a capital accumulation device—albeit unfunded. Assuming tax treatment is favorable, executives may find these arrangements superior to any otherwise available options such as annuities, cash value life insurance, taxable investments, and the like.

CONSTRUCTIVE RECEIPT

As noted, an individual is generally not subject to income tax on deferred amounts until they are actually paid out. However, the IRS has long taken the position that an individual may be taxed with respect to a deferred amount that he or she has "constructively" received, even if no actual payments have been made. This position—the doctrine of constructive receipt—is one of the most important factors affecting the design and administration of nonqualified deferred compensation plans.

IRS Regulations provide that:

> Income although not actually reduced to a taxpayer's possession is constructively received by him in the taxable year during which it is credited to his account, set apart for him, or otherwise made available so that he may draw upon it at any time, or so that he could have drawn upon it during the taxable year if notice of intention to withdraw had been given. However, income is not constructively received if the taxpayer's control of its receipt is subject to substantial limitations or restrictions.[2]

Whether or not this doctrine applies depends on choice—more specifically, the executive's choice. Whenever an executive can elect to receive a payment currently or defer receipt to a future date, the doctrine is potentially applicable. It will trigger taxation unless the executive has made his or her deferral election sufficiently in advance of the scheduled payment date, or unless the right to elect payment is subject to a substantial limitation or restriction.

What constitutes a sufficient period of time before the scheduled payment date, or a substantial limitation or restriction, must be deduced from a patchwork of published and private IRS rulings and case law. Some of the principal guideposts are summarized below.

Bear in mind that the doctrine of constructive receipt may apply to a deferred compensation arrangement at two distinct points in time: when the initial deferral election is made, and when funds previously deferred become payable and the executive has a choice as to the form or timing of payments. The relevance of the authorities discussed below will depend on which of these two situations is being analyzed.

Election Prior to Rendering Services

The seminal published IRS ruling on the doctrine of constructive receipt is Revenue Ruling 60-31,[3] where the IRS said that unfunded deferral arrangements will result in deferred taxation for the participating executive as long as the executive makes the deferral election before he or she renders the related services. The IRS added embellishments in two subsequent revenue procedures, setting forth the conditions that must be satisfied to obtain a private letter ruling that a deferred compensation arrangement does not result in constructive receipt.[4] According to these revenue procedures, a deferral arrangement will not result in constructive receipt provided that the executive's election to defer is made before the beginning of the period of service for which the compensation is payable. The period of service for this purpose is generally regarded by the IRS as a calendar year.

Suppose an executive wants to defer the receipt of 10 percent of her salary otherwise payable in 1994. In order to obtain a ruling that she will not be in constructive receipt of the funds, the executive's deferral election should be made before the start of 1994.

The IRS has expressly provided two exceptions to its general policy that elections must be made before the start of a year:

1. In the year in which a deferred compensation plan is initially implemented, eligible executives may make an election to defer compensation for services to be performed subsequent to the election within 30 days after the plan becomes effective.

2. A newly eligible participant in an existing plan may make an election to defer compensation for services to be performed subsequent to the election within 30 days after the date the employee first becomes eligible to participate.[5]

Note that neither of these exceptions permits an executive to defer the receipt of compensation not yet paid but relating to services already performed.

The IRS requirement that a deferral election must be made before the start of a year should not be considered an absolute legal standard that, if breached, will automatically result in constructive receipt. Even the General Counsel of the IRS has indicated that outstanding court cases call into question the Service's ability to defend the position it espoused in Revenue Procedure 71-19 in litigation.[6] Nonetheless, executives and their employers who want to avoid any risk of constructive receipt of nonqualified deferrals should adhere to the 71-19 standard.

Election Prior to Determination of Amount

Some taxpayers take the view that deferral elections need not be made until the amount of income subject to deferral is determined. This is particularly relevant for elections to defer bonuses, since amounts may vary with such subjective and/or objective conditions as profitability, individual efforts, and the like. In these situations, the executive may have already started performing the services to which the deferral relates.

Suppose an executive will receive an annual bonus based on company profits during 1994. The bonus is determined after the end of the year and is paid on March 15, 1995. Rather than electing to defer the bonus before the start of 1994, following the 71-19 standard explained above, the executive might be permitted to make the election at any time before the close of 1994.

There is some authority supporting the view that such elections will be effective for tax purposes. In this regard, Revenue Ruling 60-31 (discussed above) indicates that an author is not in constructive receipt of book royalties deferred by agreement with the publisher when the royalty contract was signed. While the book had already been written, the IRS concluded that the royalties were not yet earned at the time of the deferral election. Because the author had apparently performed all of the services he was going to perform with respect to the book, the ruling can perhaps be interpreted as an indication that compensation is not earned so long as there is still uncertainty as to the exact amount to be paid.

There are also several court cases in which taxpayers have avoided constructive receipt when they made elections before the amount of compensation was known. In *Veit* v. *Commissioner,*[7] for example, an executive was entitled to receive a share of his employer's 1940 profits payable in 1941. Late in 1940 after most of the services giving rise to the bonus had already been performed, the executive and the employer agreed to defer the receipt of the bonus until 1942. The Tax Court concluded that the executive was not in constructive receipt of the bonus in 1941 because the amount of the bonus was indefinite at the time of the deferral election. Similarly, in *Oates* v. *Commissioner,*[8] an insurance agent successfully deferred the receipt of renewal commissions after he had performed the services that gave rise to the payments because the election was made with respect to indefinite future payments.[9]

Election Prior to Scheduled Payment

Structurally, it is possible for an executive to elect to defer the receipt of compensation at any time before it is scheduled to be paid. If the services giving rise to the compensation have already been performed and the amount is determinable, however, there is little authority supporting a favorable tax outcome. A second Veit case—*Veit* v. *Commissioner*[10]—can be read as an endorsement of this approach. In this case, an executive who had previously elected to defer receipt of a bonus for one year made a second election to receive the bonus in installments over five years. The court concluded that the deferral was effective because it was made before the compensation was scheduled to be paid and was part of a bona fide agreement with the employer; that is, it was not just a sham to avoid taxes. Nonetheless, most tax planners do not consider this second Veit case sufficiently weighty authority; thus, they structure their plans to require a deferral election to be made before the related services have been performed and/or before the amount of compensation to be deferred is determined.

Payout Elections: General Considerations

Some deferral arrangements specify the time and manner in which previously deferred amounts will be paid out—as a single sum at termination of employment, for example. If an executive is not given a choice in this regard, the payout of prior deferrals will not be subject to the constructive receipt doctrine. And even though an executive may decide to terminate employment at any time, a plan that provides for payments to commence at termination of employment will not be considered to involve an election.[11]

The doctrine of constructive receipt may apply in plans that do offer an executive a choice as to the time when payments will commence or the form in which amounts will be paid. Assume, for example, that an executive previously elected to defer bonuses under a nonqualified deferral arrangement, with payments to commence on termination of employment as either a single sum or in 10 annual installments. An executive who elects to receive his balance in the form of 10 annual installments may be taxed as if he had received an immediate lump sum. That is, under the standard set forth in the IRS regulation quoted above, the lump sum would have been "made available" so that the executive "could have drawn upon it during the taxable year if notice of intention to withdraw had been given . . . "

Payout Election with Deferral Election

An executive's election as to the form of payout could be made at the same time the executive initially elects to defer the compensation. This would seem to satisfy the IRS conditions to obtain a private letter ruling with respect to the application of the constructive receipt doctrine and can thus be considered a safe approach. Note in this regard that Revenue Procedure 92-65 does not explicitly recognize an executive's ability to make this sort of election. It simply indicates that the deferred compensation plan must define the time and method for payment of the deferrals for each event that triggers a payment of benefits. A plan that is governed by an executive's election in this regard presumably will satisfy this standard, however.

Payout Election after Initial Deferral Election

If an executive can elect when to receive a deferred amount and that election can be made after the initial deferral election, the arrangement will not meet the standards specified by the IRS in order to obtain a private letter ruling as to constructive receipt, with two exceptions.

The first exception is that such an election may be made where the deferred compensation is forfeitable by the executive during the entire period of the deferral.[12] The forfeiture condition must impose on the executive a significant limitation or duty that will require a meaningful effort to fulfill, and there must be a definite possibility of forfeiture. Because deferrals are rarely subject to forfeiture, particularly over the entire period of the deferral, this exception is of little practical value.

The second exception is more useful. A nonqualified deferred compensation arrangement may provide for payment of benefits in the case of an unforeseen emergency—defined, for this purpose, as an unanticipated emergency that is caused by an event beyond the control of the participant and that would result in severe financial hardship if early withdrawal were not permitted. The amount withdrawn must be limited to the amount needed to meet the emergency.

Despite these exceptions (or perhaps because of them), some deferral arrangements are designed to provide an executive with a postdeferral election as to when previous deferrals will be paid. Whether such a provision will cause an executive to be in constructive receipt of the income at the earliest time he or she could have elected payment is, at best, uncertain in most cases.

An executive's postdeferral payout election will not trigger constructive receipt where access to the amount is subject to a substantial limitation or restriction. This is particularly applicable when deferred compensation is invested (on a phantom basis) in employer stock or other equities that may appreciate in the future. The courts and the IRS have recognized that forfeiture of the right to future appreciation without risking capital in order to receive payment of a deferral is a substantial limitation on access to the deferral and thus will prevent constructive receipt.[13]

The IRS has attempted to limit the application of this principle to situations where the amount of cash that could be elected is insufficient to allow the executive to purchase a duplicate investment.[14] The distinction it is making is best illustrated by an example. Assume an executive may receive a payment in respect of a share of phantom stock currently worth $50. If, after receiving the cash, the executive wants to continue to benefit from future stock appreciation, he can theoretically purchase the stock with the cash he receives, and has thus not forfeited the right to future appreciation.

It may be possible to subject an executive's access to deferrals to a substantial limitation or restriction so as to avoid constructive receipt by imposing a penalty on any withdrawal. For example, a deferral arrangement may permit an executive to elect to receive a lump sum instead of the installments specified by the arrangement, but only if he forfeits 25 percent of his account balance. There is some authority for this approach in the IRS regulations, although not in the context of compensation.[15]

Even in the absence of a substantial limitation or restriction on an executive's payout election, application of the constructive receipt doctrine is not a certainty. While the second *Veit* case involved a postdeferral election of installments rather than an immediate lump sum, for example, the court held that no constructive receipt occurred.

Similarly, the court in the *Martin* case found that executives who elected installments instead of lump sums were not in constructive receipt of the lump sums, noting that the election as to the form of distribution was made before payments were due. But the court also relied on the fact that the amount payable was not yet ascertainable and, as discussed above, an election to receive payment triggered forfeiture of the right to future appreciation. Thus, it is not clear how much weight the court placed on the timing of the election.

Some tax planners believe the IRS regulations on constructive receipt imply that a postdeferral election to receive payments will not cause constructive receipt if it is made at least one year before payments are otherwise scheduled to begin. This position is derived from the following phrase in the regulations:

> Income . . . is constructively received by [a taxpayer] in the taxable year in which it is . . . otherwise made available . . . so that he could have drawn upon it *during the taxable year* if notice of intention to withdraw had been given.[Emphasis added.][16]

Under this approach, payout under a deferral arrangement will be specified by an executive at the time of deferral. Thereafter, the executive may change his election as to the time or manner of payout, but the change will only become effective 12 months later. If a payout is triggered within 12 months, it will be made pursuant to the prior form of distribution.

As an example, assume that an executive elects to defer a future bonus until termination of employment and specifies that it will be paid in an immediate lump sum at that time. On December 1, 1994, she changes her election and chooses instead to receive the deferral in the form of 10 annual installments at termination. If she terminates prior to December 1, 1995, her deferral will be paid as a lump sum. If she continues employment beyond that date, any subsequent distribution will be in 10 annual installments.

DESIGN ISSUES

In designing deferred compensation arrangements for executives, employers need to consider each of the issues addressed below.

Term of Deferral

Nonqualified amounts are most commonly deferred until termination of employment—including voluntary and involuntary termination, retirement, death, or disability. To qualify for a private letter ruling from the IRS on constructive receipt, the plan must define the time and method of payment for each such event and may either specify the date of payment or provide that payments will begin within 30 days after the occurrence of the event.[17]

As an alternative, deferrals may be made for a specified number of years or until attainment of a stated age. An executive who is interested in deferring taxes for a long time period might favor the period-certain approach to protect the deferral opportunity in the event employment is terminated after an unexpectedly short time. For example, compensation might be deferred until the later of 10 years or termination of employment. An employer might not be interested in an arrangement that continues long after an individual has left the company, however.

Performance Criteria

The amount of deferred compensation payable to an executive may be based on the satisfaction of specified performance criteria, though this approach is not common. The criteria specified in the contract may relate to individual performance, company performance, or some combination thereof.

Forms of Payout

Nonqualified deferred compensation is generally paid to an executive in a lump sum or in installments for a fixed number of years. Payments in the form of a life annuity are rare. This is probably due to nature of these plans, which are typically individual accounts credited with fixed amounts but not funded. Most employers are unwilling to underwrite the life expectancies of their executives.

ERISA Concerns

If a deferred compensation arrangement is designed to delay payments until termination of employment, or provides retirement income to the executive, it could be construed as a pension plan for purposes of ERISA.

Whether a plan fulfills these criteria is a question of fact. However, a deferral arrangement that expressly defers payments until termination of employment will generally be treated as a pension plan subject to ERISA's detailed standards.

If the plan is a *top hat plan*—an unfunded plan maintained for the purpose of providing deferred compensation to a select group of management or highly compensated employees—it will be exempt from most ERISA requirements. These plans must comply with a one-time filing requirement with the Department of Labor, however.[18] These issues are discussed in detail in Chapter 4.

Investment Returns

Deferred compensation arrangements almost universally credit the deferred account balance with some sort of investment return—usually interest.[19] While the rate of interest may be fixed in advance, employers may consider a floating rate to be more appropriate in cases where the deferral period is expected to be relatively long. The rate can be tied to such external indexes as the prime rate of a named bank, the employer's cost of borrowing, rates on federal government debt, the rate credited under the fixed income fund under the employer's broad-based employee savings plan, or the rate credited under a company-owned life insurance policy maintained in connection with the deferral plan.[20]

More recent deferral arrangements credit account balances with gains or losses on a hypothetical investment in, for example, employer stock or a designated mutual fund. Regardless of the investment, it is the employer who pays the deferred compensation. Thus, the company might want to consider hedging its risk where it offers hypothetical mutual funds by purchasing shares of the mutual fund as a corporate investment. Note, however, that mutual fund dividends credited to the employer and sales of mutual fund shares by the employer will generate a tax liability for the employer.

RELATIVE TAX TREATMENT OF EMPLOYER AND EMPLOYEE

A deferred compensation arrangement that results in deferral of taxation for the executive also results in deferral of the related tax deduction available to the employer. An executive who defers a $50,000 bonus until termination of employment will not be taxed until he or she receives the bonus. And despite the employer's unconditional legal obligation to pay the bonus in the future, its deduction will also be delayed until payment.[21]

Thus, the *overall* tax implication of these deferrals depends on the relationship between individual and corporate income tax rates. As of 1993, the top marginal individual rate is 39.6 percent and the top marginal corporate rate is 35 percent, making the executive's tax deferral worth more than the cost of the corporation's deferred deduction. An executive in the 39.6 percent bracket would defer $19,800 of Federal income tax on a $50,000 bonus. Disregarding interest credited on the deferral, this same bonus would reduce the employer's federal income tax by only $17,500 (at 35 percent).

FICA/FUTA TAXATION

Deferral arrangements are generally *not* effective in delaying the application of Social Security taxes. IRC Section 3121(v)(2) provides that:

> any amount deferred under a nonqualified deferred compensation plan shall be taken into account [as wages for FICA tax purposes] as of the later of when the services are performed or when there is no substantial risk of forfeiture.

A similar provision applies for FUTA tax.[22]

At present, there is little guidance as to what constitutes a deferred compensation plan. It is very likely that any definition eventually promulgated by the IRS will include elective deferrals of current compensation unless the deferral is for a short time. While not directly relevant, the IRS might use the standard it developed in the context of deductions for deferred compensation plans. Under this standard, a deferral for more than a brief period after the close of the employer's tax year is treated as deferred compensation, and any deferral for longer than 2½ months after the close of the year is presumed to be more than brief.[23]

Note that the application of Social Security taxes to nonqualified deferrals prior to the date they are paid will often minimize the amount of such taxes that arise. This is because the old age, survivors, and disability income (OASDI) part of the FICA tax (6.2 percent) only applies to wages up to a specified limit—$60,600 for 1994. An executive who has current salary and other compensation in excess of the applicable wage limit will not generate any added OASDI tax on a nonqualified deferral that is earned or vests in that year. What's more, a deferral treated as wages in a prior year (and any income credited thereto) is exempt from FICA tax in any later year, including the year or years in which paid (at which time the executive may have no other FICA wages.).[24] FUTA tax applies in the same way, except that the wage limit is only $7,000.

The only exception to this perverse situation—where it is advantageous to have Social Security tax apply sooner (during employment) rather than later (after termination)—involves the hospital insurance (Medicare) portion of the FICA taxes. This 1.45 percent tax applies to all wages without limit starting in 1994. Thus, a nonqualified deferral will be subject to this tax regardless of the amount of other current income the executive receives.

AMENDING PRIOR ARRANGEMENTS

The terms of a deferral arrangement will generally govern whether the employer, the employee or both may later amend the agreement. It may be dangerous to give an executive the unilateral right to amend an agreement so as to accelerate the payment of deferred amounts, since such control is likely to cause the executive to be in constructive receipt. Giving the employer the unilateral right to terminate a deferral arrangement, while somewhat unusual, does not pose the same tax concerns. Special care should be taken where the executive is a controlling shareholder of the employer, however.

SHORT-TERM DEFERRALS

Executives often consider short-term deferrals of income when tax rates will drop from one year to the next, either because of legislative change or because the executive stops working and expects to be in a lower marginal bracket. In such instances, an executive may seek to defer the receipt of his or her year-end salary or other payments until early in the next calendar year.

The IRS has evinced particular hostility toward tax-motivated short-term deferrals. In Announcement 87-3, it said it would closely scrutinize deferrals measured in months or shorter periods that are intended to take advantage of a scheduled drop in tax rates. It also said that an individual who executed a short-term deferral might be held to be in constructive receipt of income where the deferral was not bona fide or lacked business substance. The IRS did not cite any particular authorities in support of this position, however, and the case law to date shows no evidence of any stepped-up IRS enforcement efforts directed at these sorts of deferrals.

NOTES

1. For an illustration of the after-tax cost to the employer of a deferral, see Table 6–3 in Chapter 6. Costs are also discussed at length in Chapter 9.
2. IRS Reg. Section 1.451-2(a).
3. 1960-1 C.B. 174.
4. Rev. Proc. 71-19 and Rev. Proc. 92-65.
5. See Rev. Proc. 92-65.
6. See GCM 35196, January 16, 1973.
7. 8 T.C. 809 (1947), acq. 1947-2 C.B. 4.
8. 18 T.C. 570 (1952), acq. 1960-1 C.B. 5
9. See also *Olmstead* v. *Commissioner,* 304 F.2nd 16 (CA 8 1962), aff'g 35 T.C. 429 (1960), nonacq. 1961-2 C.B. 6.
10. 8 T.C.M. 919 (1949).
11. See Rev. Rul. 60-31, described above. The requirement that an individual give up his employment to receive payments is probably also a "substantial limitation or restriction" on the person's access to prior deferrals sufficient to avoid application of constructive receipt under the IRS standard.
12. See Rev. Proc. 71-19.

13. See Rev. Rul. 80-300, 1980-2 C.B. 165 and *Martin* v. *Commissioner*, 96 T.C. 814 1991.

14. PLR 8829070 4/27/88.

15. See IRS Reg. 1.451-2(a)(2) and (b). See also PLR 8142058 7/21/81, in which a qualified plan participant was determined not to be in constructive receipt of his withdrawable account balance where a withdrawal would trigger a 6 percent penalty imposed on future employer contributions. It is questionable whether the IRS is willing to extend its position respecting qualified plans to nonqualified plans.

16. See IRS Reg. Section 1.451-2(a).

17. Rev. Proc. 92-65.

18. DOL Reg. Section 2520.104-23.

19. This issue is also discussed in Chapter 6.

20. See Chapter 12 for a discussion of corporate-owned life insurance.

21. In *Albertson's* v. *Commissioner*, 12 F.3d 1529 (CA9 1993), the Ninth Circuit ruled that an employer may take a current deduction for interest accrued on nonqualified deferred compensation. As we go to press, the court has agreed to rehear this controversial decision. A bill to overturn *Albertson's* has also been introduced in Congress.

22. See IRC Section 3306(r)(2).

23. IRS Reg. Section 1.404(b)-1T.

24. IRC Section 3121(v)(2)(B).

Chapter Four

Executive Benefit Arrangements under ERISA

The Employee Retirement Income Security Act (ERISA) of 1974 contains a panoply of rules governing employer-sponsored benefit plans. Many executive benefit arrangements are exempt from, or can be designed to avoid the impact of, some or all of these rules. This chapter provides an overview of ERISA's requirements and the treatment of various executive benefit arrangements under ERISA.

PENSION PLANS

ERISA defines *pension plan* broadly to include any plan, fund, or program that provides retirement income or results in the deferral of income until termination of employment or beyond. This definition does not necessarily encompass every plan that defers the receipt of compensation or provides retirement income, however. Certain of these plans receive special treatment under the statute and DOL regulations, as discussed below.

Excess Benefit Plans

An excess benefit plan provides benefits that cannot be provided through a qualified plan solely because of IRC Section 415 limits on benefits and contributions. If it is unfunded, an excess benefit plan is completely exempt from Title I of ERISA. If it is funded, it is subject to Title I's reporting and disclosure, fiduciary responsibility, and enforcement provisions. (Summaries of various ERISA requirements appear later in this chapter.)

A supplemental retirement plan that provides benefits a qualified plan cannot provide for reasons *other* than the 415 limits—including the limit on compensation under Section 401(a)(17) and the dollar limit on elective deferrals ($9,240 in 1994)—would not fall within the excess benefit plan exemption. But such a plan might be considered a top hat plan, as discussed in the following paragraphs, and would, provided it is unfunded, be exempt from most ERISA requirements.

Top Hat Pension Plans

A plan that is "unfunded and is maintained by an employer primarily for the purpose of providing deferred compensation for a select group of management or highly compensated employees" is an ERISA Title I pension plan but is *not* subject to the participation and vesting, funding, or fiduciary responsibility provisions of Title I.[1] The enforcement and reporting and disclosure requirements do apply to these top hat plans. (Note that *top hat plan* is an informal designation; the term does not appear in ERISA or in any regulations.) Under the enforcement provisions, a top hat plan must comply with ERISA's claims review procedures and provide participants with access to federal courts to pursue a claim for benefits. The reporting and disclosure requirements that apply are simplified; the employer need only file a letter with the DOL setting forth its name, address, and tax employer identification number, the number of top hat plans it maintains, and the number of employees in each.[2]

Early DOL opinion letters were fairly liberal in interpreting the "select group" requirement (to include, for example, key employees earning at least $18,200[3]). Since the issuance of ERISA Proc. 76-1, the DOL has declined to rule on whether or not a plan is a top hat plan.[4] (Nonetheless, it did conclude that the top hat exemption was *not* available to a specific plan in view of the broad range of salaries and employees covered.[5])

The DOL *has* indicated that it would now view the $18,200 pay cutoff referred to above as much too low. It was rumored for a time that the DOL would propose regulations limiting the top hat group to those employees with compensation in excess of three times the FICA wage base who were among the top-paid 2 percent or 3 percent of employees.[6] These regulations have not been promulgated, and the DOL has removed them from its regulatory agenda.[7]

Despite its failure to issue regulations or a definitive advisory opinion, the DOL has clearly *not* adopted the IRC Section 414(q) definition of highly compensated employee for purposes of the top hat exemption.[8]

(HCEs are generally employees earning $75,000 [indexed] or $50,000 [indexed] and among the employer's top-paid 20 percent.) The preamble to the IRS regulations defining HCEs for purposes of the nondiscrimination requirements notes that a broad extension of the IRS definition to a determination of what constitutes a select group for purposes of ERISA "would be inconsistent with the tax and retirement policy objectives of encouraging employers to maintain tax-qualified plans that provide meaningful benefits to rank-and-file employees."[9]

In its most recent pronouncement on the subject, the DOL expressed the view that the top hat exemption would be available only for those employees who "by virtue of their position or compensation level, have the ability to affect or substantially influence, through negotiation or otherwise, the design and operation of their deferred compensation plan, taking into consideration any risks attendant thereto, and, [who] therefore, would not need the substantive rights and protection of Title I."[10]

The DOL also said that the term *primarily,* as used in the phrase "primarily for the purpose of providing deferred compensation for a select group of management or highly compensated employees," refers to the purpose of the plan (i.e., the benefits provided) and not the participant composition of the plan. Thus, if a plan extended coverage beyond a select group, the DOL would not consider it a top hat plan.

At least one court has favorably cited this opinion letter. In *Hollyshed* v. *Buford Equipment Co.,*[11] the court held that the top hat exemption was not applicable because the plan extended coverage beyond the select group encompassed by the exemption. Given that employees at every level of the company were potentially eligible for participation, however, it is hard to imagine any other result. Thus, *Hollyshed* need not be read as necessarily dispositive of the issue of whether a top hat plan must cover *only* management or highly compensated employees.

Few other courts have dealt with the top hat exemption. In *Belka* v. *Rowe Furniture Corp.,*[12] the Maryland district court concluded that the top hat exemption applied to a plan that covered between 1.6 percent and 4.6 percent of company employees where the *average* salary of covered employees was substantially greater than the company-wide average. The plaintiff had sought to establish that a number of covered employees were not management and that some others were not highly compensated. The court rejected plaintiff's argument, specifically noting that the exemption applies to those plans that are primarily designed for individuals who are *either* management or highly compensated. The court also noted the lack of guidance on this subject from other courts or the DOL.

In 1988, the Oklahoma Supreme Court had occasion to consider the issue in *Loffland Brothers Company* v. *C.A. Overstreet*.[13] It concluded that participants in a plan covering less than 1 percent of the company's employees constituted a select group. Citing *Belka* and undertaking a plain analysis of the statutory provision, the court also concluded that the exemption does not require that participants be both management and highly compensated.

Belka was again cited favorably in *Starr* v. *JCI Data Processing*,[14] although the district court concluded on the facts (38 percent of those covered were nonsupervisory clerical employees and their salaries ranged as low as $12,000 in 1989) that the plan was not a top hat plan. Neither Opinion Letter 90-14A nor *Hollyshed* was discussed by the New Jersey district court.

The issue in both *Belka* and *Loffland Brothers* was whether nonhighly compensated management employees and nonmanagement highly compensated employees could constitute part of a select group. These cases did not squarely address whether nonmanagement, nonhighly compensated employees could participate without the loss of the top hat exemption. Assuming, *arguendo*, that a top hat plan can cover only management or highly compensated employees, there is still a question as to which employees are "management" or "highly-compensated" for this purpose. While the DOL's view seems overly constrictive, a court would not necessarily take a more expansive view of the exemption, given ERISA's remedial purpose and the likelihood of a sympathetic plaintiff.

In addition to limiting participation to a select group, a top hat plan must also be unfunded. The DOL has expressed the view that any determination with respect to the funded or unfunded status of a plan must be based on the surrounding facts and circumstances, including the status of the arrangement under relevant non-ERISA law. In this regard, the DOL has indicated that, in the absence of pertinent legislative history defining the term *unfunded* for purposes of Title I of ERISA, significant weight will be accorded to the positions adopted by the IRS.[15]

A plan's ERISA status has important implications for both employers and executives. Proceeding under one of the exemptions to Title 1 could result in a significant level of unsecured benefits—benefit promises that are not backed with irrevocably committed assets. Further, compliance with the "select group" provision would obviously require that the plan be limited in terms of its coverage. The reduction in the Section 401(a)(17) pay limit to $150,000 has made the coverage issue more troublesome, as discussed in more detail in Chapter 6.

Electing to comply with Title I provisions would provide some level of benefit security, but it could also produce undesirable income tax results (at least for deferred compensation plans) and would limit plan design choices.[16] An exemption from Title I requirements gives the employer considerable flexibility in plan design in such areas as participation requirements, vesting, and the forfeiture of otherwise vested benefits under certain conditions.

Severance Benefits

In general, a severance pay plan or severance policy comprises scheduled payments made to employees who terminate for qualifying reasons after satisfying applicable service requirements.

Under ERISA, a severance pay arrangement such as a golden parachute would generally be considered a pension plan because it results in the deferral of income until termination of employment or beyond.[17] An arrangement that provides severance benefits is exempt from the definition of pension plan if it meets the requirements set forth below, however. A severance arrangement that satisfies these requirements is considered a welfare benefit plan.[18] As such, it is not subject to ERISA's participation, vesting, and funding rules.[19] The other provisions of Title I (reporting and disclosure, fiduciary responsibility, and administration and enforcement) are generally applicable. Note, however, that an unfunded welfare benefit plan maintained primarily for the purpose of providing benefits for a select group of management or highly compensated employees is exempt from the reporting and disclosure requirements.[20]

Under DOL regulations, a severance pay plan is not a pension plan if it meets the following conditions:[21]

- Payments must not be contingent, directly or indirectly, upon the employee's retiring.

- The total amount of all payments made may not exceed two times the participant's annual compensation (including the cost of fringe benefits) for the 12-month period before separation from service.

- All payments made to a participant must be completed within 24 months after the participant separates from service. If termination occurs in connection with a "limited program of terminations," payments can be stretched out, as long as they are completed within 24 months after normal retirement age (if that is later than 24 months after separation from service). For this purpose, a

> limited program of terminations is a program that, when it was begun, was scheduled to be completed on a date certain or upon the occurrence of one or more specified events; specifies in advance the number, percentage or class(es) of employees to be terminated; and sets forth this information in writing.

As indicated by the regulation and its preamble and in various DOL opinion letters on the subject, this regulation is a safe harbor: while a severance pay plan that meets all of the conditions of the regulation would be deemed not to be a pension plan, a severance pay plan that does not meet all of those conditions might also not be pension plan. The status of a non-safe harbor severance pay plan as either a pension or welfare plan depends upon the relevant facts and circumstances. The DOL does not generally render an opinion if the plan does not fall within the safe harbor.[22]

The DOL has usually taken the position that severance plans with age or service eligibility requirements that effectively restrict benefits to employees of retirement age are pension plans.[23] Furthermore, a plan that is conditioned upon a participant's taking benefits under the pension plan if such a plan is available—although not itself conditioned on age or service—is also considered a pension plan.[24]

On the other hand, the DOL has indicated that the status of severance payments under the safe harbor does not depend upon whether the employee has retired so long as he or she is not *required,* directly or indirectly, to retire in order to receive the payments.[25] Thus, the imposition of a service requirement in and of itself need not result in the plan being characterized as a pension plan. For example, the DOL has advised that a plan requiring employees to have worked at least 200 days in each of the 10 calendar years prior to termination or to be at least age 55 with 20 years of service was not a pension plan.[26]

The DOL would not rule that a plan effectively requiring 18 or more years of service was not a pension plan, however. Its decision was based on the fact that it was possible under the plan "that the eligible employees may constitute a group at or near retirement age, and therefore, the severance benefits, as a factual matter, may be contingent upon the employees' retiring."[27] Note that, unlike the situations discussed previously where the plan imposed both an age and service requirement, the DOL did not conclude here that the plan was in fact a pension plan.

Further, while a service-based eligibility requirement may be problematic, it is permissible to tie the *level* of severance benefits to service without making the plan a pension plan. Thus, a severance plan that provides one month's pay for each year of service is not considered a pension plan.[28]

In light of the foregoing, an employer that wants to use a severance pay plan as part of an executive benefit arrangement has a number of options:

- *The safe harbor plan.* It may be possible to structure the severance pay plan so that it would be payable to all executives who have a stated number of years of service, (e.g., 10 years). Such a requirement should result in the plan being considered a welfare plan rather than a pension plan.

- *The nonsafe harbor plan.* It can be argued that even a plan outside the safe harbor nonetheless constitutes a welfare benefit plan in that it merely provides a temporary cushion against loss of income rather than retirement income.

- *The nonplan.* Where severance is paid in a lump sum under a one-time arrangement (e.g., a change-in-control plan), it can be argued that there is no plan because there is no ongoing administration requirement. This argument relies heavily on the U.S. Supreme Court decision in *Fort Halifax Packing Co.* v. *Coyne,* which involved the payment of a one-time lump sum benefit to employees pursuant to Maine's plant closing law.[29] The Supreme Court rejected the company's ERISA preemption argument, holding that because a one-time lump sum payment triggered by a single event requires no ongoing administration, no ERISA plan was involved. As a result, the employer had to pay employees the benefits prescribed by the Maine statute.

While *Fort Halifax* has spawned a number of seemingly diverse decisions, one thing seems relatively clear. The decision should be viewed narrowly, focusing on the nature of the employer's obligations rather than the mere fact of a lump sum payment. To the extent the obligation is ongoing, involving determinations of eligibility as well as the form of payment, an ERISA plan will likely exist. The consequences of a successful *Fort Halifax* argument must also be considered (see the paragraphs that follow). Remember, the decision in *Fort Halifax enabled* employees to pursue their state law claims against their employer.

Nonexempt Plans

If an executive pension plan is a funded arrangement (e.g., a SERP with a secular trust) it will not qualify for either the excess benefit plan or top hat plan exemptions discussed above. It then must comply with the rules of Title I of ERISA governing reporting and disclosure, participation and vesting (including the accrual rules and joint and survivor annuity rules), and funding, as well as ERISA's fiduciary requirements. The drawback of compliance with ERISA's vesting, funding, and trust requirements is the current tax consequences to executives.[30]

Reporting and disclosure requirements. An Annual Report, including financial statements (Form 5500 series), Summary Plan Description (SPD), Summary of Material Modifications (SMM), and Summary Annual Report (SAR) are all required for nonqualified pension plans. The employee benefit statement and claims procedures rules also apply. These requirements, particularly the annual report and audit (for plans with 100 or more participants), can be burdensome.

Participation requirements. ERISA Section 202(a)(1)(A) provides that no pension plan can condition participation on attaining an age greater than 21 or on service of longer than one year (though a plan that provides full and immediate vesting can require two years' service). A plan in which an employee cannot participate until retirement (as is the case for a window plan offering enhanced benefits to encourage early retirement) fails to meet this test.[31] (Regulatory authority under this section of ERISA lies with the Treasury Department and the IRS.) But the regulations go on to state that a plan providing *supplementary benefits* to a pension plan—qualified or nonqualified—that meets the participation requirement will also be deemed to meet the participation requirement. While the example given in the regulations is of a cost-of-living supplement for retirees,[32] it is likely that a plan providing bridge-type benefits (e.g., until Social Security and/or pension benefits become payable) will also qualify.

In this regard, the IRS has discussed the application of the minimum funding rules to a plan providing cost-of-living increases and Social Security supplements. The plan in question is characterized as one providing benefits that merely supplement benefits paid to employees under a qualified plan, as contemplated by the regulation discussed above. This supports the notion that Social Security supplements (i.e., until Social Security eligibility) are acceptable. The availability of that exception in cases where nonsupplementary (basic) benefits are provided is more tenuous.

Vesting requirements. Typically, rights to payments from nonqualified plans are fully vested, and such plans would thus meet the vesting requirements of ERISA.[33] However, the vesting rules also place restrictions on mandatory distributions and cash-outs and would forbid non-compete clauses that call for forfeitures.[34]

Joint and survivor rules. Nonqualified plan benefits are subject to ERISA's requirement that benefits be offered on a qualified joint and survivor basis.[35] These rules do not apply to Social Security supplements and other ancillary benefits.

Funding requirements. ERISA sets forth minimum funding standards, which would be applied separately to fund the benefits of those employees who elect to participate in a nonqualified plan.[36] The basic requirement for a defined benefit plan is to amortize over 30 years the unfunded liabilities for past service benefits arising from a new plan.[37] If a plan has no accumulated assets, this requirement will be overridden by the deficit-reduction contribution, which calls for immediate funding of 30 percent of the unfunded liabilities for remaining past service benefits.[38] It will normally not be possible for a nonqualified plan to meet the minimum funding requirements merely by paying current participant benefits through a dry trust, unless the benefits consist almost entirely of immediate lump sums.[39] The employer must also make quarterly contributions to meet the minimum funding requirement.[40]

Fiduciary requirements. The assets of a nonqualified plan must be held in a trust (or annuity contracts).[41] Because plan assets must be held for the exclusive benefit of participants,[42] a grantor or rabbi trust (i.e., a trust that is not considered a separate entity for federal income tax purposes) cannot be used, although a secular trust satisfies this requirement.[43] Failure to maintain a trust or to meet the minimum funding requirements may result in prohibited transactions on the basis that such failures amount to an indirect extension of credit to the employer from the plan or use of plan assets by the employer.[44] Breaches of general fiduciary duties could also result.[45]

Accrual rules. Under Title I of ERISA, nonqualified pension plans are subject to accrual rules identical to those found in IRC Sections 411(b) and (d).[46] Social Security supplements and other ancillary benefits are not subject to these rules.

Failure to Comply

Assume that an employer designs and implements what the DOL or a court concludes is really a pension plan and, further, that it is not a top hat plan. What is the downside?

While the employer may have violated a number of ERISA rules, there are two issues that may involve significant money: the joint and survivor (and involuntary cashout) rules and the funding requirements, which impose a cash outlay on the employer and accelerated taxation on participants. Failure to offer benefits in the form of a qualified joint and survivor annuity could result in significant additional costs. While an employer can raise an equitable defense against a claim by an employee for double payment, such a defense may carry significantly less weight where the claim is made by the employee's spouse who neither waived the joint and survivor annuity (because none was offered) nor consented to the distribution. This issue is most likely to come up in the context of a pending or future divorce proceeding.

This is not to minimize other potential ERISA violations such as the failure to prepare and file reports and disclosure documents. ERISA Section 502(l)(1) authorizes the DOL to impose a civil penalty against a fiduciary or any other person who violates, or knowingly participates in a violation of, Part 4 (Fiduciary Responsibility) of ERISA in an amount up to 20 percent of any amount recovered from the fiduciary or other person with respect to such breach. (A breach of fiduciary duty could, for example, be found in the failure to offer annuities, since the plan provision providing solely for lump sums would be inconsistent with Title I,[47] or in the failure to establish a trust.) Dollar penalties may also apply in the event of noncompliance with ERISA's reporting and disclosure provisions. Criminal penalties may be imposed upon conviction for a willful violation.

EXECUTIVE WELFARE BENEFITS

Welfare plans must comply with ERISA's reporting and disclosure and fiduciary responsibility provisions. Under DOL regulations, a welfare plan that covers a top hat group of employees is exempt from the reporting and disclosure requirements of Title I, except for the requirement to provide plan documents to the Secretary of Labor on request. Thus, for example, a split-dollar life arrangement,[48] a medical reimbursement plan, or a disability plan[49] that covers a select group would be exempt from Title I reporting requirements.

IS IT A PLAN?

One question that frequently arises is whether a particular executive benefit arrangement constitutes a plan under ERISA. The law is unclear as to whether an individual employment contract between one employee and his or her employer is considered a plan under ERISA. Some DOL advisory opinions have taken the position that a particular participant arrangement was not a "plan, fund, or program" under ERISA, while others have gone the other way.

In *Williams* v. *Wright*,[50] the Eleventh Circuit Court of Appeals determined that a letter promising monthly benefits for life to a terminating general manager, in addition to continued group life and medical coverage, constituted an ERISA pension and welfare plan. The court, evidently at the urging of the DOL (which filed an amicus curiae brief), ruled that the promise tailored for one individual constituted an ERISA plan.

Under the facts of the case, James Williams, general manager of Wright Pest Control Co., retired in accordance with the terms of a letter from the company president. The letter, which followed discussions between Williams and his employer, provided that Williams would receive $500 per month from company assets to supplement his Social Security benefits, plus life insurance and medical coverage for life, in addition to continued country club membership, a company car, and continued use of his office. While the agreement provided that the payments were in exchange for Williams' acting as a consultant advisor, the company intended the payments to constitute retirement pay, and Williams performed minimal, if any, consulting services. When the business was sold four years later and payments and benefits stopped, Williams sued, alleging that his payments and benefits were subject to ERISA's protection.

The district court concluded that the arrangement was not an ERISA "plan, fund, or program," but was instead an individual employment contract that included postretirement compensation. The Eleventh Circuit disagreed, finding that the $500 monthly payments constituted an ERISA pension plan and that the health and life benefits constituted ERISA welfare benefits. According to the court:

- Payment of benefits from general corporate assets is not relevant to whether ERISA coverage applies.
- The continuing obligations to Williams involved administrative procedures characteristic of ERISA plans, based on the *Fort Halifax* decision discussed above. [51]

- Nothing in ERISA prohibits its application to an arrangement for a single employee. The court noted that DOL regulations refer to a plan "covering one or more common law employees," in addition to self-employed individuals, as covered by ERISA. It also relied on the various DOL Opinion Letters, indicating that ERISA coverage is "not affected by the fact that the arrangement is limited to covering a single employee, is negotiated between the employer and the employee, or is not intended by the employer-plan sponsor to be an employee benefit plan for purposes of [ERISA] coverage."

In so ruling, the court distinguished this case from other cases that reached opposite results. Here, the court noted, Williams' payments were primarily retirement income, resulting from the agreement made immediately prior to his retirement, as opposed to deferred compensation payments incidental to an employment agreement.

The Williams case indicates that supplemental retirement income negotiated at the time of termination may well constitute an ERISA pension plan (and that supplemental welfare benefits may well constitute ERISA welfare benefits). Note that if payment is made as an equivalent single lump sum rather than an annuity, the single payment would not involve an ongoing administrative scheme. Under *Fort Halifax*, it could then be argued that the single-sum payment is not an ERISA pension plan.

If payments are made as an annuity, the employer may still be able to argue that ERISA's requirements do not apply because the plan is an unfunded top hat plan. In that case, only ERISA's enforcement provisions would apply, which would allow the participant to sue in federal court.

NOTES

1. ERISA Sections 201(2), 301(a)(3) and 401(a)(1).
2. DOL Reg. Section 2510.104-23.
3. DOL Opinion Letter 75-63A
4. Section 5.03(c) of ERISA Proc.76-1 and (e.g., DOL Opinion Letter 79-107).
5. Opinion Letter 85-37A.
6. The FICA wage base is $60,600 for 1994.
7. 57 Fed. Reg. 16977, April 27, 1992.
8. See Chapter 10, footnote 13.
9. IRS Reg. Section 1-414(Q)-1T.

10. DOL Opinion Letter 90-14A.

11. 13 EBC 1302 (M.D. Ala. 1990)

12. 4 EBC 2169 (D. Md. 1983).

13. 758 P.2d 813 (1988).

14. 757 F. Supp. 390 (D. N.J. 1991).

15. See letter from Elliot I. Daniel, assistant administrator for Regulations and Interpretations, Pension, and Welfare Benefits Administration, to Richard H. Manfreda, Chief, Individual Income Tax Branch, Internal Revenue Service, dated December 13, 1985. See also DOL Opinion Letters 92-13A and 90-14A. Thus, because the IRS considers a SERP for which a rabbi trust has been established to be unfunded for tax purposes (see Chapter 10), the SERP would also be considered unfunded for ERISA purposes and, provided it covered a select group, would be entitled to the top hat plan exemption.

16. See Chapter 6 for a detailed discussion of design issues.

17. See Chapter 15.

18. ERISA Section 3(1)(B); DOL Reg. Sections 2510.3-2(b) and 2510.3-1(a)(3).

19. ERISA Sections 201(1) and 301(a)(1).

20. DOL Reg. Section 2520.104-24. See *Top Hat Pension Plans* in the preceding paragraphs for a discussion of what constitutes a select group. Also, compare the reporting and disclosure exemption afforded top hat pension plans under DOL Reg. Section 2520.104-23.

21. DOL Reg. Section 2510.3-2(b).

22. For example, see DOL Opinion Letter 92-3A, where in the DOL would not opine on a plan pursuant to which benefits could extend beyond 24 months following termination. (But see DOL Opinion Letter 91-20A, concluding that a plan was a welfare plan even though plan benefits would exceed two times annual compensation under certain circumstances.)

23. See, for example, DOL Opinion Letters 80-37A (age 55 with 10 years of service); 80-72A (age 65 or age 62 with 15 years of service); and 81-8A (age 60 with 5 years of service).

24. DOL Opinion Letter 81-75A.

25. See March 2, 1979 Preamble to DOL Reg. Section 2510.3-2(b).

26. DOL Opinion Letter 79-40A.

27. Opinion Letter 84-15A.

28. DOL Opinion Letter 82-60A.

29. 482 U.S. 1, 18 EBC 1729 (1987).

30. See Chapter 10.

31. IRS Reg. Section 1.410(a)-(3)(e).

32. IRS Reg. Section 1.410(a)-3(e)(2), Example 5.
33. ERISA Section 203(a).
34. ERISA Section 203(e).
35. ERISA Section 205.
36. ERISA Section 302.
37. ERISA Section 302(b)(2)(B)(ii).
38. ERISA Section 302(d)(4).
39. A dry trust is merely a conduit for funds and has no ongoing investments.
40. ERISA Section 302(e).
41. ERISA Section 403.
42. ERISA Section 403(c)(1).
43. See Chapter 10 for a discussion of these trusts.
44. See ERISA Sections 406(a)(1)(B) and (D).
45. Under ERISA Section 404(a).
46. See ERISA Section 204.
47. ERISA Section 404(a)(1)(D).
48. See Chapter 12.
49. See Chapter 7.
50. 927 F.2d 1540, 13 EBC 2137 (1991 CA11).
51. See footnote 29, supra.

Chapter Five

General Design Considerations

In designing an executive benefit program, an employer must address most of the issues that arise in connection with any employee benefit plan, including who is eligible to participate and under what conditions, what type and level of benefits will be provided, and what happens at retirement, death, disability, or termination of employment. The employer must also develop supporting plan provisions, including the definition of compensation for calculating benefits, what constitutes length of service, benefit distribution provisions, and so forth.

This chapter covers general design considerations and specific plan features common to all types of executive benefit plans. Chapter 6 focuses on issues unique to retirement and capital accumulation plans; Chapter 7 covers life insurance, health care, and disability income benefits.

GENERAL DESIGN CONSIDERATIONS

Many factors can influence the structure of executive benefit programs—beginning with the employer's objectives.[1] Before designing or modifying a plan, an employer should articulate those objectives and, if necessary, rank them in order of importance, to ensure that they are supported by the actual plan provisions.

If the employer wants to facilitate midcareer recruiting, for example, it should probably impose relatively short service requirements for eligibility to participate in its plans and liberal vesting requirements. In addition, it will probably make sense to use a benefit formula that either recognizes service with the prior employer or provides for relatively generous accrual rates during the executive's first few years of employment. Employers that are interested in *golden handcuff* retention devices may want to impose stringent vesting requirements and limit (or not provide) posttermination welfare benefits until an executive has met stipulated service and age requirements.

As noted in Chapter 1, the employer's basic views on executive compensation and benefits, as well as the environment in which the company operates, will also influence plan design, as will the factors summarized below.

Internal Equity

Many plans provide the same (or close to the same) level of benefits (particularly retirement benefits) for all executives, imposing relatively short service requirements. Long-service executives might consider such plans inequitable, since their benefits will not be proportionately greater than those of their shorter-service colleagues. Concern over this issue often prompts employers to include additional service-related benefits—perhaps additional pension accruals at a lower rate for service in excess of some stipulated period such as 20 or 25 years.

Cost and Accounting Considerations

As with any employee benefit plan, the ultimate cost of an executive benefit plan will equal the sum of the benefits paid plus any expenses associated with plan administration. Benefit amounts will, in turn, reflect eligibility requirements, the pay base, service requirements, and other plan design elements. If the benefits are not prefunded, as is typically the case with executive plans, there is no investment income on plan reserves to offset these costs.

Although employers can and should consider plan costs from a cash flow perspective, they should also consider charges to the company's financial statement (both profit and loss and balance sheet) made in accordance with relevant accounting requirements. Supplemental executive retirement benefits generally fall within the scope of FAS 87, while postretirement death and health care benefits come within the purview of FAS 106. Certain other postemployment benefits are governed by FAS 112.[2]

Employers should also take care in selecting the actuarial assumptions used to estimate costs—assumptions that will not necessarily parallel those used in estimating costs under broad-based plans. Assumptions as to future salary growth, turnover, and retirement age for an executive group might very well differ from those used for rank-and-file employees, for example.[3]

Tax Considerations

Tax results, including both the deductibility of employer contributions and the taxation of contributions and benefits, will also differ for broad-based and executive benefit plans. In an unfunded retirement plan, for example, the employer is generally entitled to a deduction only when benefits are paid or become taxable to the executive; by contrast, the employer's contribution to a tax-qualified plan is generally deductible when made.[4]

Remember, too, that the employer cost of providing a given amount of supplemental executive retirement benefit could be higher than the cost of providing the benefit under a broad-based, tax-qualified plan, because investment income under a tax-qualified plan accumulates tax free.

Another important point is that retirement benefits for executives will be treated as ordinary income, with no special treatment for lump sum distributions. But these benefits will not be subject to early or excess distribution taxes, as are qualified plan payments.

Disclosure

Welfare plans for executives are generally not subject to ERISA's disclosure requirements (except for the requirement to provide plan documents to the Secretary of Labor upon request).[5] While these requirements do apply to executive retirement plans (other than unfunded excess benefit plans limited to restoring benefits lost by reason of Section 415 of the IRC), the sponsor of an unfunded plan need only notify the DOL of the existence of the plan and the number of employees it covers (and provide plan documents to the Secretary of Labor on request).[6]

SEC disclosure requirements, which are the subject of Chapter 13, are also relevant. Information on executive benefit plans should be included in the proxy statement.[7] Concern over public and shareholder reaction to proxy disclosures could influence the design of an employer's executive benefit program.

GENERAL PLAN FEATURES

Some features are common to all executive benefit plans, including eligibility requirements, the definition of compensation used to determine benefits, and the determination of what constitutes service for plan purposes.

Eligibility Requirements

Establishing which executives are to be covered is an important first step in designing any type of benefit plan. Regardless of the criteria, there will probably be some executives, at mid- to-lower levels, who will be excluded. Thus, employers should be clear about the rationale behind their choice of eligibility requirements.

In general, this rationale will reflect plan objectives. If a retirement plan exists solely to restore benefits lost by reason of the Section 415 limits, a requirement limiting plan eligibility to those earning over $500,000 would obviously be inconsistent with that objective. Many executives earning less would have difficulty understanding why they were excluded from participation in such a plan. The criteria used in setting eligibility requirements for an executive benefit plan typically include one or more of the following: minimum age, length of service, job grade or title, income level, and/or management or board approval.

Minimum age.   Although it is possible to specify a minimum age for plan participation, such a requirement is rarely found in an executive benefit plan. Administrative concerns often support postponement of participation in broad-based plans until employees are beyond the high turnover stage of employment. Because this is rarely a concern in the executive group, a minimum age requirement would be of little value.

Some employers do require that executives attain some minimum age before benefits, particularly retirement benefits, vest and/or become payable. No benefits might be paid unless an executive terminates after age 55 or 60, for example, regardless of length of service. Because the benefit is generally not prefunded, participation, in the usual sense of the word, is not relevant. What is relevant is that the executive must have attained some minimum age before benefits are available if he or she terminates employment.

An employer that wants to impose a minimum age requirement must observe EEOC age discrimination requirements.[8] These requirements would, among other things, forbid the use of a maximum age to exclude individuals from participation. There are no tax law or ERISA restrictions on executive welfare plans and no tax law restrictions on retirement-type benefits involving age. ERISA restrictions could apply to any retirement-type plan that does not qualify for an exemption (either as an excess benefit plan or as an unfunded plan for a select group of management or highly compensated employees).[9]

Length of service. It is possible to require that an executive have completed some minimum period of service before becoming eligible to participate. As is the case with minimum age requirements, however, this practice is relatively uncommon in executive benefit programs. In fact, any significant service requirement would be inconsistent with such common plan objectives as midcareer recruiting. Nonetheless, some employers want newly hired executives to complete a probationary period of service before they extend supplemental and oftentimes significant benefits to them. Again, no ERISA or tax law requirements stand in the way of a minimum service requirement, although a one-year service requirement is the maximum generally allowed for a retirement-type plan that does not qualify for an ERISA exemption.

As is the case with a minimum age requirement, some employers view the use of a service requirement in a broader sense—that is, the minimum service required before retirement benefits (including postretirement health care) vest or become available.

Job classification. Job classification is probably the most common eligibility requirement for executive benefits, defined by title (e.g., the plan covers the CEO, COO, executive vice presidents), by job grade or classification, or both.

The eligibility requirement is critical because it determines the number of executives covered by the plan and thus the cost of the plan. It may also determine whether an unfunded retirement plan qualifies for an ERISA exemption as a plan maintained for a select group of management or highly compensated employees—a top hat plan.[10] It is extremely important that the job classification reflect the employer's objectives in sponsoring the plan.

Income level. Some plans cover only executives who earn in excess of a stipulated amount—for example, $200,000 per year.[11]

Employers who use such a requirement should take care to update the minimum pay level from time to time to reflect inflation and growth in executive pay levels in general. Absent such updating, the covered group could grow too large to conform to employer objectives, and in the case of a retirement plan, to qualify for a top hat exemption under ERISA.

Employers who want to use a minimum pay requirement will have to decide what elements of pay they will measure. Will the minimum apply to base salary only, or will short-term incentives be included? If bonuses are included, will they be measured over some averaging period to smooth out the volatility of payments from year to year? Will the plan use the same definition of pay used under the broad-based plan for benefit accrual purposes?

Employers may find that job grades offer a simpler solution than specifying minimum compensation for eligibility purposes; job grades encompass pay levels, and they are usually updated to reflect inflation and pay growth.

Other criteria.   Plans may also require that an otherwise eligible executive be approved for participation by some senior officer (e.g., the CEO) or committee (e.g., the compensation committee of the board of directors or the company's executive management committee). Approval may be the only eligibility requirement in some plans.

Eligibility requirement(s) may also be a direct function of the plan's objective. If a plan exists solely to restore benefits lost by reason of the Section 415 limits, eligible executives might include any individuals who have lost qualified plan benefits because of these limits.

Eligibility can also be conditioned on such factors as participation in specific compensation programs (a long-term incentive plan of some type, for example) or employment at a particular location (e.g., corporate headquarters or certain specific subsidiaries).

Prevalence.   Table 5–1 shows the prevalence of various eligibility provisions in the executive benefit programs of companies in the Towers Perrin Executive Benefit Data Base.

Compensation

Executive life insurance, disability income, and retirement benefits are pay-related. Two factors must be considered in defining the compensation

TABLE 5-1
Executive Benefit Eligibility Requirements

Criteria	Defined Benefit SERPs*	Disability Income	Life Insurance
Bonus eligibility	12%	18%	14%
Top management approval	56	30	18
Salary level or grade	27	39	33
Title	—	20	—

Note: Because some plans use more than one requirement, numbers do not add up to 100 percent.
*Excluding SERPs that are restoration plans

on which these benefits will be based: the elements of pay that will be included, and the period of time (if any) over which compensation will be averaged.

Elements. Base salary and short-term incentives are typically included as compensation elements in executive benefit plans. In fact, providing benefits related to short-term incentive pay is frequently a key plan objective, since broad-based plans often base benefits only on basic salary or wages. Such limits in the broad-based plan usually reflect employer concerns about costs, administrative simplicity, and the practice of replacing irregular income such as overtime. Many employers do not want to extend this approach to executives who place part of their compensation at risk with the expectation that they will be rewarded for superior performance.

Moreover, bonuses are usually viewed as an integral part of executive compensation that should be replaced or maintained in the event of retirement or death. Some employers feel the same way about disability and include bonuses in the compensation base for disability income benefits. Because bonuses are paid to incent current performance, others believe it is inappropriate to continue any incentive pay when an executive is unable to work and, as a result, to contribute to current profitability.

The definition of pay may also include compensation that the executive has deferred (either voluntarily or involuntarily) for payment at some future time.[12] A broad-based welfare plan can be amended to include deferred compensation in the definition of pay without necessitating a separate plan for executives. Generally, deferred compensation amounts cannot be included to establish contributions and/or benefits under broad-based retirement plans. Thus, the definition of compensation in an executive retirement program usually includes any deferred amounts that have affected broad-based plan benefits or should otherwise be taken into account.

While it is also possible to include the value of long-term incentive compensation in the pay base, this practice is relatively uncommon. Long-term incentive plans are basically capital accumulation programs that are not considered part of regular, year-to-year compensation and thus need not be replaced when the executive is no longer working. Further, it is extremely difficult to value these plans and arrive at an amount to replace.

Other elements of executive pay such as perquisites and other forms of imputed income are typically disregarded in establishing the pay base for executive benefits.

Of the 283 SERPs in the Towers Perrin Executive Benefit Data Base:

- 139 use the definition of pay from the underlying base plan; 64 use base pay only, and 75 use base pay plus bonus.
- 62 use a definition of pay that adds bonuses (i.e., the underlying plan uses base pay only while the SERP uses base pay plus bonus).
- 80 add deferred compensation.
- 4 add long-term incentive compensation.
- 33 percent of disability income plans define pay to include bonuses; the remainder use base pay only or a combination of base pay plus deferred compensation.
- Of 72 life insurance plans:

    65 percent use base pay only.

    14 percent use base pay plus bonuses.

    11 percent use base pay plus bonuses and deferred compensation.

    10 percent use other definitions or provide benefits that are not pay-related.

Averaging period.   Disability income plans typically determine the amount of benefits payable on the basis of the executive's current pay, however it is defined. The same is true of life insurance, although usual practice is to use the pay in effect as of a specific date (e.g., the beginning of the plan or calendar year), and to adjust the level of benefit periodically (e.g., annually).

Because bonus amounts can vary substantially from year to year, plans that include bonuses in the definition of compensation often use averaging; an executive's 1994 plan compensation might be the sum of his 1994 base pay plus an average of bonuses paid during 1991, 1992, and 1993, for example. Longer averaging periods may be appropriate where bonus payments vary significantly over the years.

Current compensation is also appropriate for determining the contributions credited to the executive's account each year under defined contribution or capital accumulation programs. In a conventional defined benefit plan, benefits are typically based on final average pay over a three- or five-year averaging period. Bonuses may be averaged over the same or an even longer period.

Although many executive defined benefit plans use the same averaging period as that used in the broad-based plan, some use a shorter period to produce a relatively higher level of income replacement for the executive group. In fact, some executive plans base pension benefits on the final year's pay without averaging (with the possible exception of bonuses).

Postretirement inflation considerations may be the impetus for such an approach. Social Security provides substantial inflation protection for rank-and-file employees through automatic cost-of-living adjustments. While an executive's Social Security benefit is also adjusted, that benefit represents only a small part of total retirement income. Thus, use of a shorter time period to determine pensionable pay produces additional benefits to compensate for the fact that the largest part of the executive's retirement benefit will not be automatically increased for inflation.

Service

An executive's service is relevant for determining initial eligibility to participate, vesting rights, benefit accruals, and eligibility for benefit payments. For example, an employer might require an executive to complete 10 years of service and attain age 55 to receive retirement benefits and to be eligible for postretirement health care benefits.

In most situations, an executive's service will be defined as the period of employment with the employer, measured from date of hire to date of termination (for whatever reason). Like broad-based plans, executive benefit plans should specify whether time on leave (paid or unpaid and/or on account of disability) will be counted as service and whether broken periods of service will be aggregated for various purposes.

There are no ERISA or tax law requirements governing the determination of service for welfare benefits or for retirement benefits that qualify for an ERISA exemption. If Title I of ERISA applies with respect to retirement benefits, the plan must comply with rules on determining service for purposes of eligibility to participate, vesting, and eligibility for benefit accruals.[13]

Though it is not common practice, a plan may limit service to the period of time an individual is employed as an executive. If a person has been an executive for 10 years out of a 30-year career with the same employer, for example, he or she would be credited with only 10 years of service for executive benefit plan purposes.

It is also possible, though unusual, to limit service to the period of time that the executive participates in the plan. While this also limits service to time spent as an executive, it is broader in scope, since it also excludes executive service before the plan was initiated. Some employers impose these limitations to eliminate benefit distortions that might otherwise result from recognizing different amounts of service prior to adoption of a plan. Others want the executive plan to reflect current contributions and performance rather than to reward prior service.

When an executive switches jobs, his or her accrued pension benefit will be frozen at the then-current pay level. To address this concern, and thus assist in recruiting executives in midcareer, some plans define service to include service with a prior employer.[14]

NOTES

1. See Chapter 1.
2. The accounting treatment of executive benefits is covered in Chapter 8.
3. See Chapter 9 for a discussion of plan costs.
4. The tax consequences of various nonqualified approaches to providing executive retirement benefits are discussed in Chapter 10.
5. DOL Reg. 2520.104-24. See Chapter 7.
6. DOL Reg. 2520.104-23. See Chapter 4.
7. These requirements are discussed in Chapter 13.
8. These requirements prohibit any discrimination on the basis of age, including the use of a mandatory retirement provision. A limited exception permits an employer to force a bona fide executive to retire at age 65 if the annual employer-provided retirement benefit for such executive is $44,000 or more.

9. ERISA exemptions are discussed in Chapter 4.

10. As discussed in the previous chapter, the term *highly compensated employees* has never been defined by the DOL, with the result that employers have been left on their own to determine, with advice of counsel, whether the group they wish to cover is within the meaning of this term. The definition of highly compensated employee found in the IRC and supporting IRS regulations applies for tax purposes only and is not determinative when applying the labor provisions of ERISA.

11. The lowering of the limit on pay that can be taken into account for purposes of tax-qualified retirement plans (to $150,000 for 1994) will obviously influence the decision-making process when it comes to eligibility to participate. This issue is discussed in more detail in Chapter 6.

12. See Chapter 3 for a discussion of deferred compensation arrangements.

13. See Allen, Melone, et al., *Pension Planning*, pp. 123–127 for a complete discussion of these rules.

14. Providing benefits for this prior service could result in a doubling up of credits if the executive has a vested benefit with his prior employer. Thus, when prior employer service is recognized in this fashion, it is customary to subtract the amount of any such vested benefits from the benefits being provided under the new employer's plan.

Chapter Six

Plan Design: Retirement and Capital Accumulation

Retirement and capital accumulation plans are, in many ways, the most significant of the benefits made available to executives. This chapter begins with a general discussion of the key concepts that influence the design of executive retirement and capital accumulation plans and continues with an overview of the features unique to these plans. The chapter concludes with a discussion of the impact of OBRA '93 on plan design, communication, and administration.

KEY FACTORS

By its very nature, a retirement plan covers an expanse of time with respect to individual executives. The benefit usually accrues over a lengthy period—15, 20, or even 25 or more years—and it can be paid over an equally long period. These plans also involve substantial sums of money for both the employer and participating executives—considerations that underscore the need for thoughtful plan design that supports employer objectives.

There are a number of threshold issues an employer must consider before turning to specific plan features, including whether it prefers a defined benefit or a defined contribution approach to providing benefits, how the plan will operate under the Employee Retirement Income Security Act of 1974 (ERISA) and tax law, and how executive plans will be coordinated with any underlying broad-based plans.

These issues are discussed later in this chapter. To set the stage, we will begin with a brief review of the key characteristics of executive retirement plans and the terminology used in connection with them.

Tax and Legal Environment

As discussed in Chapter 2, the acronym *SERP* (short for supplemental executive retirement plan) is used broadly to include all types of executive retirement arrangements. Some SERPs simply restore benefits lost under qualified plans due to various Internal Revenue Code (IRC) restrictions; other SERPs provide distinctly supplemental benefits for the executive group.

SERPs can be funded or unfunded. A plan is funded when assets are irrevocably committed to provide benefits. Some plans may earmark assets for the payment of benefits (as is often the case with corporate-owned life insurance), or may conditionally transfer assets to a trust (as with a so-called rabbi trust), but these plans are not considered to be funded.[1] Most SERPs are unfunded.

The design and administration of a SERP should recognize that the tax and legal environment for these plans differs from that applicable to broad-based programs. The impact of ERISA and the tax law can also differ depending upon whether a plan is an excess benefit plan (restoring only benefits lost under the qualified plan as a result of the Section 415 limits) or a more all-encompassing SERP, and on whether it is funded.

These differences are discussed in greater detail in other parts of this text; for purposes of this chapter, key differences are recapped below.

- SERPs are not tax-qualified plans. As a result, SERP design is not restricted by the qualification and nondiscrimination requirements that apply to broad-based plans.
- Because they are not tax-qualified, certain of the tax advantages of qualified plans are not available to SERPs. For example, any investment income on plan assets will generally be taxable, lump sum distributions will not be accorded special tax treatment, and the doctrine of constructive receipt will apply.
- If the SERP is unfunded, the general rule is that an executive will not be taxed on benefit values until they are paid, even though these values are vested.
- If the SERP is funded, the general rule is that an executive will be taxed on benefit values as soon as they become vested, even though benefits are not yet payable.
- The employer will generally be allowed a tax deduction only when and to the extent the executive has reportable income.

- Early and excess distribution taxes do not apply to benefits payable under a SERP.
- Funded SERPs may become subject to the provisions of Title I of ERISA (minimum participation, funding and vesting, and so forth), but Title I does not contain any provisions that limit benefits (e.g., such as Section 415 of the IRC), nor does it contain any provisions that prevent discrimination in favor of highly compensated employees.
- Title IV of ERISA (plan termination insurance) does not apply to SERPs.

Defined Contribution versus Defined Benefit

While the relative merits of defined benefit and defined contribution plans receive considerable attention when it comes to rank-and-file employees, the differences between these two approaches are less significant in the executive arena. Potential coverage under the plan termination provisions of ERISA often deters a company from establishing a broad-based defined benefit plan, for example, but defined benefit SERPs are not subject to these rules. Similarly, a defined contribution SERP can be structured to avoid one of the key characteristics of a broad-based plan—the transfer of investment and inflation risks to employees.

Most SERPs have been established on a defined benefit basis, particularly in cases where the SERP builds on an underlying broad-based defined benefit plan, by applying the base plan benefit formula to short-term incentive pay that is otherwise excluded when calculating plan benefits, for example.

The defined benefit approach works well when a SERP is unfunded because it can accommodate most employer objectives and serve to coordinate benefits from all sources. It is also easy to explain and administer.[2]

With a funded defined benefit SERP, difficulties may arise when executives have to include the value of their accrued and vested benefits in taxable income, since these values will be based on assumptions as to future pay growth, inflation rates, investment returns, mortality, and the like. If the assumptions prove to be too conservative, the plan may have created more value than is necessary. Because executives will already have been taxed on this value, it cannot be taken away (except on a prospective basis to the extent future accruals and/or compensation can be adjusted).

The use of more aggressive assumptions or less-than-full funding to provide a margin can avoid or minimize such problems.

As an alternative, employers can adopt a defined contribution approach to establishing benefit levels and, as a result, funding levels. The defined contribution approach is attractive for a number of reasons, whether or not a plan is funded. For example:

- Executives are accustomed to dealing with the idea of capital accumulation and might feel more comfortable with this approach than with conventional income replacement concepts.

- The defined contribution approach more readily coordinates with the use of company stock and the role of stock in overall executive compensation.

- Any imputed rates of return (where benefits are not funded and otherwise invested) can be tied to company performance measurements such as growth in profits, company stock prices, dividend growth, or return on assets.

- Several design issues are easier to deal with, such as offsets for vested benefits from prior employment, making additional contributions sufficient to attract executives in midcareer, and so forth.

Hybrid approaches also warrant consideration. Under a target benefit plan, for example, the employer uses a defined benefit formula to establish a projected retirement benefit, converts the benefit to a lump sum value, and establishes the annual contribution or credit necessary to fund to this lump sum value at some assumed interest rate. Once the contribution level has been established, the plan operates like a defined contribution plan.

The cash balance approach is another alternative. A cash balance plan is a defined benefit plan that looks like a defined contribution plan. A participant's account is credited with a specified percentage of pay each year, and the account earns interest at a specified rate; the participant's ultimate benefit equals contributions plus earnings. Annual contributions may be weighted to reflect age or age and service (e.g., 8 percent of pay before age 50 and 12 percent at or after age 50, or 6 percent when age and service total 30 to 39, 9 percent when they total 40 to 54, and so forth).

An employer establishing a new SERP should evaluate the advantages and disadvantages of defined benefit, defined contribution and hybrid arrangements in light of its specific plan objectives.

Coordination with Broad-Based Plans

By design, a SERP will have many provisions that differ significantly from corresponding provisions in the employer's broad-based plan—the definitions of pay and service, for example, and benefit accrual rates and early retirement provisions. In other areas there is little need for different treatment, and consistency is in fact desirable.

One such area is the form and manner in which benefits are distributed. The law requires a broad-based plan to provide a joint and survivor benefit as the normal form of distribution for a married employee. The benefit payable to the employee will typically be reduced to reflect the value of the benefit that might be continued to the survivor, although this is not always the case. In any event, the SERP should specify the form in which its payments will be made and whether the offset for base plan benefits (as discussed in the following section) will be made before or after any reductions called for by the joint and survivor provision.

Other optional forms of payment should also parallel the broad-based plan, although the SERP should be structured to avoid constructive receipt by the executive of the entire value of his or her SERP benefit.

Other provisions where some coordination with base plan provisions might be desirable include: the right to name and change beneficiary designations; facility of payment authority (if the payee is mentally or physically incapable of accepting payment); what will happen if a beneficiary cannot be located; which state law will govern plan interpretation; and the right to amend or terminate the plan.

Along these same lines, it may be advisable to coordinate SERP and base plan administration and communication, though confidentiality considerations may dictate that the plans be handled separately.

PLAN FEATURES

Before turning to such major plan features as retirement ages, benefit structure, vesting, and disability and death benefits, the employer must decide whether the SERP will be a stand-alone plan or a wrap-around plan. A stand-alone SERP is self-contained, and the executive's total benefit is the sum of whatever is payable under each plan (qualified and nonqualified), determined in accordance with each plan's provisions. A wrap-around SERP establishes a gross benefit and then offsets actual benefits payable under the base plan.

A wrap-around plan requires careful thought as to its relationship with the broad-based plan. Depending on how it is structured, the SERP can provide significant additional benefits for executives. Suppose, for example, that the SERP applies the base plan benefit formula to total pay, including bonuses, while the underlying plan uses base salary only. Suppose further that the base plan has full actuarial reductions for early retirement, but the SERP provides for unreduced benefits as early as age 60. An executive retiring at age 60 will not only receive a SERP benefit that reflects his bonus; he will also receive a supplemental SERP benefit equal to the actuarial reduction of his base plan benefit. At age 60, this additional early retirement SERP benefit could be worth as much as 50 percent of the benefit payable under the base plan.

Retirement Ages

Retirement age is not critical for defined contribution or capital accumulation SERPs; an executive's benefit equals the account balance at termination—whether for normal, early, or deferred retirement; death; disability; or any other reason. Thus, such a SERP can be designed without any specific reference to retirement age. As a practical matter, however, many defined contribution SERPs do specify normal, early, and deferred retirement ages. One reason for defining normal retirement age is to make it clear when the employer expects executives to retire. Another is to tie the definition to other plans (defined benefit pension, postretirement health care, and life insurance) so as to have a consistent approach to retirement and eligibility for benefits under both the base plans and the SERP.

Normal retirement age. Most broad-based plans establish 65 (or the completion of five years of service, if later) as normal retirement age. Many SERPs do the same, though some employers prefer that executives retire earlier and thus specify an age such as 60 or 62 as normal retirement age for the SERP.

With one exception, Equal Employment Opportunity Commission (EEOC) requirements prohibit the use of a mandatory retirement age. The exception relates to individuals who have been employed for at least two years as "bona fide" executives or in "high policy-making positions," and whose nonforfeitable employer-provided retirement benefit from all sources is at least $44,000.[3] An employer can force any such individual to retire at or after age 65. Thus, employers need to consider whether they want to take advantage of this limited exception and mandate retirement at age 65 to the extent allowed.

Early retirement age. Many SERPs define early retirement eligibility in exactly the same way it is defined in the underlying broad-based plan—typically, the attainment of age 55 and the completion of at least 10 years of service. Some SERPs are more liberal in this regard, particularly when encouraging early retirement is a plan objective. In either case, it is customary for the early retirement service requirement to at least equal the service required for full vesting.

Employers who want to create "golden handcuffs" may want to be more restrictive, perhaps requiring that executives attain age 62 to be eligible for SERP benefits, even though the base plan permits early retirement as early as age 55. Another approach (with or without a higher age requirement) is to permit early retirement under the SERP only with employer consent.

Benefits available at early retirement can be designed in a conventional manner—that is, with benefits actuarially reduced if they begin before normal retirement age. Employers can also subsidize SERP early retirement benefits, in line with base plan subsidies or to a greater extent. For example, the SERP might make full, unreduced benefits available at age 60 or 62 (with a limited service requirement such as 10 years), with only minimal reductions for retirements before this age, while the base plan would make actuarial reductions at all ages.

As noted, a wrap-around SERP can provide a significant supplemental benefit equal to the amount of actuarial reduction that applies to the executive's base plan benefit. Of 197 defined benefit SERPs in the Towers Perrin Executive Benefit Data Base, 105, or 53 percent, provide for unreduced early retirement benefits. Table 6–1 shows the criteria required for unreduced benefits in these plans.

Clearly, the design of a SERP's early retirement provisions as to both eligibility and benefit levels will reflect the employer's preferences with respect to the continued employment of older executives.

Deferred retirement. Deferred retirement refers to an executive's right to remain employed after his or her normal retirement date. With the exception noted above for mandatory retirement at age 65, EEOC regulations apply to SERPs and, as a result, exert significant influence on this plan provision. Thus, individuals who are not bona fide executives

TABLE 6–1
Unreduced Early Retirement Benefits

Criteria	Number of Plans
Age only*	34
Age and service**	66
Other	5

*Typically 60 or 62.
**Typically 60 or 62 with 10 years of service.

or who are not in high policy-making positions must not be discriminated against on account of age, as discussed below. Even those individuals who come within the scope of the exemption must not be discriminated against on account of age if the employer does not use the exemption.

Compliance with EEOC regulations means there can be no mandatory retirement prior to age 65 for bona fide executives, and no mandatory retirement at any age for individuals who do not fall within the exemption. Further, benefit accruals must continue until an executive actually retires. This will require additional "contributions" or credits to a defined contribution SERP. It will require additional benefit accruals in a defined benefit SERP to reflect pay levels (and changes, for example, in final average pay), as well as additional accruals for service up to any maximum service period stipulated by the plan.

Because defined benefit SERP accrual rates are often generous, many employers cap recognized service to control benefit levels and costs for employment beyond stipulated periods of time. Such a cap, which is permissible under the Age Discrimination in Employment Act (ADEA), can also encourage executives to retire early—or at least by the plan's normal retirement age—if that is an employer objective.

Benefit Structure—Capital Accumulation Plans

The benefit structure of a defined contribution or capital accumulation SERP is relatively straightforward. The employer establishes a contribution or credit amount, accumulates the contribution or credit with actual or imputed investment income, and pays out the accumulated amount at some future time, usually retirement, death, disability, or other termination of employment. The plan may be unfunded (as is typically the case) or funded. Some employers earmark or conditionally contribute amounts in the executive's name, but these arrangements are usually not considered to be funded as contemplated by ERISA and the tax law and do not involve irrevocably committed assets.

Contribution levels.   Many defined contribution SERPs exist solely to restore benefits lost under broad-based plans due to IRC provisions—most notably Section 415, the $7,000 (indexed) deferral limit, and the $150,000 (indexed) pay limit. In these plans the amount of employer contribution or credit simply reflects the provisions of the base plan and the tax law.[4]

Other defined contribution SERPs go further, providing more substantial employer credits or contributions, sometimes as an alternative to conventional defined benefit arrangements. Employers have several options for establishing contributions, including the target benefit approach described earlier. Contributions may be incentive-oriented, reflecting employer profits, or they may represent a fixed percentage of pay (a money purchase plan). If assistance in midcareer recruiting is a plan objective, additional contributions may be made in the early years of an executive's participation to compensate for the potential loss of benefits under a prior employer's plan.

Deferred compensation arrangements can be considered another type of defined contribution SERP.[5] The amount credited or contributed to an executive's account each year may simply consist of deferred compensation amounts. These deferrals may be automatic under some incentive compensation plans; under others, they may be totally voluntary or both automatic and voluntary.

As noted in Chapter 3, whether an executive is better off taking current cash or deferring it (and thus risking higher future tax rates) depends, in large part, on the rate of return the employer will credit to deferred amounts (which will "accumulate" on a before-tax basis) relative to the after-tax rate of return the executive could earn on deferred amounts if they were taken as current income. See Table 3–1 for an example.

Investment return.   Determining the rate of return on credits or contributions made under a defined contribution SERP is a key design consideration. If the plan is funded, this rate of return will obviously

TABLE 6-2
After-Tax Cost to Corporation of Deferring $10,000

Deferral Period	Amount Payable To Executive	Corporate Rate of Return		
		10%	*15%*	*20%*
10 years	$25,937	$ 4,658	$ 379	($–5,205)
20 years	$67,271	$20,825	$1,945	($–31,171)

reflect actual investment results.[6] If the plan is unfunded, the employer must establish some method of imputing investment return. Some companies determine this rate with reference to one or more prime rates; others tie the rate to their own return on capital or their own cost of borrowing. Still others use an external base such as a Moody's Bond Index.[7]

Special issues arise if the defined contribution SERP is a restoration plan, because the underlying plan will typically permit several investment choices. Will the rate of return on amounts credited under the SERP mirror the investment results of the choices the executive made under the base plan, the composite result of all funds under the base plan, the rate of return under a designated fund of the base plan, or something else?

Some observers have suggested that the IRS might consider participants in a nonqualified, unfunded plan to be in constructive receipt of income if participants are given investment authority. Discussions with an IRS official indicate that this does not accurately depict the IRS' attitude in this regard, and that a participant may be permitted to direct the investment of his or her account balance in an unfunded plan without being in constructive receipt of the account balance for tax purposes. This is consistent with the position that the IRS has taken in a number of private letter rulings on this issue.[8] It may be prudent to include an express provision in the plan document stating that the employer is under no obligation to make any investments or to segregate any of its assets in any way in response to a participant's "investment elections" in order to ensure that the plan maintains its status as unfunded for both tax and ERISA purposes. While an employer might actually make investments to match the participant's elections, it should be under no legal obligation to do so.

The employer cost of an unfunded defined contribution SERP will be sensitive to the before-tax rate of return credited to deferred amounts relative to the gross rate of return the employer can achieve with respect to these amounts. This is illustrated in Table 6–2, which shows the after-tax cost of deferring a $10,000 payment for 10 and 20 years, respectively, and crediting this deferred amount annually with a 10 percent before-tax return. The table assumes the company pays a 35 percent tax rate and that it could earn, before-tax, either 10, 15, or 20 percent per year. The higher the corporate rate of return and the longer the period of deferral, the more favorable the results for the corporation.

Benefit Structure—Defined Benefit Plans

The benefit formula in a defined benefit plan should reflect the employer's income replacement objectives. Key factors include:

- The percentage of pay to be continued in retirement and whether this percentage will vary by income level.
- The definition of what constitutes pay.
- The length of service required for full (or optimum) benefits under the plan.
- The retirement age at which full (or optimum) benefits are provided.
- Sources of income recognized in determining whether income replacement objectives have been met.

Whether or not the employer wants to link benefits to performance, as discussed later in this chapter, is also a factor.

      Replacement percentages. The typical broad-based plan replaces a relatively high percentage of preretirement income for lower-paid employees, dropping that percentage as income levels increase. Such a plan typically seeks to replace about 80 to 85 percent of pay for employees earning less than $25,000 (with Social Security), with these percentages grading down to perhaps 55 to 60 percent for the highly paid.

      If the SERP is strictly a restoration plan, it has the same income replacement objectives as the broad-based plan by definition. If the SERP is to provide benefits over and above those provided by the broad-based plan, the employer must decide what income replacement percentages to use and whether to use the same percentage for executives at all pay levels. The income replacement target for executives is often 55 to 60 percent of pay regardless of income level. Higher percentages could provoke shareholder criticism and even raise questions as to reasonableness of compensation from the standpoint of the deductibility of plan costs.

In designing a SERP to meet its income replacement objectives, the employer must consider how to structure and combine the four components that constitute the plan's benefit formula: (1) the accrual rate, (2) the pay base, (3) recognized service, and (4) any offsets.

Accrual rate. The rate at which benefits will accrue in a SERP may be identical to the base plan rate; this would be the case in a restoration plan or in a plan that simply applies the base plan formula to incentive pay. An employer may also choose to use a different accrual rate in the SERP, or to front- or back-load the formula, depending on its income replacement and other objectives. To facilitate midcareer recruiting, for example, the formula could specify a relatively high accrual rate (such as 3 percent per year) for the first 5 or 10 years, followed by accruals at a lower rate thereafter. A back-loaded formula would reverse the process and might be appropriate for use in a situation where the employer wants to reward length of service.

Definition of pay. As noted in Chapter 5, there are two things employers must decide in defining pay for purposes of a SERP: which elements of pay will be included, and the period (if any) over which pay will be averaged. The definition the employer adopts for the SERP may or may not be the same as the definition in the underlying broad-based plan. The most common differences are that the SERP may include short-term incentives and may average pay over a shorter period. In many situations, the sole objective of the SERP is to apply the broad-based plan formula to the executive's short-term incentive pay, thus providing a total benefit from both plans that reflects the executive's total direct pay (but still excludes such items as long-term incentives and perquisites).

The employer may want to use the SERP to apply the broad-based benefit formula to a definition of pay that is more beneficial to the executive, thus producing higher replacement percentages. Table 6–3 compares the benefit payable under the same formula applied to five-year average pay, three-year average pay, and final year's pay. Here, the executive's final pay is $500,000 and has grown at 8 percent a year for the past 10 years. The benefit formula is 50 percent of the applicable pay base.

As the table illustrates, an employer can increase an executive's benefit substantially by simply changing the pay base to which the basic benefit formula applies.

TABLE 6–3
Pay Base and Benefit Comparison

	Five-Year Average	Three-Year Average	Final Year
Pay Base	$431,213	$463,877	$500,000
Annual pension	$215,606	$231,939	$250,000
Pension as a percent of final year's pay	43%	46%	50%
Increase in pension over benefit based on five-year average			
In dollars	N/A	$ 16,332	$ 34,394
As a percent	N/A	8%	16%

Length of service.   Most defined benefit formulas specify that the accrual rate applies to each year of service recognized for plan purposes. A 1 percent accrual rate in a plan with unlimited service credit would produce a pension benefit of 30 percent of pay for an executive with 30 years of service. An employer usually chooses the accrual rate for a specific plan to produce the desired income replacement percentage after an executive completes what the employer considers to be the appropriate period of covered employment.

In broad-based plans, this period is often 25 or 30 years—a span of time that may also be appropriate for a SERP. Often, however, employers want to provide full benefits to executives after a shorter period, say 10 or 15 years. Some employers may want SERP benefits to accrue only during an individual's service as an eligible executive. Whatever the decision, the plan should specify the service required before an executive will be entitled to the full benefits contemplated by the program. This, in turn, will help determine the accrual rate used in the benefit formula.

Offsets.   Depending on its objectives, an employer may reduce or offset SERP benefits by the amount of benefits payable under the broad-based plan (in a wrap-around SERP), the executive's Social Security benefit, and/or vested benefits from a prior employer's plan.

Retirement age. Broad-based plans typically make full benefits available at the plan's normal retirement age of 65. SERPs often use a younger age (e.g., 62). Retirement before that age can result in lower benefits, because the executive will have shorter service and benefit payments will be paid over a longer period than that originally contemplated for full benefits.

Income sources. Once an employer has established its overall income replacement objectives, it needs to decide which sources of income it will take into account to determine whether those objectives have been met. Obvious sources are the SERP itself, the underlying broad-based retirement plan, and Social Security.[9] The employer may also want to take the annuitized value of any broad-based or supplemental defined contribution benefits into account.

Vesting

A funded SERP that is subject to Title I of ERISA must comply with minimum vesting standards similar to those applicable to tax-qualified plans. Thus, full vesting of values attributable to employer contributions must occur no later than normal retirement age and, before that time, under either one of two schedules: (1) full vesting after five years of service, or (2) 20 percent vesting after three years of service, increasing 20 percent each subsequent year until 100 percent vesting is achieved after seven years. Employers are free to adopt more liberal vesting provisions.

No vesting requirements apply to unfunded SERPs. Thus, an employer's options in this regard range from full and immediate vesting to no vesting at all until retirement. Even at retirement, the retired executive's rights can be made forfeitable under certain conditions—for example, if he or she goes to work for a competitor.[10]

SERP vesting often parallels the vesting provisions of the underlying base plan. In some cases, particularly in SERPs that are used for midcareer recruiting or to encourage executives to retire early, vesting provisions may be more liberal.[11] If the SERP is intended to create golden handcuffs, however, vesting may be restricted and may occur only when the executive qualifies for retirement.

An unfunded plan can provide for the forfeiture of benefits that might otherwise have been vested. For example, an executive's benefits might be forfeited if his or her employment is terminated for acts of dishonesty such as fraud or embezzlement. As noted above, forfeiture might also occur (even after retirement) if the executive goes to work for a competitor or reveals trade secrets. Such provisions are sometimes difficult to enforce, but many employers believe they provide reasonable and necessary protection. Only 24 percent of the defined benefit restoration plans in the Towers Perrin Executive Benefit Data Base include forfeiture provisions; they are found in 54 percent of other defined benefit SERPs, however.

Disability

Many SERPs treat disability in much the same way it is treated under the broad-based plan. A typical provision might continue to accrue service during the period of disability and while disability benefits are being paid to the executive under the firm's long-term disability program.

In some cases, particularly with older executives, a SERP may treat disability as early retirement without reducing the benefit for early commencement of payments. The plan might even credit the disabled executive with additional service for the period remaining until normal retirement age—in effect treating him or her as a normal retiree with full service.

Death

Most SERPs provide for some type of death benefit when an executive dies before retirement. In the case of defined contribution plans, the benefit is usually the executive's account balance. A defined benefit SERP often provides a lifetime benefit to the spouse equal to part or all of the executive's accrued benefit. Next most common is a joint and survivor benefit. A few defined benefit SERPs provide for a lump sum benefit; employers who prefer a lump sum approach generally find it more effective to provide it through additional amounts of life insurance, however.

Table 6–4 shows the percentage of defined benefit SERPs in the Towers Perrin Executive Benefit Data Base that provide preretirement death benefits.

Postretirement death benefits are less common than preretirement benefits, largely because the cost of such benefits is significant.

The design of death benefit provisions in a defined benefit SERP requires answers to many of the questions that arise in designing a broad-based plan. Should the plan require a minimum period of marriage (e.g., one year) before the spouse becomes eligible, for example? If the executive dies

TABLE 6–4
Preretirement Death Benefits

Type of Benefit	Restoration Plans*	Other SERPs**
Spouse benefit for *n* years	0%	14%
Lifetime spouse benefit		
50% of accrued benefit	13%	11%
100% of accrued benefit	3	6
Other percentage	1	6
Joint and survivor benefit		
50% of accrued benefit	55	25
100% of accrued benefit	4	3
Other percentage	4	6
Lump sum payment	6	19
Other	12	6
None	2	4

*117 plans
**72 plans

before eligibility for early retirement, will the spouse be entitled to immediate payment, or will payments commence only when the executive would have reached early retirement eligibility? Will amounts payable to a joint annuitant be adjusted if he or she is more than a certain number of years younger than the executive? These are among the issues employers must address in designing SERP death benefit provisions.

OBRA '93

The Omnibus Budget Reconciliation Act of 1993 (OBRA '93) has significant implications for executives and raises a number of important plan design, communication, and administration issues for employers. As noted in Chapter 1, OBRA '93 reduced the amount of pay that can be taken into account for qualified plan purposes to $150,000. The original IRC Section 401(a)(17) limit of $200,000 had grown through indexing to $235,840 for 1993. While the $150,000 limit is indexed, it will only rise in $10,000 increments (i.e., only when accumulated changes in the CPI amount to $10,000). OBRA '93 also "uncapped" the Medicare tax, applying it to all current income—including SERP accruals—starting in 1994.[12] We have touched on these points elsewhere, but they warrant more extensive review here, in part to underscore the issues and trade-offs employers must weigh in offering supplemental retirement plans for their executives.

Impact on Executives

As Table 1–1 in Chapter 1 illustrates, the portion of retirement benefits payable to executives outside the qualified plan arena will increase as a result of the new pay cap. The number of employees affected by the pay cap will increase as well. A Towers Perrin survey of 100 employers conducted shortly after OBRA was enacted showed a fourfold rise in the number of employees subject to the cap across the survey group. An obvious consequence—discussed in more detail in the paragraphs that follow—is the need for employers to revisit the issue of who will be eligible for SERP participation.

As more benefits become payable to more people from nonqualified plans, interest in benefit security will undoubtedly increase. At present, most nonqualified plans are unfunded and thus represent nothing more than a promise to pay on the part of the employer. As a result of the pay cap, executives may encourage their employers to take a closer look at various approaches to funding or otherwise securing executive benefits (which are discussed in more detail in Chapter 10). Because funding can have current tax consequences for executives, they may also ask to be "grossed up"— that is, made whole with respect to any additional taxes they may incur in this regard. Funding and grossing up will obviously have cost consequences for employers.

Benefit security is an issue that can extend into retirement, so executives may also be interested in receiving their benefits in the form of a lump sum, even at the price of less favorable tax treatment. Here, too, costs for employers could increase, since lump sums are typically more expensive than annuity payouts.

There are other implications for executives as well. Defined contribution plans have become an increasingly important part of the total retirement income picture, and executives are not likely to be happy missing out on the capital accumulation opportunity that is usually available through the qualified plan via salary reduction. In addition to raising individual tax rates, OBRA '93 has thus imposed an indirect tax on executives by reducing their ability to save on a pretax basis, and by lowering the portion of their retirement income eligible for advantageous tax treatment in the form of income averaging on distribution.

Shifting Liabilities

OBRA '93 also raises a number of important issues for employers with respect to their qualified and nonqualified plans. Because the lower pay cap will shift liabilities to the nonqualified, and typically nonfunded, arena, qualified plan accruals for many executives are likely to cease for a period of time, and some plans could conceivably hit the full funding limit or increase surplus as a result.

The shift in liabilities to the nonqualified arena will obviously have an impact on the balance sheet, since employers must record a minimum liability equal to the unfunded accumulated benefit obligation of each underfunded retirement plan. The extent to which this is a cause for concern may reflect the size of the unfunded liabilities an employer is already recording for postretirement medical benefits.

As noted earlier in this chapter, one issue employers must consider in designing a defined contribution SERP to restore benefits is whether the SERP will offer executives the same investment choices that are available in the underlying broad-based plan. If the choices mirror those in the qualified plan, which was the case in 42 percent of the defined contribution restoration plans in the survey group cited above, the balance sheet will be increasingly vulnerable to any volatility in investment results as the pay cap pushes more "money" into the SERP.

Eligibility Issues

As noted in Chapter 5, deciding which executives are to be covered is an important first step in designing any benefit plan. By lowering the 401(a)(17) pay cap, OBRA '93 has complicated the issue considerably by increasing the number of employees subject to the cap. To remain exempt from ERISA funding, vesting, fiduciary, and other requirements, SERPs must be maintained "for a select group of management or highly compensated employees." Because the Department of Labor (DOL) has never clearly defined this phrase, employers do not know how far below the executive ranks they can extend SERP participation without jeopardizing the top hat status of their plans.[13] Among the Towers Perrin survey group, 73 percent of respondents offering supplemental defined benefit plans

(73 companies) said they would extend plan coverage to all employees affected by the cap, compared with 68 percent of those who sponsor defined contribution SERPs (50 companies).

Implementation Issues

While the new pay cap focuses attention on various design issues associated with supplemental plans, an important first step in responding to the cap is a qualified plan review. For example, some employers may find that they still have latitude, within the confines of the nondiscrimination rules, to make plan changes that enable them to pay more qualified plan benefits to executives. Because the cap applies plan-by-plan rather than on an aggregate basis, some small employers have considered another possibility: dividing the workforce in half and setting up two qualified plans, each covering half of the business plus all executives earning over a specified (substantial) amount such as $250,000. This approach would effectively double the qualified plan benefits payable to executives covered by both plans. Whether it is administratively feasible, and will continue to pass muster with the IRS, remains to be seen.

Actual implementation of the new pay cap is governed by final regulations, issued by the IRS in June 1994,[14] which retain the main features of regulations issued after the 401(a)(17) limit was first imposed.[15] Benefits accrued or allocations made under a plan for plan years prior to the effective date of the original $200,000 limit are not subject to the limit; similarly, benefits accrued or allocations made under a plan for plan years prior to the effective date of the OBRA '93 changes are not subject to the reduced limit. Thus, for example, an employee's benefits accrued prior to the 1994 plan year that are based on compensation in excess of the $150,000 annual compensation limit under OBRA '93 need not be reduced, and these accruals based on excess compensation are not required to be offset against the employee's benefit accruals in subsequent years.

Defined benefit plans.   In order to satisfy the requirements of Section 401(a)(17) as originally implemented, a defined benefit plan had to "fresh start" the benefits of all employees with accrued benefits that were based on compensation that exceeded the then $200,000 annual compensation limit. In order to implement the reduced limit under OBRA '93, a defined benefit plan must again fresh start the benefits of all employees with accrued benefits that are based on compensation in excess of $150,000.

Transition choices for fresh starts, like those that applied to the original $200,000 limit, are as follows:

1. *Formula with wear away.* The frozen accrued benefit as of the last day of the 1993 plan year (limited by the 401(a)(17) provisions in effect on December 31, 1993) would be a minimum benefit.

2. *Formula without wear away.* A benefit calculated using service earned after the 1993 plan year and using average compensation as of an individual's termination date (limited by 401(a)(17) as in effect at termination) would be added to the frozen accrued benefit as described in "formula with wear away."

3. *Formula with extended wear away.* Take the larger of (1) and (2).

Alternative (1) produces the least amount of administrative burden and is most compatible with final average earnings plans. Alternative (2) is most suitable for career pay plans. Using alternatives (2) or (3) in implementing the change for final average earnings plans would be administratively more complicated, but the regulations provide that the fresh start rules may be applied to determine the accrued benefits of 401(a)(17) employees (i.e., employees whose accrued benefits in the years before the statutory effective date were determined by taking into account compensation in excess of the compensation limit in any year) but not the accrued benefits of other employees in the plan, without violating the consistency rules.[16]

The lowering of the 401(a)(17) pay cap to $150,000 raises the issue of the interaction between the cap and the Section 415 limits.[17] Would the 415 defined benefit limit applicable to an employee earning $200,000 who retires at age 72 in 1994 be calculated as the lesser of 100 percent of average pay up to $150,000, or the dollar limit of $118,800 increased to $167,164 for payment at age 72?

The absence of any cross references between the IRC and/or regulations covering 415 and 401(a)(17) suggests that the 401(a)(17) pay cap does not apply in the calculation of the various 415 limits. The benefit described in the above example should be calculated as the lesser of two amounts—the plan benefit and the 415 limit. The plan benefit must include the effect of the pay cap, but it could be based on a formula such as 5 percent of average pay per year of service up to 25 years. In that event, the plan benefit of a $200,000 employee with 25 or more years of service would be 125 percent of average pay up to $150,000, or $187,500. The 415 limit for such an employee retiring at age 72 in 1994 would be $167,164—the lesser of 100 percent of unlimited average pay or the dollar limit of $118,800 increased for payment at age 72. Comparing the $187,500 plan benefit and the 415 limit of $167,164, the plan would pay a benefit of $167,164, even though this is greater than 100 percent of the pay cap. Because the IRS has not formally ruled on this question, it is possible that they will reach the opposite conclusion at some time in the future.

Defined contribution plans. The final regulations clarified that the limit need not be prorated in the case of a payroll-based 401(k) plan or savings plan. Nonetheless, employers should be aware of the impact of the limit on their plans. Assume that an employee elects to contribute 3 percent of pay to a 401(k) plan at the start of the plan year to a plan that permits contributions of up to 6 percent. If the employer stops contributions when the employee's compensation hits the $150,000 cap, the employee will have contributed $4,500 for the year (3 percent × $150,000). As an alternative, the employer could specify that the employee could contribute a total of $9,000 (6 percent × $150,000) at any time during the year. As this example illustrates, it is important for employers to determine how their payroll departments should monitor the reduced pay cap.

In many cases, the $150,000 pay cap could result in smaller 401(k) deferrals for middle management and professional employees at the lower-paid end of the highly compensated group due to the operation of the ADP/ACP (nondiscrimination) tests for qualified plans.[18] It is not necessary to understand the details of ADP/ACP testing to illustrate the problem. Consider a plan with only two highly compensated employees (HCEs) in 1993—Anne, earning $90,000, and Barbara, earning $250,000.[19] Assume that both had elected to make the maximum possible 401(k) contribution in 1993 ($8,994). Dividing each salary by the elective deferrals of $8,994 would produce deferral percentages of 10 percent for Anne and 3.8 percent for Barbara, for an overall ADP of 6.9 percent for the highly compensated group.

If the test were run applying the $150,000 cap to Barbara's salary, her deferral percentage would rise to 6 percent and the overall ADP would rise to 8 percent for the HCE group.

Suppose the plan failed the test at the 8 percent level but just passed at the original 6.9 percent level. To bring the overall HCE deferral percentage down to that level, IRS rules would require the employer to reduce Anne's deferrals to 7.8 percent of pay, or $7,020. Thus, the lower-paid HCE would experience a 22 percent reduction in contributions, while the higher-paid HCE would lose nothing. In addition, any excess contributions refunded to Anne after the close of the year would probably be treated as income for 1993 and might require her to file an amended tax return if she filed before she was aware of the refunds.

If the plan sponsor is alert to this problem during the plan year, the rules provide latitude in correcting contribution levels among the highly paid group. Companies that sponsor a defined contribution SERP may choose to limit contributions by the highest paid HCEs so that lower-paid HCEs can contribute the full amount, letting higher-paid HCEs make up the difference through the SERP. If the sponsor waits until year-end testing, however, its hands are tied. At that point, the 401(k) rules require use of the *step-down* or *leveling* method that results in reduced deferrals for Anne in the example above.

Medicare Tax Issues

Executives and employers will feel an additional tax bite now that both owe 1.45 percent of pay on all current compensation rather than just the first $135,000. For employers, however, administering the tax is likely to be more burdensome than paying it. The most nettlesome issue—one on which the IRS has not provided guidance at the time of this writing—is how, when, and what amount to withhold from a SERP participant's pay to cover the tax on a SERP accruals.[20]

The requirement to withhold FICA tax from amounts deferred under SERPs and other nonqualified plans is not new. Since 1984, employers have been required to withhold the tax when deferred compensation amounts are earned or, if later, when they vest, rather than when the money is actually paid out (e.g., at retirement). As a practical matter, however, such withholding was rarely necessary before OBRA '93, since most SERP participants had annual earnings above the cap ($135,000 in 1993) and their annual SERP accruals triggered no additional tax liability.

In the past, IRS officials have indicated informally that employers generally can remit FICA tax on accruals earned on nonqualified deferred compensation arrangements once a year. Because the tax cannot be withheld from a SERP that is simply an unfunded promise or a notional account, employers will presumably have to withhold the tax from other cash compensation.

In cases where defined benefit accruals vest immediately, employers will presumably have to make annual determinations of the present value of current accruals for all SERP participants beginning with the 1994 plan year. If vesting is delayed (e.g., until age 55 with 10 years of service), the value of the entire accrued benefit will presumably be subject to FICA tax in the year the participant vests, with additional accruals subject to the tax annually thereafter.

One key complication involves the vesting date of SERP benefits such as enhanced early retirement subsidies that gradually disappear the longer an employee works. If these benefits "vest" for FICA purposes according to the plan's normal vesting schedule, employers and employees could end up paying tax on benefits that are never actually paid. An alternative might be to treat such benefits as if they do not vest until the employee actually retires.

COMMUNICATION

One reason the DOL is willing to grant exemptions from ERISA requirements for certain executive plans is that it assumes a certain level of sophistication on the part of participants. Many employers have apparently made the same assumption with respect to communicating their executive plans. While a great deal of effort is typically expended in designing executive plans and communicating them to the compensation committee of the board of directors, communication to executives themselves is often confined to contracts or other documents written by lawyers for lawyers.

For many executives, the lower pay cap will mean reduced benefits or frozen pension accruals. Further, SERP participation could increase significantly in some companies, expanding to include employees who fall into the middle management, rather than the executive, ranks. While both groups need to understand how the changes will affect them, those new to SERP participation need basic information about the difference between qualified and nonqualified plans and the implications unfunded arrangements could have for them personally. As a result, the new law may prompt employers to revisit and improve their executive communication programs.

One approach to communication that more and more employers are considering is personalized benefit statements for SERP participants. In addition to meeting the information needs of individual employees, this approach forces the employer to gather and organize information on what it is providing to whom. In many cases, corporate records on executive benefit arrangements are scattered and may consist of nothing more than copies of individual contracts. In addition to complicating administration and recordkeeping, this ad hoc form of recordkeeping may mean that employers do not have current and accurate information as to, for example, an executive's beneficiary.

To the extent that an executive benefit program is linked to performance, effective communication is even more important, since there is little incentive value to a program that executives do not fully understand.

THE PERFORMANCE LINK

As discussed in Chapter 2, executive salaries, bonuses, and long-term incentive plans have been the subject of increasing shareholder scrutiny in recent years. At issue is whether these expenditures on senior management are commensurate with senior management's performance in increasing the value of the company.

By increasing unfunded liabilities, OBRA '93 may serve to turn the spotlight toward executive benefit programs as well. If an executive's salary and bonus do not truly reflect performance, the typical executive pension plan will further weaken the pay-performance link, since it is usually salary and bonus (and not long-term incentives) that determine the level of benefits. The resulting total compensation package will reward age and service more than performance and shareholder wealth creation. (In the typical SERP, the benefit is of greatest value late in an executive's career because the value of accruals is a function of age.)

As a result, we can probably expect to see some (though by no means all) employers move to strengthen the performance link. An employer might, for example, consider a program that provides a basic retirement income safety net, avoids performance-insensitive final pay formulas, bases capital accumulation on annual performance, and links SERPs to total pay. A program that makes use of company stock will obviously provide a performance link. The stock-based SERP is the subject of Chapter 11.

NOTES

1. The use of permanent life insurance in conjunction with executive benefits is discussed in Chapter 12. Rabbi trusts are covered in Chapter 10.

2. As discussed later in this chapter, however, the uncapping of the Medicare tax raises administrative complications with respect to these plans.

3. Age Discrimination in Employment Act, Section 12(c)(1). See EEOC Reg. 1625.12 for a discussion of what constitutes a "bona fide executive" and "high policy-making position." Also, it should be noted that unlike many other dollar amounts set forth in the law, this $44,000 figure is not indexed to inflation.

4. Under Section 401(k) regulations, benefits cannot be granted based on an employee's decision to participate or not participate in a 401(k) plan. Deferred compensation falls under this rule, but the regulations permit deferred compensation so long as the employee will not receive greater benefits by participating or not participating in the 401(k) plan. Thus, it would be acceptable for an employer to offer a supplemental plan that assumed the employee deferred the maximum amount under the qualified plan and permitted nonqualified deferrals over and above that level. It would not be acceptable for the employer to offer a plan that allowed an employee to elect nonqualified deferrals in lieu of qualified deferrals. IRS Reg. 1.401(k)-1(e)(6).

5. These arrangements are discussed in more detail in Chapter 3.

6. See Chapter 10 for a discussion of how this investment income is taxed.

7. See also Chapters 9 and 10.

8. See, for example, PLR 8804057 (11/4/87); PLR 9332038 (5/18/93); PLR 9015022 (1/11/90); PLR 8822051 (3/4/88).

9. Common practice is to recognize only the executive's Primary Social Security benefit. However, the executive's total Social Security benefit, including amounts payable on account of the executive's spouse, may also be considered.

10. This discussion covers only ERISA and tax law implications. Employment arrangements that include noncompete clauses and forfeitures are subject to general legal requirements as to reasonableness and as to whether they constitute an improper restraint on trade.

11. As is the case with greater early retirement subsidies, a wrap-around SERP with more liberal vesting than the base plan can provide supplemental benefits to a terminating executive equal to the value of his or her nonvested benefits in the base plan.

12. In 1993, the Medicare tax of 1.45 percent (on employers and employees) applied only on wages up to $135,000.

13. See Chapter 4 for a discussion of top hat requirements.

14. IRS Reg. Section 1.401(a)(17)-1.

15. IRS Reg. Section 1.401(a)(17)-1, 56 FR 47603 (9/9/91).

16. IRS Reg. 1.401(a)(17)-1(e)(3).

17. As noted in Chapter 1, the Section 415 limit on annual benefits payable from a defined benefit plan is $90,000 (indexed; $118,800 for 1994); the annual defined contribution limit is $30,000.

18. See Chapter 1, footnote 4.

19. For the IRS definition of HCE, see Chapter 10, footnote 13.

20. See Chapter 11 for an additional discussion of FICA.

Chapter Seven

Plan Design: Health and Welfare Plans

The term *health and welfare plan* can encompass any number of arrangements, including perquisites and statutory fringe benefits. This chapter focuses on the three major health and welfare plans employers provide for their executives—death, disability income, and health care benefits.[1]

Note at the outset that, with the exception of self-insured health care plans, federal tax law does not impose severe nondiscrimination rules on health and welfare benefits. The tax law requirements that do exist differ for each type of benefit with respect to: (1) the definition of the group that cannot be provided with discriminatory benefits (without penalty), (2) the nondiscrimination tests that apply, (3) the mechanics of these tests, and (4) the penalties invoked if the plan is found to be discriminatory.[2]

DEATH BENEFITS

Employers have a number of options for providing death benefits for their executives. One is to pay benefits in cash out of corporate assets. This can produce adverse income and estate tax consequences, however: payments will be taxable as income to the beneficiaries and will be included in the executive's gross estate for federal estate tax purposes if the executive had the right to receive amounts while alive or had the right to name the beneficiary.

In general, income and estate tax treatment is more favorable if employers provide death benefits through some type of life insurance mechanism—typically through additional amounts of group life insurance. Use of some type of individual permanent life insurance—so-called corporate-owned life insurance (COLI) or split-dollar arrangements—is also common.

Because of the special nature of individual life insurance policies, their tax treatment and financial structure is discussed separately in Chapter 12. The following discussion of federal tax law relates primarily to group term life insurance and group universal life programs.

Federal Tax Law—Group Term Life Insurance

To fully appreciate the potential after-tax value of executive group life insurance, it is helpful to have a basic understanding of the applicable tax law, including the deductibility of employer contributions, the taxation of employees under a nondiscriminatory plan, and the penalties associated with discriminatory coverage.

Deductibility of employer contributions. Employer contributions for group life insurance premiums are deductible when made, regardless of whether the plan provides discriminatory benefits.[3]

Taxation of employees. Under Section 79 of the Internal Revenue Code (IRC), employees are considered to have taxable income each year equal to the value of any group life insurance provided by the employer's plan. If the plan meets the nondiscrimination requirements of Section 79 (both an eligibility and a benefits test), the cost of the first $50,000 of coverage is excludable from the employee's taxable income. The amount of reportable income for insurance in excess of $50,000 will be determined by rates published by the IRS, the so-called Section 79 rates, as shown in Table 7–1.

The amount of reportable income otherwise determined under Section 79 will be reduced by the amount of any employee contributions toward the cost of coverage, including contributions made for the first $50,000 of coverage. It is important to note that a fully contributory plan is not subject to Section 79 requirements. A plan will be considered fully contributory if all employees contribute, at all ages, either more or less than the Section 79 rates, and if there is no significant employer involvement.

In most situations, the actual cost of the coverage will be less than Section 79 rates. This, in conjunction with the tax liability that employees incur when Section 79 does apply, argues in favor of fully contributory coverage that escapes the application of Section 79.

Assume, for example, that a 55-year-old executive will receive $1,000,000 of employer-paid coverage, $950,000 of which is taxable.

TABLE 7–1
Reportable Income per $1,000 of Coverage
Under Nondiscriminatory Group Life Insurance

Age Bracket	Reportable Income (monthly)
Under 30	$ .08
30–34	.09
35–39	.11
40–44	.17
45–49	.29
50–54	.48
55–59	.75
60–64	1.17
65–69	2.17
70 and above	3.76

Assume further that the executive is in a 39.6 percent tax bracket, the monthly employer premium for coverage at her age is $.29, and the applicable Section 79 rate is $.75. Under this scenario, the annual employer cost for the coverage is $3,306 (950 × $.29 × 12). The executive will also owe $3,385 in taxes (950 × $.75 × 12 × .396). Thus, the total economic cost of the purchase is $6,691 ($3,306 + $3,385).

Suppose that the employer gives the executive a cash bonus of $3,306 instead of contributing that amount toward coverage. If she applies her after-tax proceeds of $1,997 toward the insurance premium, she will only need to contribute an additional $1,309 ($3,306 − $1,997) to obtain the $1,000,000 in coverage. Under this scenario, her out-of-pocket cost of $1,309 represents a savings of $2,076, and her employer's cost is unchanged.

Discriminatory coverage. If the plan fails to meet the nondiscrimination requirements of Section 79, key employees will lose the $50,000 exclusion.[4] Further, reportable income for these employees will be determined by the actual cost of the insurance if that cost exceeds the Section 79 rates. Except for very old retirees, this will rarely be the case. Thus, for all practical purposes, the only real penalty for discriminatory coverage is the loss of the $50,000 exclusion.

A 62-year-old executive in a 39.6 percent tax bracket who loses the $50,000 exclusion will have additional taxable income of $702 (the Section 79 monthly rate of $1.17 × 12 × 50), for example. This would result in an additional tax of $278 (39.6 percent of $702). Grossing up the executive's pay to cover the additional tax would require an additional but deductible contribution of $460 ($278 ÷ 1 − the employee's 39.6 percent tax rate).

This penalty is quite small relative to the potential tax advantages life insurance can provide. Life insurance proceeds are tax-free to the beneficiary, even under a discriminatory plan. While the value of life insurance is includable in the employee's gross estate for estate tax purposes, it will qualify for the marital deduction if payable to a spouse. Further, if the executive assigns all rights of ownership in the insurance at least three years prior to death, no part of the proceeds will be includable in the gross estate. Thus, life insurance gives employers a tax-deductible opportunity to provide executives with a substantial benefit that can escape both income and estate taxation. For an executive who is concerned about building and conserving an estate, this benefit can be quite significant.

Federal Tax Law—Group Universal Life Insurance

Group universal life plans (GULP) are growing in popularity, and more and more employers are using them to replace or supplement conventional group term life insurance arrangements.

Coverage.   GULP has two elements—term life insurance that is much the same as group term life insurance, plus an optional savings or cash value feature (sometimes referred to as the sidefund). GULP is fully contributory (with no employer financial support) and, if properly designed, is not subject to Section 79.

The term insurance portion is underwritten on a group basis, with premiums usually based on the underlying mortality experience of the employer's group of insured employees. Each covered employee has the option of contributing additional amounts (within statutory limits) to create a savings fund, which is credited with a competitive rate of interest that is guaranteed for a period of time.[5] If the employee dies, the death benefit is the sum of the term insurance in force plus any amount in his or her savings account (principal contributions and interest).

Key characteristics of GULP include the following:

- Coverage can be discriminatory and can, for example, be written to cover only an executive group or to provide this group with additional coverage. (The extent to which this can be accomplished, of course, depends upon the insurer's underwriting flexibility.)
- Employee contributions are made with after-tax dollars.
- The coverage is portable; employees who leave for retirement or any other reason can continue the insurance in force by paying premiums directly to the insurer. Typically, retirees will pay premiums that are supported by the experience of the employer's active employees; other terminations will pay premiums based on the insurer's pool of similar coverage. This can be of significant value to an executive who wants to keep full coverage in force after retirement to meet estate planning needs.
- Employees have significant savings flexibility (within statutory limits), including the ability to vary or suspend the rate of savings for specific periods or on an indefinite basis, and the ability to make lump sum contributions from time to time.
- Employees can withdraw all or any part of their savings at any time.
- The employee can make loans from the insurer at any time using the savings account as collateral.
- At retirement, the employee has several options, including: (1) continuing to pay premiums (for term insurance only or for both term insurance and savings), (2) using existing cash values to pay future term insurance premiums, (3) surrendering the coverage for its cash value, and (4) using existing cash values to purchase paid-up insurance.

Taxation.   Because GULP is not subject to Section 79, there are no nondiscrimination standards that must be met under federal tax law, nor is there any problem with respect to imputed income for the value of the coverage.

If the program is properly structured, interest credited to an employee's savings account will accumulate free of income tax under the general tax shelter that applies to most life insurance products. This means the coverage must meet the definition of life insurance in Section 7702(a) of the IRC. While this section limits the amount of savings relative to the amount of term insurance in force on the employee's life, the limits are high enough to create a significant savings opportunity.

TABLE 7–2
Taxation of GULP Interest

20-year results:

Total insurance premiums:		$ 76,800
Total savings value:		
Contribution		$120,000
Interest		140,460
		$260,460

Calculation of taxable gain:

Total savings value:		$260,460
Less cost basis:		
Contribution	$120,000	
Premiums	76,800	
		196,800
Net taxable gain:		$ 63,660

If paid as part of a death benefit, the interest credited to the employee's account will be treated as tax-free life insurance proceeds. This is an attractive tax shelter for the executive who does not need the savings fund for current living or other expenses; the investment income could escape income taxation completely, and it would also escape estate taxation if paid to a spouse or if the executive assigned ownership rights at least three years prior to death.

Interest accumulations paid out while the employee is alive will be taxable as ordinary income as follows:

- Under the basis recovery rules, the first amounts withdrawn will be considered a return of the employee's investment in the contract (i.e., his or her after-tax contributions).[6]
- No penalty or excess distribution taxes will apply to the withdrawal.[7]
- Any amounts contributed by the employee for term life insurance will be added to his or her investment in the contract and will thus operate to reduce the amount of the taxable gain.

Table 7–2 illustrates the potential value of this last item, showing how the otherwise taxable investment gain under GULP over a 20-year period can be significantly reduced by the amount of insurance premiums paid. The table assumes $1,000,000 in insurance coverage for an executive who

TABLE 7–3
Executive Death Benefit Insurance Schedules

Schedule	Percentage of Companies
Percent of pay	
100	10%
200	26
300	11
400	8
Other	32
Total	87%
Flat dollar amount	4%
Other	9%

was age 40 when the insurance took effect, saves $500 per month, and earns interest income of 7 percent per year. Insurance rates for this executive range from $.16 per month per $1,000 at age 40 up to $.52 per month at age 55. The total interest income of $140,460 is reduced by accumulated insurance premiums of $76,800, leaving only $63,660 subject to taxation.

This tax treatment can be an important advantage for some executives. As noted earlier, contributory coverage is in itself a cost-effective device. If contributions can also serve to lower taxes on investment earnings, it is even more cost-effective.

Benefit Structure

Of the 180 companies in the Towers Perrin Executive Benefit Data Base who maintain SERPs for their executives, only 32 percent have executive death benefit plans. These plans have been established to meet one or more objectives: to provide additional benefits, to assist in midcareer recruiting, to recognize incentive pay, and so forth.

Most plans in the Executive Benefit Data Base provide a benefit that is pay-related. A breakdown of the benefit schedules used in these plans is shown in Table 7–3.

About one-half of these companies provide a benefit that is related to base pay only; the others relate the benefit to a combination of base pay, incentive pay, and/or deferred compensation. Despite the tax advantages of contributory plans, 74 percent of these companies offer noncontributory coverage.

Split-dollar life insurance is used to fund the executive death benefit in 43 percent of the companies in the Towers Perrin Data Base. Eighteen percent of these companies use COLI; another 9 percent use group life insurance. Executive-owned life insurance and company book reserves are less common.

A key design issue is whether to continue the death benefit after the executive retires. While postretirement coverage can be expensive, it can play an important role in meeting the estate planning needs of executives. Most companies in the Towers Perrin Data Base continue executive death benefit coverage in one form or another for retirees.

DISABILITY INCOME BENEFITS

Federal Tax Law

In general, federal tax law does not require that disability income plans meet any nondiscrimination standards.[8] Further, there are no adverse tax consequences if employers provide additional or different benefits for highly compensated employees.

The tax treatment of disability income contributions and/or benefits is as follows:

- Employer contributions to pay benefits or insurance premiums are deductible when paid.[9]
- Employer contributions to pay insurance premiums or to create reasonable reserves will not be taxable to employees when made.
- Benefit payments attributable to employer contributions will be taxable as ordinary income when received.
- Benefit payments attributable to after-tax employee contributions will not be taxable.[10]

Benefit Structure

Only 25 percent of the companies in the Towers Perrin Executive Benefit Data Base offer executive disability income plans. Nevertheless, these benefits can be important and can help to achieve a number of employer objectives.

The typical broad-based disability income plan consists of two parts—a short-term plan and a long-term plan. The short-term plan usually provides for the continuation of full pay for a limited number of days or weeks. The period of full and/or partial pay typically increases with length of service, as does the total period for which benefits are paid. In most plans, short-term benefits are payable for a maximum of six months.

Benefits under the long-term portion of the plan, payable when the disability continues beyond the short-term maximum, are often set at a specified level of pay, typically around 60 percent (including Social Security benefits), and are usually limited to a maximum monthly benefit of a specified dollar amount (e.g., $5,000 or $10,000). These dollar maximums are often established by the insurer who underwrites the plan benefits. It is also common to require the employee to complete a minimum period of service (such as one or two years) before becoming eligible for long-term coverage.

This configuration presents two problems for executives. The first is that newly employed executives may not receive any significant protection—under either the short- or long-term plans—because of service requirements. Thus, most executive disability income plans provide coverage immediately upon employment. Many of them also continue full pay for a much longer period than the broad-based plan—full pay for up to six months or one year, regardless of length of service, for example.

The second problem is that the dollar maximum may produce inadequate benefits in terms of the executive's actual pay. Thus, many executive disability income plans impose no dollar maximum on long-term benefits or use a dollar maximum that is much higher than that applicable to the broad-based plan—$20,000 per month, for example.

Employer objectives in offering executive disability income plans include the following:

- Granting a benefit more generous than that available under the broad-based plan.
- Providing a benefit that reflects both base salary and short-term incentive pay (in situations where the base plan benefit relates to base pay only).
- Including deferred compensation in the definition of pay used to determine benefits.
- Extending benefit payments for nervous and mental conditions (which broad-based plans typically limit to a period such as two years unless the employee is confined to a hospital).

- Defining disability more broadly than the base plan—to include, for example, the executive's inability to do his or her own job, where the base plan might define disability as the inability to perform any job for which an employee is suited by reason of education, experience, or training.

An employer can establish an executive disability income plan as a separate plan or, as is often the case, a plan that wraps around the base plan. Most employers provide executive disability income benefits on a self-insured basis, establishing book reserves as necessary and disbursing benefits from corporate assets. Some companies use either group or individual insurance policies to provide part or all of an executive's long-term benefits.

HEALTH CARE

Employer health care plans that are insured are not subject to nondiscrimination standards. Self-insured health care plans are subject to nondiscrimination rules under Section 105(h) of the Internal Revenue Code (IRC). Note, however, that employer health care plans provided through a tax-exempt trust under Section 501(c)(9) of the IRC are subject to the nondiscrimination rules even if the benefits are insured. Similarly, insured health care plans are subject to the nondiscrimination rules of IRC Section 125 if they are part of a flexible benefits plan.

Insured plans.　　To qualify as an insured plan and avoid discrimination testing, a plan must transfer risk from the employer to an unrelated third party. The fact that an insurance company may be involved does not mean that the plan is considered to be insured. Minimum premium contracts or cost-plus arrangements with insurers with no meaningful limit would probably not be considered to be insured. Administrative-services-only contracts are clearly not insured even though an insurer handles all claims.

If a plan is considered to be insured and if it is not part of a Section 501(c)(9) or Section 125 arrangement, the federal tax situation is as follows:

- The plan can be completely discriminatory in terms of coverage and benefits without adverse tax consequences.
- Employer contributions to pay insurance premiums are deductible.

- Employer contributions to pay premiums are not taxable as income to the covered employee.
- Any benefits payable to or on behalf of an insured employee are not taxable.

Self-insured plans. Section 105(h) of the IRC establishes nondiscrimination standards for self-insured plans (including self-insured parts of a program that also involves insurance). There are two tests: an eligibility test and a benefits test. To meet the eligibility test, the plan must cover 70 percent or more of all employees, or 80 percent of those eligible if 70 percent are eligible. To meet the benefits test, each benefit available to highly compensated employees must be available to all other participants. A plan that meets both tests will be treated as an insured plan for federal tax purposes. If a plan fails the tests, federal tax treatment is as follows:

- Employer contributions will be deductible.[11]
- Employer contributions, as such, will not be taxable to employees.
- Benefits payable for nonhighly compensated employees will not be taxable.
- All or part of the benefits payable for highly compensated employees will be taxable.[12] If the plan fails the eligibility test, the taxable amount is the amount the highly compensated employee receives under the plan that is attributable to employer contributions, multiplied by the ratio of the total amount paid for all highly compensated employees to the total amount paid for all plan participants. If the plan fails the benefits test, all amounts received under the discriminatory part of the plan attributable to employer contributions are taxable. Benefits attributable to the employee's own contributions are not taxable.
- Reimbursements paid under a plan for "medical diagnostic procedures" for the employee (but not dependents) are exempt from nondiscrimination testing. This exception does not apply to expenses incurred for treatment, cure, or testing of known illnesses, nor does it apply to activities undertaken for exercise, fitness, nutrition, recreation, or the general improvement of health. An executive's annual physical examination conducted at the executive's personal physician's office is not subject to discrimination testing. If the examination is conducted at a resort, however, it will be subject to the nondiscrimination tests.

Benefit Structure

Most medical expense plans include deductibles, coinsurance features, and dollar limitations on certain procedures and provide no coverage at all for specified expenses. It is also common for these plans to restrict coverage of employee dependents to specified individuals.

Because of tax considerations, self-insured executive health care plans are not widespread. Insured plans do exist where insurers are willing to underwrite the coverage. To the extent that special benefits are provided for executives, they usually include one or more of the following:

- Coverage of medical expenses not included in the broad-based plan—for example, cosmetic surgery or certain custodial expenses associated with the delivery of otherwise qualified health care services.
- Payment of out-of-pocket costs of the base plan—deductibles, coinsurance payments, expenses in excess of inside plan limits, and the like. This can be a significant benefit in the case of outpatient psychiatric care, which is usually subject to strict limits in the base plan, and in point-of-service managed care programs where the executive chooses out-of-network treatment.
- Waiver of expenses associated with preexisting conditions at the time the executive is employed.
- Extension of coverage to dependents not covered under the base plan (e.g., dependent parents and/or children who no longer qualify as dependents because of age).

NOTES

1. See Chapter 15 for a discussion of golden parachutes, and Chapter 16 for more information on perquisites.
2. A detailed discussion of these requirements is beyond the scope of this text. For such a discussion, see Jerry S. Rosenbloom, *The Handbook of Employee Benefits*, 3rd ed. (Homewood, IL: Irwin, 1992), Chapter 50.
3. Contributions that establish excess reserves will not be deductible and, of course, there is the overriding requirement that contributions be reasonable and that they constitute an ordinary and necessary business expense.
4. A key employee is one who, at any time during the plan year or any of the four preceding plan years, is: (1) an officer with annual compensation in excess of 50 percent of the $90,000 (indexed) Section 415 defined benefit limit; (2) one of the 10 employees with annual compensation greater than the $30,000 (to be indexed) Section 415 defined contribution limit owning the

largest interests in the employer; (3) a 5 percent owner; or (4) a 1 percent owner with annual compensation greater than $150,000. A retired employee is included if he or she was a key employee at the time of retirement.

5. Some insurers may offer a group variable life product that allows the savings element to be invested in an equity portfolio. Under this type of product, there would be no guarantee of a fixed rate of return; however, there would be the opportunity for gains and losses associated with market performance.

6. These basis recovery rules will not apply if the coverage is determined to be a modified endowment contract under Section 7702(A) of the IRC, in which event amounts withdrawn will be taxed on an earnings-first basis under Section 72(2)(10). However, this result can be avoided under a properly drawn and administered arrangement.

7. A 10 percent tax could apply to distributions made under a modified endowment contract but, as noted, this result could be avoided by a properly constructed arrangement.

8. Disability income benefits funded through a voluntary employee benefit association (VEBA) must meet the nondiscrimination requirements of Section 505 of the IRC, which requires that the plan (in terms of coverage and benefits) not discriminate in favor of highly compensated employees, as defined for qualified pension plan purposes. Also, if a disability income benefit is based upon compensation in excess of $150,000 (indexed), the plan will be discriminatory. Because of these requirements, VEBAs are not used to fund executive disability income benefits.

9. As with other benefits, contributions to establish excessive reserves will not be deductible and cost must be reasonable and must constitute an ordinary and necessary business expense.

10. If employee contributions are made on a before-tax basis under a flexible benefit plan, they are treated as though they were employer contributions; thus, benefits attributable to such before-tax contributions will be taxable when received.

11. As mentioned for other plans, the contributions must be reasonable and must constitute an ordinary and necessary business expense. Further, contributions to create excessive reserves will not be deductible. It should also be noted that while the investment income on employee benefit plan reserves is generally exempt from income taxation, this will not be the case for reserves held for the purpose of providing postretirement health care benefits; here, the investment income will be taxed as though it were unrelated business income.

12. For purposes of Section 105(h), a highly compensated employee is: (1) one of the five highest paid officers, (2) a 10 percent owner, or (3) an employee who is among the highest paid 25 percent of all employees other than employees who have less than three years of service or who are under age 25.

Chapter Eight

Accounting

Accrual accounting attempts to recognize the financial effects of transactions and events that have future cash consequences for an entity when the underlying transaction or event occurs, rather than when cash is received or paid out. If an executive elects to defer a portion of his or her compensation to future periods, for example, accrual accounting requires that the company recognize the executive's full compensation—both amounts to be paid currently and the portion deferred—as an expense of the current period. At the same time, the company will reduce cash for the compensation paid currently and set up a liability for the compensation deferred for payment in future periods. Accrual accounting is required under generally accepted accounting principles.

This chapter reviews the accounting requirements applicable to various deferred compensation arrangements. In order to approach the subject from a total compensation expense perspective, it includes information on accounting for stock compensation programs as well as for benefit programs.

DEFERRED COMPENSATION

Deferred compensation is the result of an exchange agreement between an employer and one or more selected key employees or executives; the employer agrees to pay cash or benefits in the future in exchange for the executive's current service. As the key employee or executive renders the necessary service, the company accrues the expected cost of and liability for the future payments or benefits.

In some cases, individual deferred compensation contracts, considered collectively, might be equivalent to a postretirement or postemployment benefit plan. Because of the differences in accounting for individual contracts that provide a unique benefit for each individual and contracts with a group of individuals that provide a similar benefit for all the individuals (a "plan"), which are discussed later in this chapter, employers should analyze the nature of such arrangements very carefully.

Accounting Principles Board Opinion No. 12, *Omnibus Opinion—1967* (APB 12), sets forth the accounting treatment for individual deferred compensation contracts. Do not be misled by the term *contract*. In general, if an employer has a substantive commitment, written or unwritten, to provide certain compensation or benefits, the accounting should reflect the substance of the agreement (the implied *contract*).

If an employer has a practice of continuing health care coverage for retired senior executives, for example, that practice creates an implied contract that is the basis for the accounting. The fact that the practice is not documented by a formal written policy does not override the notion that, based on past practice, the company has a substantive commitment to continue to provide retiree medical coverage for senior executives. (This presumption can be overcome by clear evidence, such as written communication, that the benefit has been or will be discontinued, however.) Because payment of medical benefits during retirement is viewed as an exchange for service rendered to the company, the present value of the benefits expected to be paid is accrued ratably over the executive's relevant service period with the company.

Measurement

The amount to be accrued under a deferred compensation arrangement is measured as the present value of the amount or amounts expected to be paid in future periods. Consequently, the measurement requires estimates of the amount and expected timing of any future payments. APB 12 specifies that "such estimates should be based on the life expectancy of each individual concerned (based on the most recent mortality tables available) or on the estimated cost of an annuity contract, rather than on the minimum payable in the event of early death." Employers should review the reasonableness of the measurement assumptions (such as expected retirement date and mortality) annually, accounting for any adjustments to the liability accrued to date as a change in estimate. Note that, as with measurements for stock compensation plans, there is an underlying presumption that the individual will meet the service requirements of the agreement.

Although the measurement is to be discounted, APB 12 does not provide guidance on the selection of a discount rate. As a result, many accountants follow the guidance provided by FASB Statement No. 87, *Employers' Accounting for Pensions* (FAS 87), and No. 106, *Employers' Accounting for Postretirement Benefits Other Than Pensions* (FAS 106). Those statements, discussed later in this chapter, require employers to look to rates of return on high-quality fixed-income investments currently available, whose cash flows match the timing and amount of expected benefit payments, in developing the assumed discount rate.

APB 12 provides no guidance on how changes in the assumed discount rate should be recognized. The predominant practice is not to change the discount rate once it has been selected; as a result, future costs are measured using the rate fixed at the initiation of the individual contract. Another practice, which is consistent with FAS 87 and FAS 106, is to adjust the discount rate to reflect changes in the economic environment, with the resulting change in the measurement of the past service liability recognized as a gain or loss.

Recognition

The present value of expected payments or benefits is to be accrued over the periods of service the individual must render in exchange for the future compensation payments or benefits.

APB 12, as amended, requires that "to the extent the terms of the contract attribute all or a portion of the expected future benefits to an individual year of the executive's service, the cost of those benefits shall be recognized in that year. To the extent the terms of the contract attribute all or a portion of the expected future benefits to a period of service greater than one year, the cost of those benefits shall be accrued over that period of the executive's service in a systematic and rational manner." In other words, the present value of the cost of the expected benefits should be accrued from the date the contract is entered into until the date the executive has earned the right to terminate and receive the benefits; the cost is to be accrued in the same manner in which the benefits are earned (benefits are attributed to service following the benefit formula). The underlying notion is that the employer should have fully accrued the present value of the cost of the expected benefits at the time the executive has completed his or her part of the exchange agreement.

Because the amount accrued each period is a present-value-based measurement, interest cost on the accumulated liability also must be accrued each period. Interest cost is measured by multiplying the liability that has accrued to date by the assumed discount rate. The interest cost accrual will steadily increase during an executive's service period, reflecting an ever-increasing liability as additional benefits are attributed to the executive's service and the liability is one year closer to payment.

To illustrate, assume a company enters into an agreement to pay its chief financial officer a supplemental pension benefit of $10,000 per month, provided the CFO retires on or after attaining age 55 and has 10 or more years of service. The CFO is currently 50 years old and has worked for the company for nine years. Because the CFO will be fully eligible for the supplemental pension benefit at age 55, the present value of the pension benefits expected to be paid (based on the life expectancy of the individual) should be accrued ratably over the CFO's next five years of service. If the CFO were already age 55 and had worked for the company for nine years, the cost of the expected benefits would be attributed to the next year of service; at the end of that year, the CFO would have met the 10-year service requirement.

In addition, interest cost would be accrued each year for the remainder of the CFO's life, to reflect the time value of money on the measure of the remaining liability. If the CFO were expected to retire at age 60 and live to age 70, for example, the present value of the company's liability accrued when the CFO turned 60 would be $824,215, assuming an 8 percent discount rate. In the following year, the company would recognize interest cost of $63,910 (the average accrued liability during the year times 8 percent), which would increase the accrued liability; the accrued liability would be reduced by the $120,000 in benefit payments during the year. At the end of the year the accrued liability would be $768,125.

Elements of deferred compensation for both current and future service complicate the attribution process. APB 12 states that "if elements of both current and future compensation are present, only the portion attributable to the current services should be accrued."

Suppose a contract states that the company will provide a $2,000 per month supplemental pension benefit in exchange for an executive's past and future service and for consulting services to be provided following retirement. The executive is currently eligible to retire and would be entitled to supplemental benefits. If the company expects future benefits from the consulting services to be minimal, the present value of the expected pension benefits would be accrued in its entirety at the date the contract is entered into.

However, assume instead that a company enters into an agreement to continue an executive's base pay for five years past retirement in exchange for substantive consulting services to be provided during that period.

Because it is not reasonable to assume that an executive will continue to receive the same compensation for substantially less work, the employer must allocate the salary continuation agreement between current and postretirement service.

Let's say the executive currently receives annual base pay of $300,000, averages 60 hours of work per week, and will work five more years before retiring. During retirement, he will work an average of eight hours per week. To come up with a reasonable allocation, the employer would develop an average hourly rate based on the executive's expected service and expected pay over the next 10 years (the five years prior to retirement plus the five years after retirement covered by the contract): $300,000 × 10 years divided by 5 years (60 hours × 52 weeks) + 5 years (8 hours × 52 weeks) = $3,000,000/17,680 hours = $169.68/hour. Thus, only $352,941 (5 × 8 × 52 × $169.68) of the $1,500,000 expected to be paid during the executive's retirement is attributable to service during that period. The remaining $1,147,058 ($1,500,000 − $352,941) should be attributed ratably over the executive's next (and final) five years of full-time service.

PARACHUTES AND OTHER CONTINGENCIES

A *parachute* is an employment contract that becomes operative only when there is a change in control of the company.[1] Such a contract is intended to attract executive talent to a company that may become a takeover target, to ensure management's objectivity in addressing shareholder interests in a takeover bid by minimizing concern over personal financial consequences, and increase the cost, and thus reduce the attractiveness, of a takeover.

From an accounting perspective, parachutes need be expensed only when it is probable that a change in company control will trigger payment of the contractual liability. FASB Statement No. 5, *Accounting for Contingencies* (FAS5), precludes a company from setting up a reserve for "loss contingencies" until it is likely a liability has been incurred and the amount of the payment is reasonably estimable.

Signing Bonus

If a company pays a signing bonus to an executive recruit, and the bonus is not contingent on the individual's continued service, it should be expensed immediately. If the newly hired executive must return all or part of the bonus if he or she resigns within a stated time period, say two years, then the cost of the bonus should be accrued ratably over that two-year period. Similar accounting should be followed for reimbursed moving costs and for executive placement services.

POSTEMPLOYMENT BENEFITS

There is generally a presumption that defined benefits provided under an ERISA plan, excess benefits provided to individuals under an ERISA top hat plan, or fixed or formula-related benefits provided to executives who meet certain service or responsibility levels in the organization should be accounted for as a plan in accordance with FAS 87, FAS 106, or FAS 112 (FASB Statement No. 112, *Employers' Accounting for Postemployment Benefits*). If these conditions are not met and benefits are provided to selected executives under separate contracts, with terms determined on an individual-by-individual basis, the accounting generally should follow APB 12.

FAS 87 covers an employer's accounting for plans that provide retirement income benefits; FAS 106 covers an employer's accounting for plans that provide health and welfare benefits after retirement. The accounting specified by those statements results in accrual, over the relevant service periods of the plan participants, of the present value of the benefits expected to be provided. Because the accounting encompasses a group of individuals, actuarial probabilities are used in the measurement process, and gains and losses arising from experience different from that assumed can be recognized systematically over future periods, instead of being recognized immediately as is required under APB 12.[2]

FAS 112 covers an employer's accounting for benefits provided to former executives and to inactive executives who currently are not working, but who are expected to return to work. Included in the inactive executive category are executives on disability leave or sabbatical, and those who are receiving workers compensation benefits. Examples of postemployment benefits include short- and long-term disability income benefits, continuation of medical and life insurance coverage, workers' compensation benefits, and supplemental unemployment benefits.

In general, FAS 112 requires that an employer accrue the expected cost of service-related postemployment benefits over the relevant executive service periods if payment of the benefit is probable and reasonably estimable. Otherwise, the expected cost of the benefit must be accrued when the event triggering payment occurs. For example, if the number of weeks of salary continuation under a disability plan is based on years of service, the expected salary continuation payments (based on the probability and duration of a disabling event) should be accrued over executives' relevant service periods. On the other hand, the expected cost of a workers' compensation claim would not be accrued until an executive is injured because the amount of the benefit payment is unrelated to the executive's years of service.

LIFE INSURANCE

Accounting for life insurance benefits depends on the nature of the insurance arrangement. Term life, corporate-owned life, and split-dollar life are discussed in the paragraphs that follow.

Term Life Insurance Coverage

Term life insurance coverage for a working executive provides a lump sum benefit to a beneficiary if the executive dies. If the plan is insured, the employer expenses the premium cost over the covered period.

Opinions diverge as to how employers that self-insure should account for this benefit. The more common view is that the employer should recognize the cost of the benefit when an executive dies. This view is based on FAS 5 accounting, which requires that a loss be recognized when it is probable a liability has been incurred and the amount is reasonably estimable, and precludes anticipation of loss contingencies. The other view analogizes to FAS 87 and FAS 106, and results in the accrual, over the executive's service period, of death benefits expected to be paid on behalf of an executive who dies while in service.

Death benefits provided to retired executives are covered under FAS 87 (if the benefit is provided through the pension plan) or FAS 106 (if the benefit is provided outside the pension plan).

Corporate-Owned Life Insurance

Companies often use corporate-owned life insurance (COLI), covering the lives of key executives, to fund deferred compensation arrangements.[3] The life insurance coverage might be designed to reimburse the company for premiums paid on the policy, the deferred compensation payments to the executive, and interest on policy loans, net of the related tax savings. Because the cash surrender value of the COLI is an asset of the company, FASB Technical Bulletin No. 85-4, *Accounting for Purchases of Life Insurance* (TB 85-4), requires that the life insurance contract be accounted for separately from any deferred compensation agreement to which it may relate.

TB 85-4 requires use of the cash surrender value method of accounting for life insurance. Under this method, as premiums are paid, the increase in the cash surrender value of the policy increases the company's asset; any excess of the premium over the increased cash surrender value is expensed. Thus, the cash surrender value of the life insurance at any point in time is reported as a long-term asset of the company. When the insured executive dies, the excess of the death benefit over the cash surrender value is recognized as income.

For example, if the company pays a $5,000 insurance premium and the cash surrender value of the policy increases by $3,500, the company would expense $1,500. If the cash surrender value of a $100,000 policy is $24,000 when the covered executive dies, the company would recognize cash of $100,000, a $24,000 reduction in its long-term asset and a gain of $76,000. That gain may be sufficient to reimburse the company for expenses recognized pursuant to a deferred compensation agreement.

If the life insurance policy contains a loan feature, borrowings may be netted against the cash surrender value asset only if the company has the legal right and the intent to offset the loan against the cash surrender value rather than repaying the loan.

Split-Dollar Life Insurance

In a split-dollar life insurance arrangement,[4] the company and the executive share the premium cost of the executive's life insurance policy, with the executive designating the beneficiary for at least a part of the benefit. The advantage of this approach is that the company can provide life insurance at minimal cost to the executive.

Although the executive may pay a part of the premium cost outright, the company usually pays the full premium cost and, in effect, makes an interest-free loan to the executive for the benefits of the policy. When the executive dies, the company is reimbursed for the premiums paid through receipt of the cash surrender value of the life insurance policy and payment of the note from the insurance proceeds.

The accounting treatment of this arrangement focuses only on the balance sheet; the company recognizes no income or expense. As the company pays the insurance premium, it records the increase in cash surrender value as a long-term asset; the premium payment in excess of the increased cash surrender value is recorded as a note receivable from a related party. (Disclosure of a noninterest-bearing note from a management executive may be required in the company's annual report on Form 10-K.) When the executive dies, the company should receive an amount from the death benefit equal to its total premiums paid. All remaining proceeds go to the beneficiary.

STOCK COMPENSATION

Many companies use stock to reward current performance or as an incentive for future performance. Executive stock plans are either compensatory (i.e., the cost of the plan is accounted for as compensation expense) or noncompensatory. In order to be noncompensatory, a plan must meet all of the following conditions set forth in APB No. 25, *Accounting for Stock Issued to Employees*:

- Substantially all full-time employees meeting limited employment qualifications may participate in the plan, although employees owning a specified percentage of the stock and executives may be excluded.
- Stock options or awards granted to eligible employees are equal or are based on a uniform percentage of salary, although the plan may limit the number of shares an employee may purchase through the plan.
- The time permitted for exercise is limited to a reasonable period (generally five years or less).
- The discount from the market price of the stock is no greater than would be reasonable if the offer were made to shareholders or others (generally no more than 15 percent).

A statutory employee stock purchase plan under Section 423 of the Internal Revenue Code (IRC) is an example of a noncompensatory plan. Most plans are compensatory. But there is no compensation expense even under a compensatory plan if the exercise price equals or exceeds the market price at date of grant, as described in the following paragraphs.

Measuring Compensation Expense

At present, compensation expense is measured at the first date on which both the number of shares and the option or award price per share are known, and equals the excess of the market value of the option or award over the price the executive must pay. Note, however, that the FASB has issued an exposure draft of a proposed standard, *Accounting for Stock-Based Compensation*, that would require measurement of expected compensation cost when an option or award is granted, with subsequent adjustments to reflect the outcome of service- and performance-related conditions. The proposed standard is described later in this chapter.

If both the number of shares and the price per share are known at the grant date, then the compensation cost, if any, is fixed at that date. For example, under a traditional market value stock option arrangement, an option is granted for a specified period of time to purchase a fixed number of shares at a fixed price per share that is equal to the quoted market price of the stock at the date of grant. Since both the number of shares and price per share are known at the grant date, the measurement date is the grant date. Further, because the exercise price equals the market price at the measurement date, compensation expense is zero. Most stock option plans are fixed plans.

On the other hand, if either the number of shares or price per share is unknown at the date of grant (a "variable" plan), the company will adjust its compensation cost each reporting period to reflect changes to the then-best estimate of the final compensation cost, until both the number of shares and price per share are known (the measurement date). Stock appreciation rights are an example of a variable plan: the total compensation is not known until the executive exercises his or her right to receive cash and/or stock. As noted above, the compensation expense is measured at the measurement date as the excess of the quoted market price of the stock over the price the executive will pay. This principle applies whether the stock-based award is restricted or unrestricted.

If the employer uses treasury stock to satisfy the award, it can use the cost of the treasury stock to measure compensation expense only if the stock was reacquired during the fiscal period for which the stock is to be awarded, the award is for current service, the stock is awarded prior to or shortly after the end of the fiscal period, and certain other conditions are met. Otherwise, the employer must use the quoted market price of the stock to measure compensation expense.

Recognizing Compensation Expense

Employers should accrue compensation expense over the periods during which an executive performs services in exchange for the stock award. The aggregate value of fixed awards is to be recognized ratably or by another systematic and rational method over the relevant service period, as illustrated in the following examples.

Example 1: A company grants 12,000 stock options at $25 per share, a $20 discount from the quoted market price at the date of grant. The options are exercisable (vest) in three years. Consequently, the company's compensation cost of $240,000 should be accrued ratably over that three-year period.

Market price at date of grant	$ 45
Option price	25
Market price > option price	20
times number of options	12,000
Final compensation	$ 240,000
over vesting (service) period	÷ 3 years
Compensation expense per year (years 1–3)	$ 80,000

Example 2: Assume the same facts, except that one-third of the options vest in year 1, one-third in year 2 and one-third in year 3. The accrual should reflect that pattern. The compensation expense associated with the first one-third of the options would be recognized fully in year 1, the expense associated with the second third would be accrued over years 1 and 2, and the expense associated with the final third would be accrued over years 1 through 3.

		Year 1	*Year 2*	*Year 3*
Market price at date of grant	$45			
Option price	25			
Market price > option price at measurement date	$20			
4,000 options exercisable in year 1 times year 1—100% accrued		4,000		
4,000 options exercisable in year 2 times year 1—50% accrued		2,000		
year 2—50% accrued			2,000	

(Continued)	Year 1	Year 2	Year 3
4,000 options exercisable in year 3			
times year 1—33.3% accrued	1,333		
year 2—33.4% accrued		1,334	
year 3—33.3% accrued			1,333
	7,333	3,334	
times fixed market price > option price	20	20	20
Compensation expense per year	$146,660	$66,680	$26,660

For *variable awards*, FASB Interpretation No. 28, *Accounting for Stock Appreciation Rights and Other Variable Stock Option or Award Programs* (Interpretation 28), requires employers to recognize changes in the quoted market value of shares or awards between the date of grant and the measurement date (i.e., changes in total compensation expense related to the option or award) in the period in which the change occurs, as illustrated in Example 3.

Example 3: A company grants stock appreciation rights (SARs) for 5,000 shares to an executive. The market price of the stock is $30 at the grant date. The rights vest in three years, and must be exercised within five years. At the exercise date, the executive is entitled to receive shares with a market value equal to the appreciation in the stock since the date of grant. The executive exercises the SAR at the end of year 4. The market price at the end of each year and the compensation expense for each of the 4 years is as follows:

	Year 1	Year 2	Year 3	Year 4
Market price, end of year	$ 31.50	$ 29.75	$ 31.00	$ 32.50
Grant price	30.00	30.00	30.00	30.00
Market price > grant price	1.50	(.25)	1.00	2.50
times number of shares	5,000	5,000	5,000	5,000
Final compensation (not less than $0)	$ 7,500	$ 0	$ 5,000	$12,500
times percent accrued	33.3%	66.7%	100%	100%
Cumulative compensation expense	$ 2,500	$ 0	$ 5,000	$12,500
less: expense already recognized	0	2,500	0	5,000
Compensation expense (income) for the year	$ 2,500	$(2,500)	$ 5,000	$ 7,500

Stock Options

The most traditional stock option arrangement is the market value option described earlier. The employer grants an option to purchase a fixed number of shares during a specified time period at a price equal to the market price at the date of the grant. Because the option price equals the quoted market price at the measurement date (date of grant), compensation expense is zero.

Compensation expense is triggered if the option is granted at a price that is less than the market price at the grant date, however. If the employer grants the option in exchange for past services, compensation expense is recognized immediately. If the option is granted in exchange for future services, as evidenced by future vesting requirements, compensation expense is recognized over those future service periods.

Arrangements with No Cash Outlay

One of the disadvantages of a stock option grant is the potentially significant cash outlays that may be required for the executive to exercise the option. While this has been ameliorated for many executives through broker-sponsored cashless exercise programs, employers may choose to offer other equity reward arrangements such as stock appreciation rights and phantom stock that reduce or eliminate the executive's cash requirements.

A *stock appreciation right* entitles the executive to receive cash and/or stock equal to the appreciation in value of a stated number of shares of stock over a specified period of time. Because the final compensation expense is not known until the executive exercises the stock appreciation right, the accounting follows variable plan accounting, as illustrated in Example 3 on page 115.

The accrued compensation is reported as a liability for stock appreciation rights payable in cash and as paid-in capital for stock appreciation rights payable in stock. If the executive can elect to have rights payable in either cash or stock, accrued compensation is reported as either a liability or paid-in capital, depending on the form of payment the executive is most likely to choose.

Phantom stock plans are based on a theoretical investment in company stock. An executive is granted a stated number of memorandum account units—each equivalent to a share of stock—for a specified period of time. The executive is entitled to dividend equivalents on the units, based on the dividends paid on the company's stock. At the end of the award period, the executive receives or is credited with cash equivalent to the appreciation in the theoretical stock investment.

This deferred compensation arrangement is similar in concept to stock appreciation rights, except that the executive may also be credited with dividend equivalents. The company recognizes the dividend equivalents as compensation expense when it declares dividends on the company's stock; otherwise, the accounting is the same as for stock appreciation rights.

Restricted Stock Plans

Stock may be issued under an arrangement that conditions the executive's ownership of the stock on certain future events, such as attaining a specified return on shareholders' equity or continued employment with the company for a specified period. Such restricted stock arrangements are similar in concept to a grant of nonqualified stock options, with one major difference: the stock awarded or sold to the executive is subject to forfeiture or repurchase by the company (at the price paid by the executive, if any) if the restrictions are not met.

Restricted stock is often awarded to the executive at no cost, other than the requirement that he or she remain in employment for a specified period. Therefore, the measurement date for a restricted stock plan—the date at which both the number of shares that can be purchased and the exercise price per share are known—is generally the award date. Compensation expense is measured at that date as the excess of the market value of the award over the executive's aggregate price, if any. That expense is to be accrued in a systematic and rational manner, based on the terms of the agreement, over the period until the conditions are expected to be satisfied. Examples 1 through 3 illustrated the accrual pattern for fixed and variable plan awards; those illustrations are equally applicable in accounting for compensation expense arising from a restricted stock award.

For financial reporting purposes, restricted stock is reported in the capital accounts (at the quoted market value of the company's [unrestricted] stock on the date the stock was issued); the offsetting charge is reported as unearned compensation, which is reflected as an offset to shareholders' equity. (The company would also record a receivable equal to the price to be paid by the executive, if any). As compensation expense is recognized, unearned compensation is reduced.

If restricted stock is forfeited or repurchased because specified conditions were not met, any previously recognized compensation expense is reversed—that is, compensation expense in the year of forfeiture is reduced by the amount of the previously recognized compensation expense and recorded as part of the cost of the stock taken back by the company (treasury stock). Any remaining balance in the unearned compensation account is eliminated, with the reduction also reported as part of the cost of the treasury stock. (An adjustment of paid-in capital would be required if the market value at that date were lower than at the date of the original award.)

Example 4: A company awards an executive 2,500 shares under a restricted stock plan. The stock is issued at no cost to the executive, but restrictions on the stock require the executive to continue to work for the company for 10 years. At the date of the award, the market price of the company's unrestricted stock is $40 per share. Aggregate compensation expense is therefore measured as $1,000,000 (2,500 shares × $40 per share). The company records the award as a $1,000,000 charge to unearned compensation (a reduction in equity account) and an increase in common stock of a like amount. In each of the following 10 years, the company will recognize compensation expense of $100,000 ($1,000,000 ÷ 10 years) and reduce unearned compensation by a like amount.

In year 6 the executive leaves the company. The executive forfeits the 2,500 shares, which revert to treasury stock. The company records a reduction in compensation cost of $600,000, reverses the $400,000 remaining in the unearned compensation account, and recognizes $1,000,000 as the cost of the treasury stock. (If the market value of the shares is less than $1,000,000 at that date, e.g. $950,000, the company would reduce treasury stock by $50,000 and record an offsetting charge to paid-in capital.)

Book Value and Other Formula Plans

Under a typical formula plan, a company sells restricted stock to selected executives or key employees at a price determined using a formula such as the book value of the company's stock or a multiple of earnings per share. The executive cannot sell or transfer the stock. On retirement, termination, or the occurrence of a specified event, the employer will buy back the executive's stock, at the price determined by applying the formula at the repurchase date.

The Emerging Issues Task Force (EITF) has concluded that a book value or other formula plan for a publicly held company is a performance plan and should be accounted for like a stock appreciation right.[5] (Subsidiaries of a public company and closely held companies with publicly registered debt are considered to be public companies for this purpose.) Because the price at which the shares will be repurchased by the company is not known until the buyback, this plan is a variable plan, and the measurement date is the date the shares are repurchased. In measuring compensation expense, however, it is the formula and not the market price that is relevant. (Different rules apply for formula plans maintained by private companies, as discussed in the paragraphs that follow.)

Example 5: Assume an executive can purchase 5,000 restricted shares at the stock's book value. The company will repurchase the shares at the executive's cost if the executive leaves within two years. Otherwise, the company will repurchase the shares at current book value when the executive retires or terminates. The employee retires in four years.

	Year 1	Year 2	Year 3	Year 4
Book value, end of year	$ 15.50	$ 16.25	$ 16.00	$ 16.50
Book value, award date	15.00	15.00	15.00	15.00
Change in book value	.50	1.25	1.00	1.50
times: number of shares	5,000	5,000	5,000	5,000
Final compensation (not less than $0)	$ 2,500	$ 6,250	$ 5,000	$ 7,500
times percent accrued	50%	100%	100%	100%
Cumulative compensation expense	$ 1,250	$ 6,250	$ 5,000	$ 7,500
less: expense already recognized	0	1,250	6,250	5,000
Compensation expense (income) for the year	$ 1,250	$ 5,000	$(1,250)	$ 2,500

As is the case with book value and other formula plans, the company records stock issued and subject to mandatory redemption at market value and reports it in the financial statements just above the shareholders' equity section.

Performance Plans

Even though an executive may meet high performance standards, the market value of the company's stock may not increase proportionately. Conversely, the stock may do well even if the executive's performance is questionable. Performance plans are designed to address these problems by focusing executive performance on meeting targeted growth or other goals. For example, a performance plan may reward an executive with a fixed number of shares if he or she meets certain earnings goals. Because the number of shares to be awarded (the fixed number or none) is not known until the executive meets the target and earns the stock bonus, employers must account for performance plans as variable plans, accruing compensation expense over the executive's service period until the goals are expected to be met. This requires the exercise of judgment and is likely to result in an annual adjustment based on the then-best estimate of when the award will be earned, if at all.

Measurement will be further complicated if the plan issues awards as the executive meets a series of goals; this will necessitate the exercise of judgment to determine the number of shares, if any, likely to be awarded. Current accounting literature does not provide much guidance in this area other than the general requirement that the accrual should be systematic and rational.

Some accountants believe that when a company establishes a performance plan, it should record unearned compensation based on the number of shares it expects to award. In this situation the company would recognize the expected stock award, measured at current market value, and a contra unearned compensation account of a like amount, at the date the plan is established. As compensation is recognized, it would reduce the balance in the unearned compensation account.

Earnings per Share Implications

Stock options, stock awards, stock appreciation rights, and other similar plans could result in the issuance of company stock at a price that is less than the market price of the stock. APB Opinion No. 15, *Earnings per Share* (APB 15), requires a theoretical measure of that dilutive effect. More specifically, APB 15 requires that those below-market options and awards be treated as though they had been exercised and the company had used the funds paid by the executive (plus certain other amounts) to repurchase shares of its stock on the open market. This is referred to as the treasury stock method. The difference between the number of shares that could have been issued under these stock option or award plans and the number of shares that are assumed to be repurchased with the proceeds represents the net number of shares theoretically outstanding for purposes of calculating earnings per share.

In calculating primary earnings per share, it is assumed that shares were repurchased at the average market price of the stock during the financial reporting period; the end-of-period market price is used for fully diluted earnings per share.

Special Rules for Private Companies

Public and private companies account for stock options, unrestricted stock awards, and stock performance plans the same way, although the determination of market value may be more difficult for the private company. The accounting treatment for formula plans, such as book value plans, may differ between public and private companies. Further, private companies are subject to special "cheap stock" considerations when they go public.

Formula plans: Because stock issuance may be a significant source of capital for a private company, key employees and executives may be permitted (or required) to purchase company stock. The executive's purchase price might be book value or some other formula-based price, with the provision that the stock cannot be sold or transferred. Instead, the company must repurchase any shares the executive wants to sell at the then-current book value or based on the same formula. The accounting issue here is whether to treat this type of plan as compensatory.

In addressing this issue, the EITF (Issue No. 87-23) concluded that no compensation expense should be recognized if the key employee or executive makes a substantive investment that will be at risk for a reasonable period of time. The theory is that individuals who purchase shares under such a plan have made a substantive investment and have all the rights, rewards, and risks of other shareholders.

The EITF did not define what constitutes a substantive investment, however. Although judgment will be involved, it is fair to say that if the formula is based on book value or a reasonable multiple of earnings such that the individual is assuming the typical risks and rewards of ownership, the individual would be deemed to have made a substantive investment. If the individual is deemed not to have made a substantive investment, the plan should be accounted for as a variable plan.

Similarly, the EITF concluded that options granted to an individual by a private company at a formula-based exercise price are to be treated as stock appreciation rights. The EITF reasoned that there is no substantive investment by the individual prior to exercising the option. As a result, variable plan accounting is appropriate.

Unlike shares issued by a public company pursuant to a formula plan (i.e., with mandatory redemption by the company), shares issued by a private company pursuant to a book value plan are reported as equity if the substantive investment requirement is met.

Initial public offerings: If, after an initial public offering (IPO), formula stock continues to be subject to mandatory redemption by the company at the formula price, no compensation expense generally is recognized for any impact the IPO may have on the company's book value. However, formula shares issued in the year prior to the IPO are considered to be cheap stock issued in contemplation of the IPO, requiring a charge to compensation expense for the increase in formula value since the date the stock was issued. Subsequent to the IPO, the now-public company must recognize compensation expense for any increase in the formula-based value.

If the company eliminates the mandatory redemption requirement for formula stock when it goes public so the executive can sell the stock on the open market, and the stock is not cheap stock, no compensation expense is recognized for the increase in value as a result of the IPO. And because the company has no obligation to redeem the shares after the IPO, no compensation expense is recorded in the future.

If the shares were cheap stock, (i.e. issued within one year of the IPO), however, the company must take a charge to compensation expense to recognize the increase in the formula value since the date the stock was issued.

For formula-based options (accounted for as a variable plan), a change in the formula value as a result of the IPO is recognized immediately as compensation expense. If the options continue to be based on a formula, variable plan accounting would continue to be appropriate. If the formula-based options convert to market value options, however, a measurement date is established and fixed plan accounting would apply from that point forward.

Valuing private company stock: APB 25 does not provide specific guidance on how market value should be determined when there is no quoted market price. Consequently, judgment will be required in developing a best estimate of market value. Absent a valuation analysis by a qualified expert, a company should consider any recent arm's-length sales of the stock, its book value, and the relationship of book value and market value for comparable public companies in developing a reasonable estimate of market value.

Proposed Change in Stock Compensation Accounting

The FASB's proposed standard on accounting for stock compensation would significantly reduce the anomalous results produced by the current accounting treatment for fixed and performance options. Companies would account for options or awards that are settled by issuing equity instruments, such as stock options, restricted stock, certain stock-settled SARs, and performance plans, based on the "fair value" of the equity instrument granted to an executive. Similarly, companies would be required to recognize compensation cost for amounts payable to executives under cash settlement plans that are based on the price of the company's stock or other equity instruments.

For equity instrument awards, companies would recognize compensation cost based on the fair value of the stock option or award. The fair value of stock options and similar awards would be determined using an option pricing model, such as Black-Scholes, adjusted for expectations about the period of time the option or award is likely to be outstanding; the probable volatility, dividend yield, and risk-free rate of return on the stock over that period; and anticipated turnover during that period. (No expense would be recognized for options or awards not expected to vest.) The option's fair value would be determined at the date the option or award is granted, with subsequent adjustments to that value recognized for turnover or timing of exercise different from that assumed. The fair value of restricted stock awards would be measured at the market price of an unrestricted share of the same stock.

Stock-based awards such as stock appreciation rights that may be settled in cash would be "marked to market" until they are settled, similar to the current accounting for SARs.

The proposed standard would be effective for awards granted after December 31, 1996, but pro forma disclosure of the effects on net income and earnings per share would be required for awards granted after December 31, 1993. Because the final standard is not expected to be issued until early 1995, the proposed disclosures are not required in 1994 financial statements. However, the FASB has not ruled out subsequent disclosures about awards in 1994 and thereafter.

NOTES

1. See Chapter 19.
2. For detailed examples illustrating how accounting cost is determined under FAS 87 and FAS 106, see Chapter 9.
3. See Chapter 12.
4. See Chapter 12.
5. Issue No. 88-6.

Chapter Nine

Costs

"How much do these benefits cost?" is a fundamental question that employers must answer to evaluate alternative benefit designs, to measure their accounting impact on company profits, and—where the accounting impact is not the best measure—to assess the economic cost of the benefits to the company. Using a series of examples, this chapter covers accounting and economic cost measurement and explores the cost of unfunded supplemental retirement and executive medical arrangements.[1]

Determining the accounting cost associated with executive benefits is almost always a prerequisite to measuring the impact of these benefits on company profits. The accounting rules described in Chapter 8 give employers relatively little discretion as to calculation methodologies, but they do offer some leeway in the use of assumptions. Accounting cost is typically determined on a pretax basis; results are usually adjusted to an after-tax basis by establishing a deferred tax asset equal to the expected tax savings to the company when the benefits are paid.

In some situations, particularly where benefits are prefunded, it is also helpful to measure the economic cost associated with executive benefits. This analysis attempts to answer a variation on the cost question stated above: What do these benefits really cost the company? An economic cost analysis evaluates the cash flows associated with the benefits, recognizing the company's possible alternative use of funds. This approach may or may not produce an answer that is similar to the accounting cost, because it is not restricted by the accounting rules and often will rely on different assumptions.

SUPPLEMENTAL RETIREMENT ARRANGEMENTS

The examples and discussion that follow relate to both SERPs covering a number of executives and to deferred compensation arrangements covering individual executives.

Assumptions

Many assumptions come into play in determining both the accounting and economic cost of supplemental retirement benefits. The more important assumptions are highlighted in the paragraphs that follow. Others may be appropriate, depending on the benefits being valued.

Discount rate: Foremost in importance is the discount rate assumption used to measure the time value of money. For accounting purposes, this will typically be the pretax rate available on high-quality fixed income investments appropriate to the time period in question. For an economic analysis, the discount rate will reflect the company's own financial situation; it may represent either the company's cost of funds or the internal rate of return on company funds. The choice would depend on whether the company views marginal funds as affecting its borrowing (cost of funds) or investments (internal rate of return). The economic rate of return can be either pretax or after-tax, depending on the analysis.

Marginal tax rate: If the employer adjusts the discount rate or cost to an after-tax basis, it must make an assumption regarding marginal tax rates, which may vary over the study period if tax laws or the company's financial situation change.

Pay increase rate: Pay-related benefits require an assumption as to future pay increase rates.

Retirement incidence: The cost of retirement benefits depends on the assumed timing of retirement, particularly if benefits are related to future service or are subsidized if an individual retires early.

Mortality rates: For annuity-type benefits, mortality assumptions address the probability of individuals surviving until benefits commence and their expected life expectancy while benefits are payable. For life insurance benefits, the mortality assumption addresses the expected incidence of death.

Termination rates: Expected rates of termination of employment are used to value benefits that are dependent on an executive continuing in employment, such as service-based benefit formulas or service-based vesting.

Measuring Retirement Benefit Costs

Using a building block approach, the examples that follow illustrate in simplified form how the costs of executive retirement benefits are measured.

EXHIBIT 9–1
Projected SERP Benefit Payments

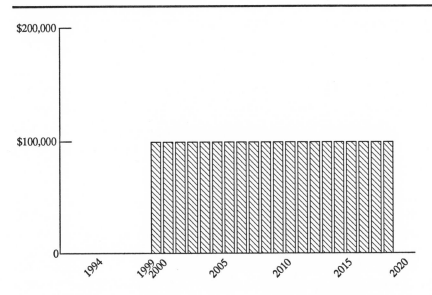

Example 1. What is the cost of covering one executive under a SERP subject to FASB Statement No. 87, *Employers' Accounting for Pensions* (FAS 87)? Assume a 55-year old executive was hired at age 42. The SERP provides a benefit of $100,000 per year for retirement at any age after age 62, with benefits payable for life. No early retirement or death benefits apply here. Assume that the executive will retire with 20 years of service at age 62 and will live for exactly 20 years more.

Our projected benefit payments are thus expected to begin in seven years (at age 62) and continue for 20 years at a rate of $100,000 per year. The discount rate for accounting purposes is 8 percent. Assuming that it is now 1993, the projected cash flows are shown in Exhibit 9–1.

Our accounting cost under FAS 87 is determined as follows:

- The total present value of expected benefits at 8 percent is $618,700 (i.e., the discounted present value of the expected cash flows at 8 percent).

- The portion of this present value allocated to prior service (the projected benefit obligation or PBO in FAS 87 terminology) is $402,200 ($618,700 total present value times the ratio of service to date [13 years] to projected service at retirement [20 years]).

- The portion of the total value allocated to the current year (the current service cost) is $30,900 ($618,700 total present value times the ratio of this year's service [1 year] to projected service at retirement [20 years]).

The annual expense is equal to the sum of three components:

- Current service cost: $30,900.
- Interest on the PBO and current service cost at 8 percent: $34,600.
- Amortization of the PBO over the average expected future service to retirement of all the SERP participants (which we will assume in this case to be 10 years): $40,200.
- Total annual expense: $105,700.[2]

When the company charges $105,700 to earnings, it can usually achieve tax effectiveness by establishing a deferred tax asset equal to the expected tax savings when benefits are actually paid. Assuming a 40 percent marginal tax rate, the deferred tax asset would equal $42,300 and the resulting net after-tax charge to earnings would be $63,400.

The economic cost analysis might examine the promise to provide benefits and seek to establish a realistic after-tax present value cost associated with the promise. Assume that a 40 percent marginal tax rate applies throughout the period, so that the $100,000 payments will cost the company $60,000 each on an after-tax basis. Assume that the company can also realize a 13 percent pretax return (7.8 percent after-tax) on invested funds, and views this as its hurdle rate in evaluating business decisions. The after-tax economic present value cost to the company of payments beginning at age 62 and continuing for 20 years, assuming a 7.8 percent discount rate, is $381,000. This represents a realistic cost to the company that it can compare to the use of corporate funds for other purposes.

The SERP examples that follow are designed to illustrate the sensitivity of the FAS 87 results to plan design, executive census data, and assumption variation. An economic cost analysis, which we have not included, would be comparably affected by these variations.

Example 2. SERP benefits are usually related to pay and service and may be offset by benefits payable under the company's qualified retirement plan. Assume the following SERP formula:

2 percent of final five-year average pay (base pay + bonus) for each year of service, less the benefit payable from the qualified retirement plan. The qualified plan benefit equals 1.25 percent of final five-year average pay (base pay only) for each year of service.

We will now determine the FAS 87 accounting cost for the 55-year-old executive, hired at age 42, whose current base pay is $200,000 per year and bonus is $100,000 per year. We will assume that his pay increases at a rate of 6 percent per year, and for simplicity we will ignore any IRS limits that apply to the qualified plan benefits. All other assumptions from Example 1 continue to apply.

The following table summarizes our executive's pay and benefits at age 62:

	SERP Benefit before Offset	Qualified Plan Benefits	SERP Benefit after Offset
Final year's pay			
Total pay	$451,100		
Base pay only		$300,700	
Final five-year average pay			
Total pay	$402,800		
Base pay only		$268,600	
Annual benefit	$161,100*	$ 67,200**	$ 93,900

*$402,800 × .02 × 20 years
**$268,600 × .0125 × 20 years

The FAS 87 calculation produces the following costs for the net benefit payable from the SERP. The calculations follow the FAS 87 rules illustrated in Example 1:

Total present value: $581,000
PBO: $377,700
Annual expense: $ 99,400

Example 3.   To illustrate the sensitivity of costs to the SERP formula, we will increase the formula to 2.5 percent from 2 percent, with no change to the offset for the qualified retirement benefit. There are no other changes from Example 2. As shown below, the 25 percent increase in the total benefit (from 2 percent to 2.5 percent) is leveraged by the fixed offset into a much larger increase in the net SERP benefit and the associated SERP costs:

	2% SERP	2.5% SERP	% Increase
Annual benefit before offset	161,100	201,400	25%
Offset for retirement plan	67,200	67,200	0
Annual benefit after offset	93,900	134,200	43
Annual FAS 87 expense	99,400	142,000	43

Example 4. In the preceding examples, we assumed a 6 percent annual rate of pay increase. We will now examine the sensitivity of our 2 percent SERP formula (Example 2) costs to a different assumed rate of pay increase. If pay were to increase at 8 percent per year instead of 6 percent, with no other change in assumptions, the benefits and costs would be as follows:

	2% SERP Benefit with Retirement Plan Offset	
	6% Pay Increases	8% Pay Increases
Projected annual SERP benefit	$93,900	$103,500
FAS 87 annual cost	99,400	109,500

If this individual were younger than age 55, the higher pay increase assumption would have a greater impact on projected benefits and costs because it would be operable for a longer period of time.

Example 5. Let us expand our examples to include two more executives at different ages. Details on our three executives covered by the 2 percent SERP (as per Example 2) are as follows:

			Service	
Executive	Current Age	Age at Hire	Current	At Age 62
A	40	32	8	30
B	55	42	13	20
C	60	30	30	32

EXHIBIT 9–2
Projected SERP Benefit Payments

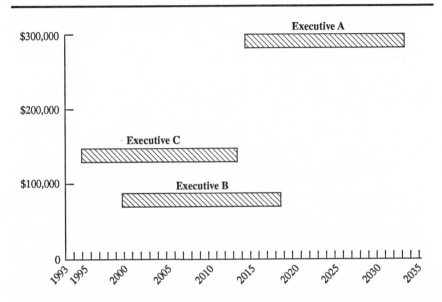

For simplicity, assume the three executives are all compensated equally (current pay equal to $200,000 base plus $100,000 bonus) and that other assumptions are uniform: pay increases of 6 percent per year, retirement at age 62, no deaths or terminations prior to retirement, and life expectancies of 20 years after retirement.

The following table summarizes projected pay and benefits at retirement and the current FAS 87 annual expense:

	A	B	C
Current age	40	55	60
Years to retirement	22	7	2
Total service at retirement	30	20	32
Projected final average pay	$965,400	$402,800	$301,000
Projected annual benefit	337,800	93,900	112,300
FAS 87 annual expense	55,400	99,400	206,700

The level and duration of the cash flows associated with these benefits are illustrated in Exhibit 9–2.

Note the following:

- Even through our three hypothetical executives now earn the same pay, their age differences produce fairly dramatic variations in projected pay and benefits at age 62 retirement.
- The annual cost for the oldest executive is higher because he has the most past service and is closer to retirement; he thus has a shorter discount period prior to the time that benefits begin.

SUPPLEMENTAL RETIREE MEDICAL ARRANGEMENTS

A company's promise to provide retiree medical benefits can be viewed as similar to the promise to provide supplemental retirement payments, with one very important distinction: retiree medical payments are not fixed at retirement, and they will increase each year as medical costs increase. An exception occurs at age 65, when an individual becomes eligible for Medicare and company costs decline significantly. Unlike retirement benefits, medical benefits are typically provided for the executive's spouse and dependent children.

Assumptions

Developing the FAS 106 accounting cost or the economic cost of retiree medical benefits requires assumptions in addition to those used for analyzing retirement benefits.

Medical cost increases: The most significant of these assumptions is the annual rate of increase in company medical costs. During the early 1990s, medical costs increased at an annual rate of about 15 percent. Most experts believe that this rate of increase will have to abate over time, or medical costs will become an unacceptable percentage of GDP.[3]

Spouse coverage: An assumption must also be made as to whether the executive will have a covered spouse or dependent children at retirement.

Per capita costs: The starting point for developing retiree medical costs is the current annual per capita cost of retiree medical coverage, which is then increased for assumed future medical cost increases. The per capita cost can be viewed as conceptually similar to the annual premium for retiree medical coverage for an individual. Typical current annual per capita company costs for retiree medical coverage are $3,500 prior to age 65 and $1,200 after age 65. Note that the FAS 106 results are based on average per capita costs and not on the actual claims experience of the executive.

Measuring Retiree Medical Costs

The following example illustrates the calculation of the cost of retiree medical benefits.

Example 6.   The promise to provide retiree medical benefits to an executive for retirement as early as age 62 would produce the expected benefit payments shown below for an individual now age 55 with an eligible spouse. This projection relies on the following additional assumptions:

- Age at retirement: 62.
- Per capita costs in 1993.

   Pre-65: $3,500
   Post-65: $1,200
- Annual rate of medical cost increases: 10 percent (assumed for simplicity).
- Spouse age: same as employee.
- Life expectancy: 20 years for employee and spouse.
- Termination prior to age 62: none assumed.

As shown in Exhibit 9–3, annual costs for the executive plus spouse are projected to be $13,600 in the year 2000, when the executive retires at age 62. They increase until both the executive and spouse turn age 65, when they drop significantly as a result of Medicare eligibility. The payments then resume an upward trend as costs continue to increase, rising to $28,600 per year.

The calculation of annual expense cost under FAS 106 is as follows assuming an 8 percent discount rate and an age 42 hire date.

- Present value of benefits (the expected postretirement benefit obligation or EPBO in FAS 106 terms) at 8 percent is $81,300.
- The portion of this present value allocated to prior service (the accumulated postretirement benefit obligation or APBO) is $52,800 ($81,300 total present value times ratio of service to date [13 years] to total projected service [20 years]).

EXHIBIT 9–3
Projected Retiree Medical Benefits for Employee and Spouse

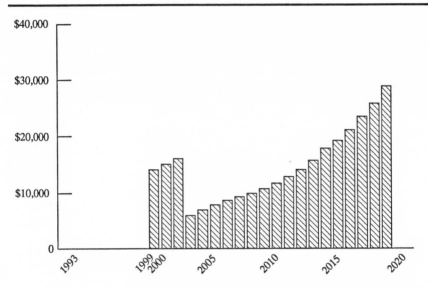

- The portion of this present value allocated to the current year (the current service cost) is $4,100 ($81,300 total present value times ratio of current year service [1 year] to total projected service [20 years]).
- The annual expense is as follows:

    Current service cost: $4,100.

    Interest on the APBO and current service cost at 8 percent: $4,600.

    Amortization of the APBO over the average expected future service to full benefit eligibility of all the SERP participants (or over 20 years, if greater, when FAS 106 first applies—which we will assume is the case in this example): $2,600.

    Total annual expense: $11,300.

The FAS 106 expense can usually be adjusted for tax effects by establishing a deferred tax asset equal to the expected tax savings when benefits are paid.

The calculation of the economic present value cost to the company of the promise to provide retiree medical benefits, assuming a 40 percent marginal tax rate and 7.8 percent after-tax internal rate of return on funds (see Example 1 for reference) produces a present value of $50,200.

The calculated FAS 106 expense and economic cost for retiree medical benefits is sensitive to the assumed rate of medical cost increases. These costs are also more sensitive than retirement benefit costs to the assumed retirement date, since medical benefits during early retirement are significant prior to Medicare eligibility. This sensitivity is illustrated in the examples below.

Example 7.   Assume our Example 6 executive will have medical coverage when he retires at age 60 with 18 years of service and that he will live for 22 years after retirement.

The increase in annual FAS 106 expense and economic present value cost associated with a change in retirement to age 60 is as follows:

	Retire at 62	*Retire at 60*
FAS 106 annual expense	$11,300	$14,900
Economic present value	50,200	59,600

Example 8.   Assume that our Example 6 executive will retire at age 62 and that medical costs will increase at 8 percent a year rather than 10 percent a year.

The decrease in annual FAS 106 expense and economic present value cost associated with the decrease in the assumed rate of medical cost increases is as follows:

	10% Medical Cost Increases	*8% Medical Cost Increases*
FAS 106 annual expense	$11,300	$ 8,600
Economic present value	50,200	33,100

NOTES

1. Chapter 10 expands the discussion of cost to funded arrangements. Employers also incur costs in administering their benefit programs. A number of administrative issues involved in executive benefit programs are covered in Chapter 6.

2. If this executive were covered under an individual deferred compensation arrangement subject to Accounting Principles Board Opinion No. 12 (APB 12), rather than a SERP subject to FAS 87, the PBO would have to be amortized over the period to the executive's expected retirement, or seven years. This would increase the amortization of the PBO to $57,500 and the total annual expense to $123,000.

3. Average medical plan cost increases among 202 *Fortune 1000* companies participating in a 1994 Towers Perrin survey declined to 6 percent for active employees, down from 12 percent the previous year.

Chapter Ten

Securing the Benefit Promise

Most executive benefit plans are unfunded and are backed by nothing more than the employer's promise to pay. As executives become more and more dependent on nonqualified arrangements for their retirement income, they have become increasingly concerned that changes in corporate ownership, or financial reverses, might mean that employers would be unwilling or unable to make good on these promises. As a result, interest in benefit security has become widespread.

Because no nonqualified approach to funding or otherwise securing executive benefits can duplicate the advantages to both employer and employee of the qualified plan, employers must consider a number of variables as they weigh their options for providing retirement income to their executives.

TO FUND OR NOT TO FUND

The decision to fund executive benefits will obviously be governed by financial as well as benefit security considerations. In evaluating financial issues, it is important to look beyond the specific transaction and examine overall implications for the company by comparing the after-tax rate of return available under a funding alternative with the after-tax rate of return available if assets are retained in the business. There are a number of ways to measure the rate of return on assets retained in the business, including the following:

- Some companies believe that the appropriate rate of return is their cost of funds—their cost of borrowing, of raising capital in the equity markets, or a combination of the two. In a low interest environment, the after-tax cost of raising capital can be on the order of 3 to 4 percent.

- Other companies believe that the appropriate rate is the after-tax return that can be realized on assets. This can be as high as 10 to 15 percent.

- Still other companies select a rate that is a composite of the above approaches.

The after-tax rate of return associated with a funding alternative may have to be risk-adjusted to reflect the underlying investments or financing scheme. With corporate-owned life insurance (COLI), for example, the expected after-tax return may have to be adjusted downward to reflect investment risk, the long-term financial viability of the insurance company or the possibility of unfavorable tax law changes affecting insurance.[1]

The financial measure a company uses will obviously affect its decision to fund or not to fund. If the company can realize an after-tax risk-adjusted return of 6 percent through a funding alternative, funding would probably make sense compared to an after-tax cost of funds of 4 percent, but not compared to an after-tax return on assets of 12 percent.

The possibility of future changes in the corporate marginal tax rate is also an issue. If rates are expected to increase, for example, employers may want to reevaluate the acceleration of a tax deduction associated with some funding schemes. In such instances it may be financially advantageous to defer funding.

Employer options for funding or otherwise securing executive benefits, including rabbi and secular trusts, annuities, and third-party guarantees, are summarized in the following pages.[2] To set the stage, we will begin with a discussion of the most common approach to providing these benefits: the book reserve.

BOOK RESERVES

Under book reserve funding, the employer books the liability for deferred compensation as it arises, and credits earnings on the deferred compensation on its books at the agreed-upon rate.[3] When the deferred compensation is payable in accordance with the terms of the agreement, the employer makes a direct payment to the employee. The arrangement is simply a promise to pay; the employer sets no money aside, and no entity other than the employer guarantees the employer's promise.

Under such an arrangement, the executive is a general, unsecured creditor of the employer. In the event of employer bankruptcy, the executive has a claim against the employer for the value of the deferred compensation, but is unlikely to have priority over other creditors. To the extent that the employer has no assets that are not pledged as security to other creditors, the executive would be unable to realize on his claim for unpaid deferred compensation.

If the employer were to *refuse* to pay deferred compensation due under a book reserve arrangement, the executive would be forced to sue the company to obtain the promised payments. This would involve an up-front expense for legal fees (which might be recoverable if the employee were successful). It might also pose the risk that the employer would claim either that the amounts were not due (e.g., because the executive violated a noncompete requirement) or that it should be entitled to offset damages it incurred as a result of the employee's actions. Such concerns are typically heightened in the event of a change in control, where new management may be unsympathetic to former executives.

While a book reserve arrangement for an executive has the advantage of requiring no current cash outlay by the company, the company must still record an expense for the deferral. Under both Financial Accounting Standards Board Statement No. 87 (FAS 87), which deals with pension benefits, and Accounting Principles Board Opinion No. 12 (APB 12), which covers individual deferred compensation contracts, deferred amounts that are to be paid to an executive in future years must typically be accrued as expenses on a current basis as the related services are performed.[4] Accounting expenses are accrued for deferred compensation as services are performed, but since a tax deduction cannot be claimed until payments are made, tax effects must be accounted for under FAS 109.

The amounts deferred, as well as earnings credited on those amounts, are not deductible by the employer until such time as they are included in the executive's gross income (i.e., typically in the year paid unless payments are determined by the end of the year and paid within two and one-half months thereafter). The entire payment would be deductible, unless it is determined to be unreasonable.

Executive Taxation

Under a book reserve arrangement, the executive receives no economic benefit from the employer's unsecured promise to pay deferred compensation, because no money is set aside for the benefit of the employee. Thus, presuming that the executive is not in constructive receipt of his or her benefit,[5] the deferred compensation will only be considered taxable, for income tax purposes, when the employee actually receives the money. Whether or not the employee is currently vested in the deferred amount is unimportant. Note that this is different from the rule that applies if the plan is funded, or if the employer is a tax-exempt organization and the plan does not meet the limits of IRC Section 457.[6] In either of these cases, taxation occurs at the point of vesting.

When amounts are distributed to employees, whether as a lump sum or in the form of an annuity, they are reported in the same manner as wages on IRS Form W-2. Like wages, these payments are subject to withholding, and the employee cannot request that nothing be withheld (which can be done with payments from tax-qualified pension plans).

Social Security Tax

Although deferred compensation does not subject the employee to income tax when earned, amounts credited under a nonqualified deferred compensation plan are subject to FICA (Social Security) tax when earned or, if later, when vested, as noted in Chapter 6.[7] The FICA tax has two components: the 6.2 percent OASDI (Old Age, Survivors, and Disability) tax on wages up to $60,600 (for 1994), plus a Medicare tax of 1.45 percent on all earnings without limit. Accordingly, the special rules of IRC Section 3121(v) will apply to every person covered by a nonqualified plan, and extra tax will generally become due earlier than the year in which plan benefits are actually paid.

As noted in the discussion of Section 3121(v) in Chapter 3, there is virtually no formal guidance from the IRS on the precise operation of the special FICA tax rules for nonqualified plans. Some issues are clear (or reasonably so) from the statute itself, but other issues are subject to varying interpretations among practitioners. Thus, employers should seek legal counsel in determining the best course of action in this regard.

The principal amount of deferred compensation credited on an employer's books for an executive for a particular year would generally be treated as the amount earned in that year for FICA tax purposes. If the executive is vested in his or her account balance, the amount earned in a year is subject to FICA tax in that year. It appears that investment earnings on prior deferrals are not subject to FICA tax.[8]

Assume, for example, that an executive elects to have her 1994 bonus of $50,000 deferred. She has previously elected to have her 1992 and 1993 bonuses (of $50,000 each) deferred, and they are being credited with interest at a rate of 10 percent (with $10,000 of total interest credited in 1994). The $10,000 of interest credited for 1994 on the balances carried forward from 1992 and 1993 is probably not subject to FICA because it is income attributable to previously earned and vested deferrals. The 1994 bonus of $50,000 will be considered deferred compensation earned in 1994. If the executive has current compensation of $150,000 for 1994, the 1.45 percent Medicare FICA tax would apply to the full $50,000 deferred in 1994, but no part of the deferral would be subject to the 6.2 percent OASDI tax because the executive's current pay exceeded the 1994 wage limit of $60,600. If the executive received a distribution of her full account ($150,000 plus accumulated interest) in 1995, none of this amount would be subject to any additional FICA tax.

Earnings on *nonvested* accruals are likely to be subject to FICA tax in the year when the earnings and deferrals vest. The exclusion for investment earnings only seems to apply to earnings attributable to previously earned and vested deferrals.[9]

In many cases, executives elect to defer bonuses they have earned for services performed in one year before the amount of the bonus is determined, usually early in the following year. While no guidance has yet been provided, the IRS may well conclude that an executive does not "earn" a bonus until the amount is fixed and determined.

In the case of a defined benefit SERP, IRS officials have indicated that FICA tax will likely apply to the present value of defined benefits in the later of the year that they accrue or vest. Increases in the present value of previously accrued and vested benefits are not taxed thereafter, even when benefits become payable. However, the present value of subsequent increases in the defined benefits themselves will be subject to tax in the year they accrue.

Assume an executive is covered by a SERP that provides a $5,000 per month life annuity at age 65. In 1994, the executive's rights become vested. At that time, the present value of the benefit is $420,000. If the executive has current compensation of $100,000, the 1.45 percent Medicare tax would apply to the full $420,000 present value of the SERP benefit in 1994; no OASDI tax (6.2 percent) would apply to this benefit because the executive's current wages exceeded the taxable wage base of $60,600.

In 1995, the executive accrues an additional benefit, attributable to additional pay and/or service, increasing the amount payable to him by

$700 per month; this accrual has a present value of $6,100. The present value of the $5,000 per month accrued in 1994 has increased by $18,000 to $438,000. In 1995, the present value of the 1995 accrual ($6,100) would likely be subject to the 1.45 percent Medicare tax but not to the OASDI tax. The $18,000 increase in the present value of the 1994 accrual is likely not subject to any FICA tax (since it represents income attributable to a previously accrued and vested amount). When the executive starts to receive payments from the SERP, no additional FICA tax will apply.

Issues on which the IRS has yet to provide guidance include:

- How to determine the present value of a defined benefit SERP accrual.
- How IRC Section 3121(v) applies to benefits payable under a SERP that are offset by benefits payable to the individual under a qualified plan, so that some of the SERP benefits may disappear over time.

As with other FICA wages, unfunded deferred compensation should be reported as wages subject to Social Security tax on the W-2. (As described above, they are not reported as taxable wages for *income tax* purposes until paid.) Because FICA tax cannot be withheld from unfunded deferrals, the employer would presumably withhold FICA tax from the employee's other cash compensation.

RABBI TRUSTS

The rabbi trust, which a company can establish to provide benefits for an individual executive or a group of executives, has two key attractions: the company can use trust assets *only* to pay promised benefits, and the executive's tax liability is deferred until benefits are actually paid, regardless of whether the executive is vested in the benefits.

Though the employer sets aside funds in a rabbi trust for the payment of benefits, those funds are not "set aside from the claims of creditors" within the meaning of IRC Section 83 and can be used to pay claims of the employer's general creditors in the event of the employer's bankruptcy. Rabbi trusts *do* provide protection in cases where the company is unwilling to pay a benefit (e.g., following a change in control).

A rabbi trust is a grantor trust, under which the employer is treated as the owner of trust income. Thus, the tax consequences to the employer are essentially the same as if the employer were the direct owner of the rabbi trust investments: the employer's deduction for trust contributions is deferred until benefits are actually paid, and the employer is subject to taxation on income earned by the trust. The income and FICA tax consequences to executives are identical to those described above for book reserve arrangements.

Rabbi trusts are named after the first such trust to obtain an IRS letter ruling, a deferred compensation fund established by a congregation for its rabbi. The IRS concluded that trust assets were not currently taxable to the rabbi because he received no current "economic benefit" from the trust and was not in constructive receipt of trust assets.

Employers typically establish rabbi trusts with a bank or other institutional trustee. The trust may require funding as benefits accrue, or may provide for funding on a "springing" basis, with employer contributions required only if a change of control appears likely. The terms of the trust usually provide that amounts contributed are irrevocably committed to the payment of deferred compensation and cannot be returned to the employer prior to the payment of all deferred compensation due, except, of course, in the event of bankruptcy. Alternatively, the trust may provide that trust funds can be returned to the company prior to a potential change in control, but that following a triggering event, amounts cannot be returned to the company without the consent of the executives affected unless all deferred compensation obligations are met.

The existence of an independent trustee assures that payments to an executive will not be stopped arbitrarily in the event of a takeover of the employer.[10] Rabbi trusts can also provide that, in the event of a change of control, the amount to be paid to an executive (for example, from a supplemental defined benefit plan) will be determined by an independent third-party administrator, who would direct the trustee as to the proper amount of payment.

A rabbi trust can be used for all types of deferred payment obligations, including payments that may be due under retiree medical plans and golden parachute arrangements and director pension and deferred fee arrangements, as well as for SERPs. Employers can establish separate trusts for different types of benefits; it is probably advisable to establish separate trusts for SERP benefits and parachute payments, for example, so that any litigation over the validity of a trust providing parachute payments to employee A will not necessarily affect the continuing provision of SERP benefits to employee B.

Responding to the growing use of rabbi trusts as security devices, the IRS has published a model trust[11] and will issue a private letter ruling for a rabbi trust arrangement only if the model trust is used. (There is no requirement that employers obtain private IRS rulings, and some employers may want to use a more flexible trust design than the IRS model.) The model trust contains both mandated and optional provisions. According to the IRS, the model language must be adopted verbatim, unless substitute language is expressly permitted. An employer may add provisions not in the model, provided they are not inconsistent with the model language.

Various IRS private letter rulings bless hardship withdrawals from non-qualified plans in connection with rabbi trust arrangements, permitting benefits to be paid in the event of an unforeseeable emergency (defined, for this purpose, as an unanticipated emergency caused by an event beyond the control of the participant that would result in severe financial hardship if the benefits were not paid). Payments must be limited to the amount necessary to meet the emergency.

Plan provisions governing hardship distributions should follow the language specified in IRS Reg. Section 1.457-2(h)(4) and (5), (relating to plans maintained by tax-exempt organizations or state and local governments), which is significantly more restrictive than the rules governing hardship distributions from qualified 401(k) plans. While a participant could receive a 401(k) plan hardship distribution for a down payment on a principal residence, for example, this would not constitute an unforeseeable emergency under the Section 457 criteria.

Various IRS private letter rulings also permit employees to direct their investments in a rabbi trust without jeopardizing the employer's status as owner of the trust, or causing employees to be currently taxed on trust amounts.

Revenue Procedure 92-64 indicates that if a rabbi trust conforms to the model, the Department of Labor (DOL) will consider the related plan to be unfunded for purposes of ERISA thus allowing the plan to qualify for the top hat exemption from most of the substantive requirements of ERISA if its coverage is limited to a select group of management or highly compensated employees.[12] Other rabbi trusts should similarly be considered unfunded for ERISA purposes if they are considered unfunded for tax purposes.

SECULAR TRUSTS

If benefit security were the only question, secular trusts (sometimes referred to as taxable trusts) would be the answer. Such trusts are irrevocable and protected from the claims of creditors. If an executive's interest in a secular trust is vested, however, he or she is subject to current taxation each time the employer makes a current contribution to the trust, regardless of when benefits are actually paid; if the executive is a highly compensated employee as defined in the IRC, which is almost always the case, the executive will be subject to tax on the growth in the value of his or her share of the assets of the trust, as discussed next.

Secular trusts remain relatively rare, perhaps because the applicable tax rules are extremely negative. Results of a 1994 Towers Perrin survey of 189 large companies with 197 plans indicate that approximately 2 percent of these nonqualified plans were funded with secular trusts, compared with approximately 41 percent funded with rabbi trusts. Most plans remain unfunded.

Unlike rabbi trusts, secular trusts designed to provide pension benefits require ongoing employer contributions in amounts sufficient to at least satisfy the minimum funding requirements of ERISA.[13]

Under a typical arrangement, the secular trust is used to secure benefits under deferred compensation plans covering executives of an employer. Contributions to the trust are for the exclusive benefit of plan participants and cannot revert to the employer until all benefit obligations are satisfied. As a practical matter, contributions are made only when participants become vested in benefits under the terms of the underlying deferred compensation plan. A separate account balance is maintained for each participant.

Each year, a participant receives a payment from the trust estimated to be sufficient to cover the federal income tax liability created by the employer's contribution to the trust. The remainder of a participant's account balance is distributed in accordance with the underlying plan (e.g., at termination of employment). Amounts distributed to participants from the trust, both annually and at termination, offset the amount the participant is otherwise entitled to under the underlying plans.

In various 1992 private letter rulings, the IRS indicated that secular trusts could not be designed so that the employer is considered the grantor of the trust, with the income generated by trust assets taxable to the employer. Instead, the trust is a separate taxable entity from the employer. Thus, to the extent that distributions from the trust each year are less than the trust's taxable income for the year, the trust itself will owe taxes. (Trusts are taxed at the same rates as individuals, although the brackets differ.)

A trust may avoid income tax liability by making annual distributions equal to its taxable income. Note, however, that this special trust deduction is limited to the trust's distributable net income (DNI). Depending on how the trust is designed and how the assets are invested, it is possible for a trust's DNI to be less than its taxable income. For example, DNI generally does not include capital gains unless they are paid, credited, or required to be distributed to any beneficiary during the current year. So to the extent a secular trust realizes capital gains that are not currently distributed or credited to beneficiaries' accounts, the trust will have to pay some taxes.

One IRS ruling suggests a way around this problem: the trust in PLR 9212024 expressly provides that capital gains are additional income allocable to the accounts of participants. Thus, realized capital gains are included in DNI.

The maximum deduction available to the employer is equal to its contributions to the trust. These are deductible in the year in which they are included in the employee's income; this means that contributions are generally deductible when made. IRS rulings make it clear that an employer is never entitled to a deduction for investment earnings on trust assets even though they are paid to participants.

In a trust covering more than one employee, the employer can deduct contributions *only* to the extent that separate accounts are maintained for each employee. This separate share rule does not require a separate trust for each employee; it does require separate bookkeeping accounts to which employer contributions, along with any income earned on the contributions, are allocated.

Surplus funds in a participant's account may be used to pay benefits to other participants, but only after the participant's entire plan benefit has been paid. Thus, surplus assets remaining in a participant's account after the participant receives a lump sum distribution in full satisfaction of his plan benefit can be reallocated to the accounts of other participants. The restriction on using surplus assets in some participant accounts to make up shortfalls in other accounts is likely to have a significant impact on the employer's funding obligation. Due to the vagaries of actuarial estimates under defined benefit plans, individual account surpluses and deficits are bound to occur. Because the trust cannot simply offset these items each year, it will tend to require more capital than a tax-qualified defined benefit plan (which is funded on an aggregate basis) to achieve a given level of funding for every participant.

Executive Taxation

If a secular trust does not meet the minimum coverage rules applicable to qualified plans under IRC Section 410(b) or the minimum participation rules of IRC Section 401(a)(26) (which is usually the case), highly compensated employees (HCEs) are subject to tax, under a special rule of IRC Section 402(b)(4)(A), on the increase in the value of their vested accrued benefits each year (i.e., the present value of their share of the trust less amounts they were previously taxed on).[14]

Each year, an employee who is 100 percent vested in his or her account balance should include in income the lesser of his or her trust account balance, or the present value of that benefit under the plan that is being secured.

This amount would be reduced by the amount already included in income in prior years (or which would have been included in income if the executive had been subject to tax).

As discussed above, a taxable trust such as a secular trust may avoid tax liability by distributing an amount each year equal to its taxable income. This avoids double taxation (to both the employee and the trust); only the employee will be taxed. Secular trusts therefore typically provide for current distributions of amounts sufficient to offset participants' tax liability resulting from employer contributions to the trust. The same distribution will satisfy both objectives—offsetting current tax liability and avoiding tax at the trust level—although a larger distribution might be required to satisfy one objective than the other. If the executive is under age 59½, however, the IRS has ruled that the 10 percent additional tax under Section 72(q) may apply. The most recent private letter ruling on the subject states that the issue is "unclear" for highly compensated employees.[15]

If a trust distributes amounts necessary to avoid incurring its own tax liability, employees may receive more in a year than they need to pay the tax they owe on the annual growth in the value of their accounts. In this situation, employees who fail to recontribute to the trust the excess of (1) what they receive from the trust during the year over (2) the amount of tax they must pay on the increase in value of their accounts may have their plan benefits reduced by the amounts not recontributed to the trust, plus assumed investment income on those funds. (In the absence of such a recontribution requirement, employees would receive the funds currently from the trust and still be credited with the deferred compensation attributable to those moneys.)

If such recontributions are required, employees will not be entitled to a tax deduction for recontributed amounts redeposited in their accounts. The IRS indicates that these recontributed amounts could eventually cause a portion of a participant's trust account to be recharacterized, however. In the event the total amount recontributed by an employee exceeds the total employer contributions to the employee's account, the employee would be treated as the owner of the portion of the account attributable to the recontributed funds. That is, that portion of the trust would be taxed as an employee-grantor trust, as described in the next section. The application of different rules to different portions of an employee's account would add administrative complexity.

Taxation of Distributions

IRS rulings indicate that participants are taxed on plan distributions according to the rules of IRC Section 72, applicable to annuities. Thus, participants who receive distributions before reaching age 59½ are potentially subject to the 10 percent penalty tax under IRC Section 72(q).

Of more significance, the rulings confirm that employer contributions on which participants are currently taxed under the special rule of IRC Section 402(b)(4)(A), described before, may later be distributed tax-free. And since this special rule essentially subjects a highly compensated employee to current taxation on all inside buildup under the trust, most distributions will be 100 percent tax-free, or virtually so. This also means the 10 percent penalty tax will not apply, although it might apply to current distributions of trust income, as noted above.

As a 1992 private letter ruling (PLR) suggests, however, administrative burdens may arise when trusts make distributions in the form of annuities to retiring participants.[16] Each payment under an annuity that includes previously taxed amounts is taxed proportionately on the basis of an exclusion ratio. This is the ratio that previously taxed amounts bear to the total amount expected to be received under the annuity (using prescribed tables to determine mortality). Normally, this exclusion ratio is calculated just once, at the annuity starting date. To satisfy the separate-share rule previously described, however, secular trust earnings generally must continue to be credited to participants' accounts, even after participants retire and begin receiving annuity payments. These allocations will be currently taxable to highly compensated employees under the special rule of Section 402(b)(4)(A). In such cases, the PLR indicates that a participant's exclusion ratio will have to be recalculated each year.

Lump sum distributions remove this administrative burden, of course. However, it is unlikely that participants can be required to take lump sum payouts from defined benefit plans due to the annuity requirements of Title I of ERISA.

Employers should keep in mind that secular trusts designed along the lines of those involved in these rulings will entail significant recordkeeping and other administrative responsibilities, particularly with respect to distributions made to participants each year before they retire.

Outside Directors

Another private letter ruling deals with the tax consequences of a secular trust, designed as previously described, used to secure deferred compensation payable to a company's outside directors.[17] In a directors' trust, the employer can actually receive trust income or reallocate it to directors' accounts. The right to receive trust income is probably attributable to the fact that a trust covering only nonemployee directors is not subject to ERISA. The IRS ruled that this outside directors' secular trust gave rise to basically the same tax consequences as the secular trust for management employees addressed earlier.

In many cases, however, the tax consequences for outside directors or other independent contractors would differ from those for employees. A trust covering only outside directors will generally satisfy the qualified plan nondiscrimination rules of IRC Sections 410(b) and 401(a)(26).[18] This is because each outside director is treated as his or her own sole employee. Accordingly, outside directors are subject to tax under Section 402(b)(1) or (2), not under 402(b)(4)(A), the provision generally applicable to highly compensated employees in a secular trust. In other words, only contributions to the trust are subject to current tax (assuming they are vested). Earnings on contributions allocated to a director's account are not subject to tax until the trust makes distributions to the director.

It is important to note that distributions from the trust to avoid taxation of the trust itself will generate additional taxable income for the directors. There is also a greater risk that the 10 percent early distribution penalty will apply to the taxable portion of the distribution.

IRS rulings may create additional interest in the use of secular trusts as security devices because they bring certainty to the tax consequences of such arrangements. As noted, secular trusts are more secure than rabbi trusts. Unlike rabbi or employee-grantor trusts (described in the next section), however, secular trusts will result in double taxation of trust earnings unless the trust invests in tax-sheltered vehicles like life insurance or tax-exempt bonds or makes current distributions equal to its taxable income.

Employee-Grantor Trusts

A variant of the secular trust, the employee-grantor trust, could pave the way toward increased use of a form of nonqualified trust to provide after-tax benefit security for executive pensions. An employee-grantor trust is created by offering the executive a choice between a current cash distribution of the benefit for which security is sought, or a contribution of those funds to a trust. In essence, an employer makes a current transfer of cash equal to the present value of pension accruals to an employee in a manner designed to discourage the employee from consuming the transferred funds prior to retirement. This approach avoids the double taxation problem encountered in secular trusts described above.[19]

The arrangement contemplates annual employer contributions each year to a segregated account (either a trust or a bank account, at the employee's choice). The annual contribution is equal to the excess of the present value of benefits under the employer's supplemental pension plan (calculated after application of assumed taxes on those benefits) over the current balance in the employee's account. Income generated by an employee's account balance is taxable to the employee. Each year, the employer makes a gross-up payment to the employee to cover the tax liability for the income and for the employer's contribution to the trust. The amount in the segregated account will be offset against the supplemental pension after it is reduced for assumed taxes.

Assume, for example, that a 50-year-old executive will be entitled to a $1 million payment from an unfunded supplemental pension plan at age 65. After deducting 39.6 percent for federal income tax, the payment will net him $604,000. At an 8 percent discount rate, the present value of $604,000 is $190,406. The executive's benefit account currently has assets of $180,000. Thus, the employer would contribute an additional $10,406 to the account. The employer would also make a gross-up payment of $6,822 to the employee to cover the taxes attributable to the contribution (39.6% × ($10,406 + $6,822) = $6,822), and a further gross-up payment to cover the employee's tax liability for any earnings on the employee's account balance. At retirement, the $1 million pension obligation will be completely satisfied if the segregated account contains at least $604,000 in assets.

It is significant that the employee-grantor trust used in connection with this arrangement is not a separate taxable entity from the employee. There is no need for the trust to make annual distributions of income to avoid paying its own tax, as is the case with the taxable trust discussed previously. Thus, the arrangement avoids double taxation of this income—once to the trust and again to the employee. The IRS has also concluded that the special rules of IRC Section 402(b), which cause highly compensated employees to be taxed on nonqualified trust income as it is earned, do not apply in this case. Because Section 402(b) does not apply, trust funds may be invested in tax-advantaged assets that will not produce any current taxable income (e.g., insurance or municipal bonds).

Prior to PLR 9235044, IRS officials had indicated that a trust could not be an employee-grantor trust unless the employee was under no duress in deciding whether to leave employer contributions in the trust or spend them currently. While the trust approved in the ruling allows the employee to withdraw the entire balance in the trust at any time, an employee who makes a withdrawal would receive no future contributions to the trust or tax gross-up payments from the employer. Thus, the individual would be left with an unfunded promise to pay a supplemental pension. Moreover, this benefit would still be offset by assets in the segregated account and by the amount withdrawn from the account plus hypothetical earnings.

For the tax treatment described above, the arrangement should conform to the following criteria:

- The accounts to which the employer will contribute cannot be limited to trusts; other types of accounts (e.g. savings accounts) should be available.

- The employee should be given the right to withdraw the full amount credited to his or her account at any time.

- The employee should establish the account. The employer may retain authority to administer the account, including the ability to remove and appoint trustees, to consent to amendments, and to direct the trustee to make payments to the employee.

The employee-grantor trust provides a high level of benefit security. To the extent the trust has assets, an executive is protected against an employer's unwillingness and/or inability to pay the supplemental pension benefit. In essence, the arrangement prepays supplemental pension benefits to a third party. Such a prepayment is at odds with the basic purpose for which the benefit is intended—to provide income to an employee at *retirement*—unless the employer is comfortable that the employee will not spend transferred funds until then. The trust in the ruling cannot be designed to guarantee this result, but it can encourage it by providing that funding will cease if the employee withdraws funds before retirement.

Like the secular trust, the employee-grantor trust is not advantageous from a tax standpoint, at least as long as the top corporate tax rate (35 percent) is less than the top individual tax rate (39.6 percent). Amounts transferred to the trust are currently deductible by the employer and includable in the employee's income. Thus, each dollar transferred saves the employer 35 cents in taxes, but costs the employee 39.6 cents in taxes. Moreover, income subsequently generated by the transferred assets is taxed at the employee's 39.6 percent rate, not at the employer's lower rate (as it would have been had it been retained in the employer's business or held in a rabbi trust).

The status of employee-grantor trusts under Title I of ERISA is unclear. Arguably, the employee-grantor trust should not be considered a pension plan under ERISA because it does not defer income until an employee's retirement: the employee is subject to immediate taxation and has the right to withdraw funds from the trust at any time. Of course, the underlying supplemental pension plan must still meet top hat requirements to avoid all but a modest ERISA reporting requirement.[20]

THIRD-PARTY GUARANTEES

Third-party guarantees such as surety bonds and letters of credit indemnify a covered executive if the employer defaults on its promise to pay deferred benefits. To avoid current taxation on the benefit, the employee, and not the employer, must arrange and pay for third-party protection from a surety company, bank, or insurance company. Because the cost and availability of a guarantee will depend on the employer's credit rating, employees with the least secure benefits may have the greatest difficulty in getting, and maintaining, adequate third-party protection.

An executive can purchase a casualty insurance policy insuring against an employer's refusal to pay an unfunded deferred compensation obligation (repudiation) or inability to pay (corporate bankruptcy) during the term of the policy. Such a policy would be tailored to the company's specific deferred compensation arrangement. The policy definition of insured event and the circumstances when benefits are due under the plan require careful analysis to make sure that appropriate payments will be made under the policy for losses. Typically, benefits would be paid under the policy for (1) the reimbursement of legal expenses in the event of a repudiation, or (2) actual replacement of lost deferred compensation in the event the employee's benefit is impaired as the result of a reorganization or liquidation following a Chapter 11 or a Chapter 7 bankruptcy filing. In the event of repudiation alone, the policy would typically pay only the cost of suing the employer for benefits allegedly due.

The coverage is written using individual policies issued to active or retired executives. The employer is not a party to the policy. (In versions of this coverage offered by Lloyds, a separate additional indemnification agreement has been required between the employer and the carrier, which raises the possibility that issuance of the policy would result in immediate taxation of the deferred compensation.)

At present, it is possible to obtain casualty insurance coverage for a term up to five years. The coverage is noncancelable and renewable. At the end of each year an endorsement attached to the policy provides for the extension of the coverage at a fixed price for another year (if the employer satisfies the underwriting requirements), therefore reinstating a five-year duration. Due to the limited term and the strict underwriting conditions as to the financial condition of the employer, this insurance may provide little protection in the face of a typically long, slow march into bankruptcy. It does protect against an insolvency triggered by a sudden catastrophe.

The premium is a function of the amount of coverage and the underwriting risks, the most important being the credit rating of the employer. For currently available coverage, the annual premium for a qualified risk falls in the range of one-fourth to one-half of 1 percent of the liability, but it could be higher and has been in the past. While this is an annual premium rate, the full premium is typically required in advance and is nonrefundable. Assuming a five-year policy term, the premium may be in the neighborhood of 1.25 percent to 2.5 percent of the liability/coverage. If an employee had nonqualified deferred compensation of $100,000 at an annual premium rate of 40 basis points, for example, the insurer would require an advance premium of $2,000 for the entire term. Premiums may be somewhat lower for executives who have already retired and started receiving benefits than for executives who are still working.

Obtaining the right amount of coverage without overpaying may be a challenge with respect to a defined benefit SERP that offsets benefits paid under the qualified plan. SERP benefits payable under such a plan may actually decrease as a working executive grows older due to the operation of the tax law limits.[21] Nonetheless, the insurer will not refund premiums and will provide coverage only for the amount of benefit payable under the plan.

Executive Taxation

The largest tax issue with respect to the various insurance products available to insure payment of deferred compensation is whether the insurance guarantee will change the unfunded nature of the promise, triggering immediate taxation of all vested benefits.

A 1993 private letter ruling makes it clear that if an executive purchases the policy without any involvement on the part of the employer, there will be no immediate taxation.[22] The letter strongly implies that any employer involvement will render the entire benefit taxable. According to the ruling, employer involvement would be found if the employer:

- Indemnified the insurer for any losses it might suffer under the policy.
- Escrowed any funds with respect to the policy.
- Participated in any negotiations respecting the terms or premiums of the policy.
- Provided the insurer with any nonpublic information about itself to help the insurer assess its underwriting risk.

The IRS makes it clear that the employer may reimburse the executive for any premiums he or she pays, but suggests the employer should not obligate itself to do so. The ruling also provides that amounts paid to the executive as reimbursement for the insurance premiums would be taxable income to the executive and would not be excludable working condition fringe benefits.[23]

Similarly, the ruling indicates that an employee could not deduct the premiums as a miscellaneous deduction or as an employee business expense.

While the issue is not addressed by IRS rulings, amounts paid by the insurer to the executive should be taxable income, regardless of who pays the premium, if they would have been taxable had they been paid by the employer (e.g., deferred compensation forfeited by reason of a business liquidation). The tax treatment of reimbursed legal expenses is not clear; an argument could be made that they are tax-free insurance proceeds, or that the executive is entitled to an offsetting deduction.

The purchase of an indemnity policy by an executive is irrelevant to the employer, who will claim deductions with respect to the deferred compensation as it is paid to the executive. If the policy triggers an immediate tax to the executive, the employer would be entitled to an immediate deduction for the same amount, provided the employer fulfills its withholding obligation.[24]

The use of an insurance contract to secure deferred compensation should not cause an arrangement to be treated as a funded pension plan subject to Title I of ERISA since the underlying benefit is still unfunded. To the extent that the arrangement is deemed unfunded for tax purposes, that treatment should also hold for ERISA, at least so long as the DOL follows the same logic it used with rabbi trusts. The DOL has not ruled on this point, however, and it is obviously a significant issue in plan design and administration.

ANNUITIES

Instead of promising to pay deferred compensation out of general assets in the future, the employer can purchase an annuity contract that will provide the same after-tax amount and transfer ownership of the contract to the executive. Various forms of payment are available. The financial integrity of the carrier and its claims-paying ability are clearly important considerations in purchasing such an annuity.

The employer typically pays a single premium to purchase the annuity contract. If an executive accrues additional deferred compensation, the employer can purchase additional contracts.

Unlike some security devices (e.g., secular or rabbi trusts), an annuity contract may not lend itself to a reversion of any funds to the employer in the event the deferred compensation for which security is sought is smaller than anticipated. This is an important consideration in a defined benefit deferred compensation arrangement.

A single premium annuity contract that is owned by the executive provides security against an employer's inability or refusal to pay deferred compensation. Benefit security under an annuity contract is thus similar to that under the employee-grantor trust described above. In both cases, the benefits being secured are immediately taxed and immediately deductible, but the annuity contract provides deferred taxation of earnings on the capital transferred by the employer. Unless an annuity can be structured with a suppressed cash value, both devices encourage, but do not ensure, that the employee will not spend the assets securing the benefit before retirement. (An employee may be able to cash in an annuity before retirement.)

An executive with a vested right in the annuity contract is taxed with respect to any premiums paid by the employer. Vesting is determined under the rules of IRC Section 83 (i.e., when there is no longer a substantial risk of forfeiture). In general, the inside buildup under the annuity contract is not taxable to the executive until distributions are made from the annuity contract.[25]

An executive with a forfeitable right in an annuity contract will be taxed on the cash surrender value of the contract when his or her interest in the annuity contract becomes vested. This delayed vesting will cause the executive to be taxed with respect to the inside buildup under the contract, assuming it has been credited to the cash surrender value. Taxes will be delayed on any postvesting inside buildup until the executive starts to receive distributions.

The employer is entitled to a deduction for any premiums it pays for a vested annuity contract.[26] If the executive is subject to delayed vesting in the annuity contract, the employer is entitled to a deduction for its premium payments only when the executive includes these amounts in income (i.e., when he or she obtains a vested interest in the contract). If more than one employee is covered by the annuity contract, the employer will lose its entitlement to a deduction unless separate accounts are maintained for each employee.

Under IRC Section 72(u), the employer, if a corporation or not otherwise a natural person, could be taxed on any inside buildup with respect to an annuity contract that it is considered to "hold." If an employer is the nominal owner of an annuity contract, the beneficial owners of which are employees, the contract will be treated as held by the employer.[27]

While the matter is not free from doubt, the use of an annuity contract to secure deferred compensation should not cause the arrangement to be treated as a funded pension plan subject to Title I of ERISA; if nominal and beneficial ownership of the contract is transferred to an executive during employment, then the arrangement does not result in the deferral of income by the executive until termination of covered employment or beyond. Even if use of an annuity contract causes the arrangement to be subject to Title I, the ERISA requirements can be satisfied fairly easily. The arrangement would have to comply with qualified joint and survivor annuity rules relating to spousal consent, for example, but, as an insured pension plan maintained by an employer for a select group of management or highly compensated employees, the plan could be exempt from the elaborate reporting and disclosure requirements that normally apply to plans subject to Title I.[28]

The following example illustrates the purchase of an annuity to provide an after-tax benefit to an employee equivalent to the employer's direct payment of deferred compensation.

If Executive A were to receive $100,000 annually in supplemental benefits directly from his employer, payable for his life, the full amount of each payment would be taxable to him when received. Assuming a 39.6 percent individual tax rate, Executive A would receive $60,400 after-tax each year.

A's employer can provide the same $60,400 in after-tax payments through the purchase of an annuity. Under IRS life annuity tables, Executive A, age 61, is expected to receive annuity payments for 23.3 years. An annuity providing monthly benefits for his lifetime can be purchased from Insurer X for $15,000 per $1000 of annual annuity. Under the "exclusion ratio" calculation of IRC Section 72, a proportionate part of each annuity payment would be deemed a tax-free return of the premium used to purchase the annuity.[29] For Executive A, $15,000 (premium) divided by $23,300 (expected return), or 64.4 percent of each $1,000 of annuity payments, would be excluded from tax when received. An annuity of approximately $70,310 would thus provide Executive A with an after-tax annual benefit of $60,400:

Tax-free portion of $70,310 benefit:	$70,310 × 64.4% = $45,280	
Taxable portion:	$70,310 × 35.6% = $25,030	
Taxable portion multiplied by 39.6 percent tax rate:	$25,030 × 39.6% = $ 9,910	
After-tax portion of $25,030:	$25,030 − $9910 =	$15,120
Total after-tax benefit:		$60,400

The employer would thus buy an annuity providing a benefit of $70,310 per year, at a premium cost of $15,000 per $1000 of annual annuity, for a total premium of $1,054,650. Because Executive A would be immediately fully taxable on the annuity purchase, the employer would also make a tax gross-up payment of $691,450 to reimburse Executive A for the income tax that A will have to pay (at a 39.6 percent marginal tax rate) on both the annuity purchase and the tax gross-up payment:

Premium treated as taxable to A:	$1,054,650
Tax gross-up also taxable to A:	691,450
Total taxable to A upon purchase:	$1,746,100
times A's tax rate:	× 39.6%
A's tax attributable to purchase:	$ 691,450

OTHER OPTIONS

Funded executive benefit plans continue to be the exception rather than the norm. With the advent of the $150,000 pay cap,[30] however, more and more employees will be dependent on nonqualified arrangements for some portion of their retirement income, and the highest-paid employees will have look to supplemental plans for the largest part of their benefit. Thus, interest in the arrangements reviewed in this chapter is likely to grow.

Other mechanisms are also available to address concerns about security. One is the employment contract. A clear and quantified contractual obligation, specifying exactly what the executive is entitled to, may provide a measure of protection. Executives who are about to retire may also prefer having a lump sum in hand rather than worrying about the security of an annuity-type distribution over 10 or 20 years.

Group universal life insurance (GULP) may offer another option. As discussed in more detail in Chapter 7, GULP includes both a life insurance element and an optional savings feature known as a sidefund. Suppose an employer is ready to spend several hundred thousand dollars over time to secure an executive benefit arrangement. If it pays the money into a trust, the payments and all earnings will be currently taxable. If it buys nonqualified annuities, all earnings will be taxable under the annuity rules as paid out. Suppose, instead, that the employer gives the executive the money to invest in the GULP sidefund. The executive will be taxed on the original premiums and on distribution will be taxed only on the earnings in excess of his or her basis in the contact. This basis includes both the executive's after-tax contributions to the sidefund and amounts used to purchase the life insurance protection. In addition, the fact that the amounts in question are in the executive's own insurance contract (instead of being part of the employer's general assets or in the hands of a third-party trustee) may provide a sense of security.

Permanent life insurance offers possibilities in the executive benefit arena as well. Corporate-owned life insurance (COLI) and split-dollar arrangements are the subject of Chapter 12.

NOTES

1. See Chapter 12 for a complete discussion of COLI.
2. Another option, the stock-based SERP, is the subject of Chapter 11.
3. The issues involved in determining the rates of return to be credited on deferred compensation are discussed in Chapter 6.
4. See Chapter 8 for a complete discussion of accounting requirements.
5. See Chapter 3.
6. See Chapter 14.
7. IRC Section 3121(v)(2), enacted in 1983.
8. IRC Section 3121(v)(2)(B) provides that income attributable to prior non-qualified deferrals is not subject to FICA tax.
9. See IRC Section 3121(v)(2)(B).
10. To recover amounts otherwise payable to an executive from a rabbi trust, an employer would typically have to sue the trustee and/or executives involved.
11. Revenue Procedure 92-64.
12. See Chapter 4.
13. Because secular trusts are funded and assets are beyond the reach of company creditors, plans using secular trusts do not qualify for an exemption from the minimum funding or other requirements of Title I of ERISA, even though they cover only a "select group of management or highly compensated employees."
14. In general, employees are HCEs for purposes of various nondiscrimination rules if they: own more than 5 percent of the employer; receive compensation from the employer in excess of $75,000 (indexed; $99,000 for 1994); receive compensation from the employer in excess of $50,000 (indexed; $66,000 for 1994) and are among the top-paid group (generally the top 20 percent of employees ranked by pay), or are officers who receive compensation in excess of 50 percent of the IRC Section 415 defined benefit limit ($118,800 for 1994). Whether an employee will be considered an HCE for the current plan year largely depends on his or her status during the prior year.

15. PLR 9417013.
16. PLR 9212019.
17. PLR 9206009. For a general discussion of compensation for outside directors, see Chapter 2.
18. ibid.
19. See PLR 9235044.
20. See Chapter 4.
21. See Chapter 1 for a discussion of these limits.
22. PLR 9344038.
23. See Chapter 16 for a discussion of working condition fringe benefits.
24. See IRS Reg. Section 1.83-6(a)(2).
25. IRS Reg. Section 1.401(c)-1(c).
26. IRS Reg. Section 1.404(a)-12(b).
27. Senate Committee Report to P.L. 99-514, Section 1135(a).
28. See DOL Reg. Section 2520.104-23.
29. This example does not attempt to account for the fact that annuity amounts paid after the employee's investment in the contract is fully recovered are 100 percent taxable, without regard to the exclusion ratio.
30. See Chapter 6.

Chapter Eleven

The Stock-Based SERP

Supplemental executive retirement plan payments are typically a function of an executive's years of service and final average pay. Today, however, more and more employers are interested in adding a performance element to the equation. One way to do so is to use company stock in the executive benefit program.

The term *stock-based SERP* covers a broad range of plans that use employer stock or related equity devices to provide retirement income. Essentially, a stock-based SERP uses equity-based compensation in lieu of or in coordination with unfunded, nonqualified cash-based deferred compensation plans. There are myriad ways to link employer stock and retirement income or other deferred compensation. In this chapter we will focus on three: the target benefit approach, the floor-offset approach and an elective approach.

OBJECTIVES

Equity-based retirement plans serve a number of different objectives. One is linking the economic interests of executives and shareholders by tying executive pay levels to company stock performance. In the case of a stock-based SERP, superior stock performance will enhance an executive's retirement income, and the executive, in turn, can afford to take a relatively longer-term approach to improving the company's stock price. Because the concept makes shareholder return over the long term a major determinant of executive wealth at retirement, it should have strong shareholder appeal.

Executives who receive stock through an option or other award program may ultimately own a significant number of company shares if they participate in a stock-based SERP as well. This may be beneficial to a company interested in demonstrating that its top executives own relatively large amounts of company stock. While large stock grants sometimes raise the ire of institutional shareholders, a company making such an award in lieu of normal SERP benefits may be in a better position to justify the size of the grant.

Many stock-based SERP designs also enhance the security of an executive's SERP benefit relative to an employer's unfunded promise to pay. As described in more detail below, stock-based SERPs may involve a current grant of shares of company stock to an executive (in lieu of or as an offset to unfunded SERP benefits). The shares are registered in the executive's name and the executive enjoys all beneficial rights of ownership except one—the stock will be forfeited if the executive terminates employment prematurely.

A plan can be designed to accelerate time-lapse restrictions in the event of a change in control of the company, giving an executive immediate access to his or her shares. An executive holding such shares is much more secure about retaining them than is an executive with an unfunded SERP who is hoping for a cash payment. A stock-based SERP obviously does not provide security against the risk of an employer's insolvency, however.

THE TARGET BENEFIT APPROACH

The starting point for this approach is the level of supplemental retirement income an employer wants to provide for its executives. The appropriate target benefit could be the amount provided by a SERP that is already in place.

Assume, for example, that an employer's qualified plan provides a benefit equal to 1.5 percent of final average pay times years of service. The company also maintains a SERP for select management employees providing a benefit equal to 2 percent of final average pay times years of service less the amount payable from the qualified plan. In this simple example, the SERP benefit is 0.5 percent of final average pay times years of service.

The first step is to calculate the value of the SERP benefit payable to an individual based on current service and final pay, expressed as a lump sum value determined as of the future date when the executive is expected to retire. This is the target SERP benefit. In lieu of this benefit, the company will grant shares of restricted stock to the executive. The number of shares granted should provide a future value equal to the future value of the SERP based on an assumption about future stock price appreciation. Each year, this process could be repeated to reflect incremental growth in the lump sum value of the target benefit.

Because stock is granted as a replacement for a cash benefit, the executive's SERP (i.e., the value of the shares at retirement) could fall short of the target if future stock price performance is lower than projected. Conversely, if future stock price performance is higher than projected, the executive's SERP will exceed the target.

Thus, the assumption as to future stock price appreciation is one of the keys to designing a stock-based SERP. The assumption should factor in dividends to be paid over the measurement period, assuming that the dividends will be reinvested in employer stock, as well as actual appreciation in the price of the stock. The higher the assumed rate of stock price growth is set, the harder it is for an executive to receive a value at retirement that equals the target benefit.

The shares granted to an executive under a stock-based SERP could be nonvested for a number of years, though a vesting schedule certainly is not critical. Because an executive who terminated voluntarily before the end of the vesting period would not be able to keep any nonvested (restricted) shares, a vesting provision—perhaps set at the same age and/or service at which the employer wants to let executives voluntarily retire—could serve as a retention device. As explained below, a vesting schedule will affect the tax consequences of the arrangement.

The shares granted under the stock-based SERP could also be subject to a contractual restriction prohibiting sale of the shares before the executive reaches the assumed retirement age or actually retires at an earlier age. The point of such a restriction is to ensure that the stock award is actually used for its intended purpose (i.e., to provide a source of supplemental retirement income to executives); it need not be imposed if this is not an employer objective. However, as discussed in more detail later in this chapter, a restriction on sales that lasts until retirement may cause problems under ERISA.

Simplicity is a primary advantage of the target benefit approach: the employer simply grants shares of company stock to replace more conventional SERP benefits. The share grant operates much like any other such arrangement in that the shares are immediately registered in the name of the executive and are held by the company or in escrow until vesting and transferability restrictions lapse. The employer no longer has any continuing obligation, as it would with a conventional SERP, to make cash payments for life to the executives starting at retirement. The concept allows for considerable freedom in designing the number of grants to make, the restricted period for each grant, the desired target benefit at retirement date, and the like.

Another benefit of this approach is that the resources available to an executive at retirement will depend on the performance of the employer's stock. The executive will have no downside protection if the stock performs more poorly than expected. Thus, the target benefit approach truly puts executives at risk with respect to a large portion of their employer-provided retirement income. This is more likely to be acceptable to institutional and other shareholders than other approaches (described in following paragraphs) that provide downside protection.

One of the shortcomings of the target benefit SERP involves the early retirement subsidy. This can be an important feature of a defined benefit-type SERP that operates like a qualified defined benefit plan, where basic benefits are determined as of an individual's normal retirement age (e.g., age 65), and benefits that commence before that are reduced to reflect the longer period over which they will be paid. If the employer does not reduce benefits to the full extent called for by interest rate and mortality assumptions, it is subsidizing early retirement. The amount of an individual's subsidy will depend on his or her age at actual retirement.

In a target benefit stock-based SERP, assumptions are made about an individual's age at retirement. Factoring in an appropriate value for an early retirement subsidy at this age to determine the number of shares of stock to award to the individual may result in an over- or underpayment of benefits, depending on the age of the individual at actual retirement.

Taxation

The federal income tax consequences of the target benefit approach to a stock-based SERP are relatively straightforward. The value of the shares transferred will be included in the recipient's income when granted or, if later, when the shares are no longer subject to a substantial risk of forfeiture. In most stock-based SERPS, the period between the option grant and vesting will be relatively long, and executives will generally include shares in income at their value when they become vested. Because shares are granted in lieu of SERP benefits, the target SERP benefit has no added tax consequences for the executive, assuming vesting occurs at the same time that SERP benefits would have been paid.

An executive who receives nonvested stock can accelerate the tax date to the date the shares are granted by making a so-called Section 83(b) election, as is the case with any property received in exchange for the performance of services. If the executive is sure the stock will appreciate significantly in value before it vests, such an election might make sense. In addition to paying tax on the relatively lower value at grant date, the executive will owe no more tax until the shares are sold. Further, any appreciation in the value of the stock after it is granted will be treated as a capital gain upon sale.

Most recipients of nonvested shares do not make an 83(b) election, because they are not certain the stock will appreciate in value and because they want to delay taxation for as long as possible. In addition, executives who forfeit the shares after making such an election and incurring a tax liability will not be entitled to any sort of offsetting deduction.

An employer is able to claim a deduction for the shares granted at the same time the executive includes the shares in taxable income and in the same amount (i.e., the value of the shares on the tax date). As with any property provided as compensation to an employee, the deduction is contingent on the employer withholding income tax in respect of the executive.[1]

An Example

The following example illustrates how a target benefit SERP might work using two grants of restricted company stock:

- Jim Smith is 52 years old on January 1, 1994. His normal retirement date is the year 2007, when he will be 65.
- The projected lump sum value of the total target retirement benefit is $6,000,000 at age 65; 67 percent of the target benefit will be paid from the SERP ($4,000,000), and the rest will be paid from the qualified plan.
- The current price of company stock is $25 per share; no dividend is currently paid or anticipated in the future.[2] Based on the company's projected share price growth (which, in turn, is based on an evaluation of historical performance and other considerations), it is assumed that the price of the company's shares will increase by 11 percent per year.
- Jim Smith's tax rate at age 65 is assumed to be 39.6 percent, with a 28 percent capital gains rate.
- Smith will receive the first grant of company stock in 1994, with restrictions lapsing in 10 years at age 62 (year 2004); he will receive the second grant in 1996, with restrictions lapsing at age 64 (year 2006).

- The target benefit is calculated as follows:

$4,000,000	Calculated pretax SERP benefit at age 65
× .604	1 minus tax rate assumed at age 65 (39.6 percent)
$2,416,000	Target after-tax benefit at age 65 from restricted stock SERP
$1,208,000	After-tax benefit to be available to Smith at age 65 from the first grant
$1,208,000	After-tax benefit to be available to Smith at age 65 from the 2nd grant

- The two restricted stock grants will fund to 100 percent of the after-tax target benefit of $2,416,000.
- The first grant of restricted shares will be for 22,276 shares, occurring in 1994. The second grant will be for 21,187 shares, occurring in 1996. Taken together, the two grants are projected to give Jim Smith sufficient shares at retirement (in 2007) to equal, on an after-tax basis, the target SERP benefit of $2,416,000.
- The size of the grant has been adjusted to provide the executive with sufficient shares to settle his tax liability. In 2004, when restrictions on the shares granted on January 1, 1994 lapse, the share price is projected to be $70.99. Smith will have a taxable event at this time, owing tax on the full value of the award in 2004. At this point, he will be free to sell sufficient shares to settle his tax liability, since the shares are now no longer subject to restriction. He will also have a capital gain on the share price appreciation at retirement based upon the growth in share price from 2004 to 2007, and will again sell shares to satisfy his tax liability. Smith will reach an after-tax basis at age 65 equal to 50 percent of his target SERP benefit, or $1,208,000.

Value of First Restricted Stock Grant

(1)	22,276 shares @ $70.99 on 2004:	$1,581,373
(2)	Tax liability due at 2004 (39.6%):	$ 626,224
(3)	Shares sold to meet tax liability [(2)/$70.99)]:	8,821
(4)	Shares remaining after meeting tax liability (22,276 − 8,821)	13,455
(5)	Value of 13,455 shares in executive's ownership in year 2004 (13,455 × $70.99):	$ 955,157
(6)	Value of 13,455 shares in executive's ownership in year 2007 (13,455 × $97.09):	$1,306,346
(7)	Capital gain on share appreciation from 2004 to year 2007 [(6) − (5)]:	$ 351,189
(8)	Capital gain tax paid on capital gain ($351,189 × 28%):	$ 98,333

(9) Shares sold to meet tax liability [(8)/$97.09]:   1,013
(10) Shares remaining after meeting tax liability (13,455 × 1,013):   12,442
(11) Value of shares owned by executive at target retirement age 65
     (12,442 × $97.09) (rounded): $1,208,000

The second grant will result in an additional projected $1,208,000 in after-tax basis. The net result is that the executive could own shares of company stock at normal retirement age worth $2,416,000 on an after-tax basis—the portion of his total retirement package payable from the SERP.

THE OFFSET APPROACH

Under the offset approach to designing a stock-based SERP, employers also grant stock to executives long before retirement, but the value of these shares merely offsets cash benefits otherwise payable to the executives under a conventional SERP. If the shares are worth less than the lump sum value of the SERP benefit, the executive will be entitled to receive the difference in the form of cash payments. If the value of the shares exceeds the lump sum value of the SERP, no cash payments will be made.

Here, too, the number of shares granted to an executive will be governed by assumptions about future stock price appreciation (including reinvested dividends). Because SERP benefits and share grants are coordinated at retirement, the number of shares granted under this approach will typically be based on the *projected* SERP benefit (i.e., assuming future service with the company and future salary increases). The share grant and the expected SERP benefit are coordinated on an after-tax basis as of an age at which covered executives are expected to retire. The value of the shares is offset against the promised SERP benefit at an executive's assumed retirement age. Thereafter, the value of the stock will not affect payments under the SERP.

Assume, for example, that a company that has already established a SERP implements a restricted stock grant program for covered executives. The company estimates the SERP benefit that would be payable for each participant at a reasonable retirement age. One of the covered executives is currently age 51 with a salary of $300,000 and a 50 percent bonus award of $150,000, and is expected to retire at age 63 after 22 years of service. His projected monthly benefit under the SERP is $241,200 (due to projected salary increases and future service credits) payable on a single life annuity basis. The present value of this annuity commencing at age 63 is $2,049,000. If the participant is in a 43.6 percent tax bracket at retirement (39.6 percent federal tax plus 4 percent state tax), the tax adjusted value of the SERP benefit is $1,156, 000. The $1,156,000 or some fraction thereof (say 80 percent) becomes the target for the accumulated after-tax value of the stock grants.

The employer's stock is currently trading at $70 per share. If the employer assumes a total annual yield (including dividends) of 11 percent and intends to make two share grants, one currently and one in four years, it will grant the executive 4,983 shares now and 5,771 shares later. Assume the executive will hold 10,100 shares at age 63 (12 years from now), after reinvesting after-tax dividends and selling some shares to pay taxes on other shares as they vest (four years from grant). If the company's original 11 percent assumption was correct, these shares would now be worth $1,332,000—exactly the same as the targeted SERP benefit after-tax lump sum value. At the assumed retirement age, the stock value is off-set against the after-tax SERP value. In this example, no benefits will be paid from the SERP, regardless of future stock performance. If the shares had appreciated at only 7 percent per year, the executive's shares would have been worth only $1,070,000 at age 63. In this event, the executive would also receive a cash payment of $403,000 ($262,000 on an after-tax basis) from the SERP to restore the promised after-tax benefit.

The offset approach allows an employer to ensure that executives will have a basic level of retirement income without regard to the overall performance of the company's stock. This will appeal to those who ascribe to the philosophy that an individual who has spent a career with a company should be sure to receive sufficient retirement income to maintain some targeted lifestyle. This SERP design can also provide an executive with an early retirement subsidy based on the executive's age at actual retirement. That is, the SERP can actually provide benefits with a greater subsidy than that contemplated in granting the stock if, for example, the executive retires earlier than assumed.

Under this approach, the stock grant provides some upside potential to align an executive's interests with those of shareholders; the executive's retirement benefit will be larger if total stock returns exceed the rate assumed by the company in determining the size of the share grant.

A principal disadvantage of this approach is that it could subject the company to criticism for a "heads you win, tails I lose" compensation plan that imposes no downside risk on executives.

Taxation

The tax consequences of the floor-offset approach are the subject of some debate. Conventional wisdom suggests this design should yield the same tax results to an executive and an employer for any shares granted as those described above for the target benefit approach. That is, the shares will generally be included in an executive's income at their value when they become vested and will be deductible by the company at the same time and in the same amount. Assuming the SERP is an unfunded promise to pay benefits, an executive will only include any residual SERP benefits in income for tax purposes as payments are made.

Despite the conventional wisdom, there may be grounds for taking a more aggressive approach with respect to floor-offset taxation.

Under applicable Treasury Department regulations, a recipient of stock or other property is not subject to tax until the property has been transferred. According to these regulations, a transfer of property occurs when the recipient acquires a beneficial ownership interest in the property, which is determined on the basis of all relevant factors. One factor listed in the regulations is the risk of loss. A transfer is not deemed to occur to the extent an individual does not incur the risk of a beneficial owner that the property will decline substantially in value.[3]

In a floor-offset stock-based SERP, declines in the value of the shares granted to an executive will be made up through the SERP because the stock offset will be reduced. But it is possible to interpret the regulations as focusing on the risk of loss only where the shares are subject to the requirement that they must be resold to the employer at termination of employment or some other event that is certain to occur. This is not the case in a typical stock-based SERP.

Conversely, there may be cause for concern that a floor-offset stock-based SERP will trigger immediate inclusion of the value of the stock in an executive's income. This concern is premised on the idea that the existence of the SERP that will make up for losses in stock value causes the shares to be considered immediately vested. The Treasury regulations provide that property is not subject to a substantial risk of forfeiture to the extent the employer is required to pay the fair market value of the property to the employee upon its forfeiture. This might occur in the context of a floor-offset stock-based SERP if an executive terminates employment prior to the vesting of shares, but recoups the value of those shares through a vested SERP benefit (that is no longer subject to a stock offset).

However, an employer's SERP benefit obligation will not typically be couched as an express obligation to pay the covered executive an amount equal to the fair market value of the shares forfeited. Thus, it may be possible to distinguish the regulations in this regard.

THE ELECTIVE APPROACH

Under the elective approach, covered executives can choose whether to receive shares (or stock options) in lieu of their normal SERP benefits. Except for the elective feature, such an arrangement operates like the target approach described above.

If stock options are granted in lieu of SERP benefits, an employer must value the options to determine how many to grant to replace a unit of SERP benefits. Black-Scholes or a similar method for determining the current value of the option is a possibility, as is making an assumption about the future appreciation in a company's share price to determine the cash value an executive might ultimately receive. Whatever the option valuation methodology, an employer will face a challenge in communicating it to affected executives, and executives who are skeptical about the valuation may opt for conventional SERP benefits.

The elective approach firmly links the retirement resources of executives to the future performance of company stock, if executives so elect. Executive choice may be perceived as either a positive or a negative feature of the plan, depending on the company's perspective.

Any arrangement that introduces choice also introduces a higher level of administrative complexity, of course. Employers must design and distribute election forms and educate covered individuals about their choices.

Use of stock options in lieu of SERP benefits will provide significant accounting advantages, at least under existing accounting rules. This aspect of these plans is described in more detail in Chapter 8.

Use of stock options in lieu of SERP benefits will not provide a greater degree of benefit security than an unfunded, conventional SERP. Unlike a share of restricted stock, in which legal title to a valuable property right is transferred to an executive up front, a stock option is merely another unfunded contractual arrangement, giving the executive the right to purchase stock from the company for a (presumably) below-market price. A company may be just as unlikely to fulfill its commitment under an option contract as under a SERP.

As explained in more detail in the next section, stock options are not subject to the doctrine of constructive receipt. Thus, it is possible to provide an executive with completely discretionary access to the value underlying a stock option with no concern about premature taxation.

Taxation

If an executive can elect to receive shares of stock or stock options in lieu of SERP benefits, the election should only relate to SERP benefits not yet credited to the executive. Otherwise, the executive might be subject to accelerated taxation under broad interpretations of the constructive receipt doctrine or the assignment of income doctrine.

Stock options are subject to relatively favorable tax rules. In general, an individual recognizes no taxable income when an option is granted and recognizes income only when the option is exercised. The amount of income is simply the excess of the market value of the shares on the day they are acquired over the option exercise price. Note that these tax consequences are not affected by the fact that an option holder may exercise an option whenever he or she chooses; taxation is still delayed until the option is actually exercised.

By contrast, an executive cannot be given unfettered access to conventional SERP benefits whenever he or she chooses. Such access would cause the executive to be taxed on the SERP payments, under the constructive receipt doctrine, when the payments could have first been elected. Thus, replacing a standard SERP benefit with stock options gives an executive a great deal of flexibility.

ERISA

In any stock-based SERP design, it is important that the stock portion of the arrangement not be considered a pension plan for purposes of ERISA, primarily to avoid the ERISA requirement that pension assets (the shares of stock in this case) be held in trust and fully vested under relatively short vesting schedules. The stock portion of the plan would also be subject to ERISA's elaborate reporting and disclosure requirements.

ERISA defines a pension plan as any plan that by its terms or through its operation provides retirement income to employees or results in a deferral of income by employees for periods extending to employment termination or beyond. Because this definition is so broad, it is possible that stock grants in which shares do not vest or cannot be sold until the recipients retire might be considered a pension plan.

Based on advisory opinions issued by the Department of Labor, the date at which a substantial number of shares under the plan become vested is an important factor in determining whether a restricted stock plan is treated as an ERISA pension plan. This should occur a considerable time before the anticipated retirement age of plan participants (e.g., five years) to avoid ERISA pension status. It is also helpful to be able to demonstrate that the stock grants *in fact* tend to be vested before participants retire. Finally, executives holding shares awarded under a stock-based SERP should be free to sell the shares after they vest.[4]

Note, however, that the parameters of ERISA pension plan status in the context of grants of company stock are ill-defined. Some advisors believe that ERISA status may be avoided even where most shares vest only at or near retirement age and individuals are barred from selling shares until retirement. Proponents of this approach argue that where all rights of ownership in stock (e.g., the right to vote and the right to receive dividends) are transferred to an executive except that the stock is not vested and cannot be sold, it is as if the executive received payment under the plan at the date the stock was granted. Thus, the plan is not deferring the receipt of compensation. Moreover, the rights in the stock retained by the company until retirement (i.e., the right to get the stock back if the executive terminates before vesting and a restriction on selling the shares to a third party) cannot be funded in any sense of the word.

It is particularly important to avoid ERISA status for the stock portion of a floor-offset arrangement. If the ERISA pension rules applied, the arrangement would constitute a prohibited transaction under ERISA. In this regard, ERISA generally allows eligible individual account plans, like a restricted stock plan, to invest up to 100 percent in employer stock. But there is a prohibition against investing in employer stock where benefits under the individual account plan are taken into account in determining benefits payable to a participant under any defined benefit plan.[5] Unfortunately, this is precisely what happens in a floor-offset stock-based SERP: the value of company stock is taken into account in determining SERP benefits. Moreover, ERISA defines the term *defined benefit plan* such that all types of nonqualified, unfunded supplemental plans are likely to be included, even those that might be target benefit or pure defined contribution type plans if they were funded. The only way to avoid this serious problem is to ensure that the stock portion of the arrangement is not subject to ERISA.

SECURITIES LAW ISSUES

Stock-based benefit plans bring various provisions of the federal securities laws into play, including the proxy disclosure rules, the registration requirements, and restrictions on insider trading. Stock exchange and NASDAQ rules and state corporation laws also have an impact on stock-based plans. These issues are covered in detail in Chapter 13.

ACCOUNTING

A target benefit arrangement is accounted for like any other restricted stock award: the value of the shares on the date they are granted will be charged as a compensation expense ratably over the vesting period.

Two methods of accounting will apply to the elective approach. For executives who elect to receive shares or options rather than a SERP, the arrangement should be accounted for like any grant of shares or stock options. For executives who elect to receive conventional SERP benefits, the arrangement generally will be accounted for under FAS 87 (if the plan covers a group of individuals). However, APB 12 would apply if the arrangement is an individual-by-individual contract. The fact that there is an election by executives will not alter this result because there is no point in time when any executive will have a tandem right to receive either equity awards or a SERP except initially.

If a floor-offset approach is used, it would be accounted for as two plans—a restricted stock plan and a cash benefit plan. The accounting for the restricted stock portion of a floor-offset arrangement would be exactly like that for other restricted stock plans, as described previously. The underlying SERP (i.e., the cash benefit) is accounted for in accordance with FAS 87 or APB 12 in accordance with the benefit formula, recognizing that the SERP benefit will be offset by the value of the restricted stock. In practice, this means that the PBO (projected benefit obligation) of the SERP would be offset each year by the then-current value of stock earmarked to offset the SERP benefit. In determining the plan's annual cost, the stock is not considered to be a plan asset. This type of accounting may actually produce a favorable result compared to the accounting for a standard, unfunded SERP in that market appreciation of the restricted stock will reduce SERP expense, but is not charged against earnings.

NOTES

1. See Treas. Reg. Section 1.83-6(a)(2). Shares are treated as wages for FICA purposes at the same time as for income tax purposes—and in the same amount. Rev. Rul. 79-305.
2. If the company's stock pays a regular dividend, the dividend stream should be factored into the share grant calculation. Dividends paid during the restricted period can be used to purchase additional company shares to reach the target benefit level.
3. Reg. Section 1.83-3(a)(6).
4. See DOL Advisory Opinions 80-29A and 85-04.
5. ERISA Section 407(d)(3).

Chapter Twelve

Permanent Life Insurance—Individual Policies

Employers often receive proposals to use permanent life insurance to "fund" benefits for their executives. Coverage may be written as corporate-owned life insurance (COLI), where the corporation is owner and beneficiary of the insurance; it can also be written on a split-dollar basis, with ownership and beneficial interests split between the corporation and the executive. In either situation, leveraging may be involved through the use of policy loans.

This chapter begins with a brief description of COLI and split-dollar arrangements. After a review of various general concepts, the chapter concludes with a discussion of some of the financial issues employers should consider in evaluating proposals to use permanent life insurance to provide executive benefits.[1]

CORPORATE-OWNED LIFE INSURANCE

The purchase of COLI is separate and distinct from the employer's plan or agreement to provide benefits for the executive. While the plan or agreement might, for example, provide for ERISA excess benefits, the restoration of other benefits lost because of the tax law, deferred compensation, or other supplemental retirement and/or death benefits, there is generally no legal link between the policy value and the employer's benefit promise.

With COLI, the employer is both owner and beneficiary of permanent life insurance purchased on the lives of participating executives. The amount of insurance is usually related to the benefits expected to be paid on the basis of current pay, although it is not unusual for initial amounts of

175

insurance to anticipate some future pay increases. Typically, the corporation makes policy loans (observing the rule requiring payment of four out of the first seven premiums other than by policy loan) to obtain maximum tax leveraging.[2] Because the employer owns the policy, the arrangement does not provide benefit security for the executive.

Upon death, the employer collects the proceeds of the policy and pays a death benefit to the executive's beneficiary. Any benefit payable to a living executive is paid from employer assets, with the employer recovering the funds through policy loans or from insurance proceeds payable when executives die. Because funding largely flows from the payment of generally tax-free life insurance proceeds, it is important that insurance be kept in force until executives die. Thus, most COLI programs continue insurance on the lives of executives who have retired or otherwise terminated employment.

Federal tax treatment of COLI is as follows:

- Premiums paid by the employer are not tax-deductible.
- Interest paid by the employer on policy loans is generally tax-deductible, but only to the extent of loans that do not exceed $50,000 per life insured.[3]
- The employer generally receives insurance death proceeds free of income tax, though proceeds are considered in determining whether a company must pay the corporate alternative minimum tax.
- The inside buildup of cash values is considered in determining whether a company must pay the corporate alternative minimum tax.
- If the employer surrenders the policy before it matures as a death claim, any excess of the gross cash surrender value (without regard to any outstanding policy loans that might reduce the cash surrender value actually available) over the premiums paid will be considered a taxable gain.
- The value of the death benefit protection provided to the executive each year does not create imputed income for the executive.
- Payments made by the employer to the executive or beneficiary under the separate benefit plan are generally tax-deductible.
- Payments received by the executive under the separate benefit plan are taxable income.
- Payments received by the beneficiary under the separate benefit plan are taxable income and are generally includable in the employee's estate for estate tax purposes.

The death benefit may qualify for the marital deduction if paid to a spouse. In large estates, this may serve only to defer estate taxation since the benefit may remain in the spouse's estate and be taxed on his or her subsequent death.

An income tax deduction for the estate tax attributable to the distribution can mitigate but not eliminate the combined effect of federal income and estate taxes.

State income and estate or inheritance taxes vary. In most situations, however, it is reasonable to assume that state tax treatment will be consistent with that of federal tax law.

It is important not to underestimate the impact of taxes on benefits. Suppose a corporation pays a $1,000,000 death benefit to an executive's beneficiary. Assuming a 39.6 percent income tax bracket and a maximum estate tax bracket of 55 percent, federal income and estate taxes would be as follows (without the marital deduction):

Estate tax	$550,000
Income tax (after estate tax deduction)	178,200
Total tax	$728,200

After taxes, only $271,800 of the gross benefit remains. Any state taxes would reduce the net benefit even further.

If the benefit qualifies for the marital deduction, an estate tax would not be payable by the executive's estate. As noted earlier, however, this might only defer the estate tax until the spouse dies. Moreover, if the marital deduction were claimed, the deduction for estate taxes would be lost, thus raising the income tax to a maximum of 39.6 percent or, in this example, $396,000.

Because insurance proceeds are generally received income-tax free by the employer and payments to the beneficiary are deductible, companies often gross-up benefits to compensate for the fact they are taxable. Nonetheless, the size of the after-tax benefit and the cost-efficiency of this approach relative to various benefit delivery alternatives may still be an issue.

In essence, corporate-owned life insurance should be viewed as a long-term corporate investment. Rates of return available in the short term are relatively low and may even be negative under some circumstances. While rates usually improve over the long term, this result is heavily dependent on the insurance policies maturing as death claims.

SPLIT-DOLLAR LIFE INSURANCE

Split-dollar is a generic term that covers a variety of funding procedures using permanent life insurance. The employer usually purchases permanent life insurance on the life of an executive, and ownership of the policy (death proceeds and cash value) is split between the employer and the executive. Premiums may be paid entirely by the employer, or they can be split between the employer and executive. The split of ownership can be handled in two ways: (1) the employer can own the policy and create the executive's interest by endorsement, or (2) the employee can own the policy and collaterally assign a portion of the proceeds to the employer.

In one typical split-dollar arrangement, the employer pays all premiums and ownership is split by assignment. The employer's interest in the cash value or the death proceeds, as the assignee, is usually limited to the amount of its premium payments (with or without an additional credit to reflect the time value of money). When the executive retires, the employer withdraws its interest from the cash value of the policy; any excess values belong to the executive. If the executive dies, the employer receives its interest through the payment of part of the insurance proceeds, with the executive's beneficiary receiving the balance. As with COLI, the transaction can be leveraged through the use of policy loans.

The major federal tax aspects of split-dollar insurance are as follows:

- The employer's premium payments are not tax-deductible except to the extent they are used to provide current life insurance protection.
- The executive will have imputed income each year equal to the cost of the term insurance that is provided—that is, the difference between the face amount of the policy and its cash value—unless the executive pays this part of the premium from his or her after-tax income.[4]
- The employer will not be allowed a deduction to the extent any portion of the policy's cash value becomes the property of the executive.
- The employer will not be allowed a deduction for the proceeds payable to the executive's beneficiary.
- Interest paid by the employer on any policy loans will be deductible as described for COLI coverage.
- If, prior to the executive's death, the employer receives payment of any part of the cash value that exceeds the premiums it paid, this excess will be taxable as income.

- Death proceeds paid to either the employer or the executive's beneficiary (including that part of the proceeds that consists of cash values) will generally not be subject to federal and state income taxes.
- Federal estate taxes (and state inheritance or estate taxes) will apply to any death proceeds payable to the executive's beneficiary, but the marital deduction will be available; proceeds can be entirely excluded from the gross estate if the executive's ownership rights are assigned at least three years prior to death, however.
- The inside buildup of life insurance cash values is generally not taxable until withdrawn from the policy, and it is assumed by most practitioners that this rule will apply to the cash value buildup under split-dollar coverage. If the executive is entitled to cash values created by employer contributions, however, there is some risk that the Internal Revenue Service will treat the arrangement as tantamount to an interest-free loan rather than insurance, in which event the buildup would become currently taxable to the executive (and deductible by the employer).

Split-dollar coverage offers potential security for executive retirement benefits over the long term under a favorable tax shelter (if the cash value buildup is not currently taxed). As noted earlier, however, the employer will not receive a deduction for cash value or retirement benefits received by the executive in this fashion. Also, use of the pension values of the split-dollar arrangement to offset benefits under the employer's SERP could reduce the accounting cost of the SERP program.

ANALYZING PROPOSALS: GENERAL ISSUES

COLI and split-dollar arrangements are complicated, and they warrant careful scrutiny and analysis. General considerations are summarized below, followed by an analysis of financial issues.

Tax Treatment

Insurance proposals typically project financial results that reflect current tax law. Changes in tax treatment are always a possibility, however, and any such changes, whether by statute or by administrative and even judicial rulings, could have an adverse impact on projected results. (Recent legislative changes have in fact been unfavorable.)[5] Future changes could include the following:

- Taxing the inside buildup of all cash values for regular income tax purposes, both for corporations and for individuals.[6]
- Treating typical split-dollar coverage as involving an interest-free loan to the executive.
- Taxing the executive on the inside buildup of cash values under a split-dollar arrangement (to the extent the values exceed the employer's interest in the policy) on the grounds the executive has received an economic benefit.
- Denying any interest deduction in connection with leveraged permanent insurance, either on an outright basis or on the grounds that interest deductions should not be allowed on loans that are used to create tax-free benefits.
- Restricting the deductibility of interest to loans held only for actively employed executives—that is, denying deductions for interest payments made on outstanding loans for executives who have terminated employment with the employer.[7]
- Taxing death benefit proceeds in situations where the beneficiary (e.g., the employer) has no insurable interest in the life of the insured individual at the time of death.

While no one can predict whether any of these changes will come about, prior legislative and administrative activity suggests that COLI and split-dollar insurance are not viewed with complete favor when used as discussed in this chapter. Changes like those described above could obviously have a major and negative impact on projected financial results.

Time Period

It is very important to recognize that COLI and split-dollar arrangements are long-term programs that produce maximum financial advantages only when policies mature as death claims. Thus, it could take 50 years or more for a program to come to fruition. Projected results of COLI and split-dollar programs typically reflect several long-term assumptions (in addition to the assumption that the tax law will not change), including the following:

- Interest will be credited for the entire period at the rate specified in the proposal.

- There will be no loss or deferral of projected tax benefits due to changed circumstances of the employer.
- Mortality will occur in accordance with the table used in the proposal—typically, the insurer's mortality table for that class of business.

Each of these assumptions deserves additional comment.

Interest rates.   The interest credited under an insurance policy has two components: the guaranteed interest rate and the excess or nonguaranteed dividend interest rate. The interest rate typically used in a COLI or split-dollar proposal is based on a total rate of return that includes projected dividends. Prior experience tells us that interest rates will vary over time and that long-term projections should take this into account. Thus, projected financial results under a COLI or split-dollar proposal should be analyzed with several different assumptions as to future interest rates. In this regard, it would be helpful to look at the insurer's investment performance for prior years as well as the history of interest rates it has credited for dividend purposes.

Loss or deferral of tax benefits.   In addition to facing possible changes in the tax law, employers cannot be certain that they will receive expected tax benefits from a COLI or split-dollar arrangement in any given year or years. Proposals typically assume that the employer will always pay taxes at regular corporate tax rates. This may not always be the case. If the employer becomes an alternative minimum taxpayer, for example, it will have to include life insurance proceeds and the inside buildup of cash values in determining its alternative minimum tax exposure. An employer may also suffer tax losses. Thus, it is important to assess the implications of losing or deferring tax benefits at various periods of time.

Mortality rates.   Projections of the tax-free life insurance proceeds that will be payable to the employer are usually based on the insurer's mortality table. An employer whose actual mortality rate is lower will collect death proceeds more slowly. Employers should carefully consider the likelihood that they will have more favorable mortality experience, because this factor alone can often turn short-term cash flow projections from positive to negative.

Employer Objectives

Insurance proposals often focus on program funding rather than program design and objectives. In fact, cash flow analyses and projected financial gains often obscure program objectives. Thus, it is important for an employer contemplating the purchase of insurance to determine exactly what it wants to accomplish. Once the employer has set its objectives, it can evaluate an insurance proposal against them and consider and compare other alternatives that may be available.

Assume, for example, that the employer's primary objective is to prefund an executive's supplemental retirement benefits—amounts that cannot be provided under the employer's qualified plan because of tax law restrictions. These benefits could be quite substantial for a highly paid employee. As a result, the amount of life insurance required to generate sufficient cash values might far exceed the employer's objectives in terms of providing death benefits. Other alternatives, including a rabbi or secular trust or a stock-based SERP,[8] might prove to be much more efficient because they would eliminate the purchase of unneeded insurance and would permit more aggressive investment of plan assets.

Benefit Security

Advocates of split-dollar insurance claim that these arrangements can provide a measure of benefit security for executives. This is true to the extent that the buildup of cash values exceeds the employer's interest in these values, which is usually limited to the premiums it has paid, with or without an additional amount representing some investment return on those premiums. Insurance products are basically front-loaded for acquisition and other expenses, however, so cash values will not build to any significant level in excess of premiums paid until the policy has been in force for an extended period of time. An employer needs to consider whether, and to what extent, this potential advantage will materialize, particularly in cases where benefit security is a key objective.

Former Executives

As noted earlier, reasonable after-tax rates of return under a COLI program are heavily dependent on the employer's receipt of substantial death proceeds on an income-tax free basis. If a policy is surrendered for cash or otherwise disposed of before the insured's death, returns may be unattractive and financial loss is a possibility.

To make a COLI program work and to avoid financial loss, the employer will have to keep insurance policies in force on executives who change jobs or otherwise terminate. This, in turn, raises the following issues:

- Keeping insurance in force on former employees and collecting the proceeds when they die (particularly if they left the organization long ago) may have public relations and human resource implications.

- The employer will have to keep track of terminated executives and obtain proof of death (e.g., death certificates).

- While insurable interest questions are normally resolved by the relationship of the parties at the time insurance is purchased, the question of whether there is any socially acceptable basis for an employer to continue paying premiums on a former executive and to collect life insurance proceeds when the executive dies might be raised in court by the executive's heirs or other interested parties.

- If the insurance policy has been leveraged through policy loans, there is also the question raised earlier in this chapter—whether interest payments will be deductible with respect to terminated employees.

Liquidity

Even though cash surrender values may be available very quickly under some policies, permanent life insurance in the form of COLI or split-dollar is relatively illiquid when viewed as an investment. If policies are surrendered before they mature as death claims, the investment return to the employer will be diminished or may even be negative; any gain when policies are surrendered will also be taxable as income.

There are a number of reasons a program might terminate early, including adverse legislation or IRS rulings, the loss or deferral of anticipated tax benefits, public disapproval (and possible legal ramifications) of collecting insurance proceeds upon the death of former executives, or the administrative burden of keeping the program in effect for extended periods of time, particularly if the program was established by prior company management. Any analysis of a permanent life insurance proposal should include an assessment of the after-tax financial implications of early termination. The fact that it will take many years for reasonable returns to emerge should be considered in light of alternative investment options available to the company.

Administrative Issues

COLI and split-dollar programs involve a great deal of administrative effort. Tasks include keeping appropriate records, establishing loan amounts each year, processing the loans, tracking former executives, testing the overall operation of the program periodically against initial and/or revised projections, enrolling new executives, factoring in pay increases, paying premiums, establishing appropriate accounting entries and so forth.

It is imperative that all parties have a clear understanding of exactly what is involved in program administration and who is to perform specific functions. It is particularly important to specify the role of the insurance agent or broker, along with the amount, form, timing, and source of the compensation the agent or broker will receive. Insurers pay first year and renewal year commissions at different rates and for different periods. Overriding commissions (to the office through which the insurance is placed) may also be payable, in effect adding to the writing agent's commission. Service fees may be payable as well. In addition, the writing agent or broker may expect to be paid fees directly by the employer.

A number of important issues are to be considered with respect to the compensation paid to an agent or broker. Will the compensation be adequate, inadequate, or excessive relative to the services he or she is expected to perform, for example? Will it be the same or different for the initial and subsequent years the program is in effect?

Note, in this regard, that commission payments are front-loaded when viewed relative to the total length of time the program will be in effect, even though the payments may be spread over several years. Thus, commission levels may bear an inverse relationship to the administrative effort; payments in early years may be disproportionately high relative to the work involved and become relatively smaller as the program matures and administrative work increases.

It is also important to determine who will continue providing services if the original agent or broker leaves the business, particularly since there will be little financial incentive for someone else to shoulder the administrative responsibilities.

ERISA Compliance

Executive retirement plans fall within the purview of Title I of ERISA. While pure excess benefit plans (limited to benefits lost by reason of Section 415) are generally exempt, other plans must comply with all of Title I's requirements unless they are limited to a select group of management or highly compensated employees and unfunded. Because the Department of Labor has yet to identify who is "highly compensated" for purposes of Title I, employers should limit eligibility and avoid anything that can be construed as funding. It is not clear whether split-dollar plans will be considered funded pension plans when the executive receives the value of tax-deferred increases in the cash value of the policy. Alternatively, these arrangements might be treated as welfare plans for purposes of ERISA due to the death benefits being provided.

Tax and Legal Considerations

Various tax and legal issues covered earlier in this chapter warrant an additional mention because they are so important in the evaluation process. These include:

1. The risk that split-dollar arrangements will be viewed as currently taxable interest-free loans to the executive.

2. The potential denial of deductions for interest paid on policy loans where the insured is no longer an employee.

3. The need to recognize that tax benefits may be lost or deferred in some years if the employer is in a tax-loss position or is an alternate minimum taxpayer.

4. The inability to deduct the cost of benefits provided to an executive through increases in the cash value of a policy held under a split-dollar arrangement.

5. The combined effect of income and estate taxes on death benefits provided from corporate assets when the benefit is funded through COLI.

6. The possibility of insurable interest issues being raised where insurance is continued on the lives of terminated executives.

7. The likelihood of federal tax law changes that could adversely affect COLI and split-dollar plans.

FINANCIAL CONSIDERATIONS

One of the difficulties in analyzing proposals for COLI or split-dollar coverage is that they often combine and thus may confuse issues of plan design and funding. The cost of the plan itself should be separated from the financial aspects of funding.

Plan Costs

From a cost standpoint, an executive benefit plan is the same as any other employee benefit plan: in general, the cost of the plan will ultimately equal the sum of the benefits actually paid plus the expense of plan operation. If the plan is funded, this outlay of principal will be reduced by any investment income on plan assets. If the investment income is less than the company could earn investing the funds elsewhere, however, funding could create additional costs. If a company can earn a 10 percent after-tax return on retained assets, but plan assets (an insurance policy, a pension fund, etc.) earn only 8 percent, the company should acknowledge a cost of 2 percent for the opportunity loss associated with the choice of investment vehicle.

If an employer buys permanent life insurance for a group of executives and maintains this insurance in force, actual mortality experience over the long run may or may not parallel that used in the insurer's table. The larger the insured group and the longer the plan is in effect, the more likely it is that actual experience will track the table. If so, the cost of the program should reflect the cost formula referred to above—the cost will equal the sum of benefits paid and expenses of operation, adjusted for investment considerations. Put another way, amounts paid to the insurer, together with investment income (and less the insurer's expenses and profit), will be returned to be paid as benefits. This principle has long been recognized in group life insurance, where experience-rating formulas develop costs in this fashion.[9]

If this formula correctly expresses the long-term cost of an executive benefit plan, it follows that the benefits paid to the executives or their beneficiaries will be a function of the actual mortality experience of the covered group and the effect of plan provisions on amounts payable.

Many proposals claim that there is no cost for executive benefits funded with permanent life insurance because "money advanced by the company to fund the program will be returned to the company together with a factor for the use of money"—a statement that often finds its way into proxy statements. This claim warrants close examination, because it may arise from a confusion of basic accounting concepts.

Suppose, for example, that an employer agrees to pay Executive A the sum of $1,000 in exactly one year. In order to have funds on hand to meet this obligation, the employer invests $909 in a 12-month certificate of deposit yielding a 10 percent annual rate of return. At the end of one year, the certificate matures for $1,000 and the employer uses this amount to pay Executive A.

Most people would agree that the employer in this simple example incurred a cost of $1,000 to provide Executive A with a benefit in that amount even though it invested only $909 for the certificate and did not have to expend any current income to meet the obligation when it came due. The interest earned during the year that became part of the total payment made to Executive A was the employer's property. The fact that the employer used an existing asset to make the payment (rather than current income) does not mean that it did not incur an expense.

This is basically what happens when an employer purchases life insurance. The employer assumes an obligation to pay benefits to the executive (or his or her estate); this obligation will produce a cost. The fact that insurance proceeds may become available to provide liquid funds that can be used to pay benefits does not mean that the benefits cost nothing. The insurance proceeds, over the long term, represent employer assets, partly a return of the principal amounts advanced and partly the investment return that could have been realized if the employer had otherwise invested the principal. In other words, setting aside an asset to meet a future cost does not eliminate that cost; it is a separate and distinct transaction.

Financial Analysis

Employers should view the purchase of permanent life insurance primarily as an investment. Thus, the effective rate of return that will be credited to the funds invested—a rate that is highly sensitive to the amount of tax leverage generated—is a critical consideration.

A discounted cash flow analysis, incorporating the time value of money, can be used to compute the employer's after-tax yield on an insurance product. Employer cash flow would include the following elements:

- *Income to the employer:* annual policy loans and net death benefits received from the insurer (i.e., gross policy death benefits less policy loans outstanding at date of death).

- *Outgo from the employer:* annual premiums and after-tax interest on policy loans.

Annual dividends typically are not considered as cash flow because they are usually used to purchase additional death benefits, which are included in the total proceeds received at death.

The discounted cash flow analysis includes these steps:

1. First, each year's income and outgo are adjusted to reflect the probability of occurrence (i.e., either survival or death).
2. Second, the adjusted annual amounts are discounted to determine the highest interest rate for which the current value of the income equals the current value of the outgo.

The interest rate determined in this manner is called the internal rate of return. This rate is often used to compare investment alternatives. If an employer can realize a higher rate of return elsewhere, the policies have a cost—the loss of the excess earnings otherwise available.

Several factors should be kept in mind when making this type of analysis.

Tax Implications.   Permanent life insurance can be a very effective tax-sheltered investment. As noted, the payment of policy proceeds at death will not be subject to income tax, and investment income that accumulates (through cash value buildup and/or dividends) over and above premiums paid will be tax-deferred—taxable only when and if the policy is surrendered. Further, investment income will not be subject to income tax at all if paid as part of the policy's death proceeds. The major exception is that both the inside buildup and the death proceeds will be considered in determining the corporate alternative minimum tax.

It is important to clarify one aspect of the claim that life insurance proceeds payable at death are income tax–free. While the basic statement is true (except for the corporate alternative minimum tax), the tax advantage only applies to part of the proceeds. To the extent the employer receives back an amount equal to the premiums it paid, there is no advantage. These amounts were after-tax or tax-free when paid to the insurer (i.e., they were not tax-deductible). Returning them tax-free does not enhance their original tax-free status.

Further tax advantages may accrue to the extent that policy loans are made (within permissible limits). This occurs when the after-tax cost of borrowing is less than the after-tax rate of interest credited by the insurer.

If a corporation borrows money from the insurer at a 6 percent interest rate, for example, its after-tax cost of borrowing (assuming a 35 percent tax bracket) is 3.9 percent. If the insurer is crediting interest to the policy with the equivalent of a 5 percent return, there is a difference of 1.1 percent. The effect of this can be illustrated by the following analysis of a $1,000 loan using the assumptions in this example:

Cost of Borrowing	Guaranteed plus Dividend Interest	Tax Saving	Net Gain
$−60	$+50	$+21	$+11

The greater the difference between the two rates, the greater the amount of leveraging.

Time value of money.   Any financial analysis should take into account the opportunity cost or time value of money associated with the proposed plan. It is not uncommon for the proposed plan to require that substantial amounts of employer capital be tied up for extended periods of time. This is illustrated by the example that follows, which is based on an actual proposal.

Executive A is currently age 55 and will be entitled at age 65 to an annual SERP benefit of $200,000 for life. The proposal calls for the employer to purchase an insurance policy with a face amount of $7,500,000 that has an annual premium of $512,000. The results at age 65 are as follows:

Cash value	
Guaranteed	4,048,000
Accumulated dividends (estimated)	2,820,000
Total	$6,868,000
Less total premiums (employer paid)	5,120,000
Net cash value	$1,748,000

The net cash value of $1,748,000 is equivalent to the required reserve for a $200,000 annual pension at age 65 using an interest rate of 7.8 percent.

In this example, which does not involve leveraging, the employer is tying up $5,120,000 (at the rate of $512,000 per year) for a 10-year period. If the same annual premium were invested each year in an investment yielding an after-tax return of, say, 8 percent, the accumulated investment return after 10 years would be $2,890,000.

This example underscores something noted earlier—the fact that it is often necessary to purchase very substantial amounts of life insurance to generate cash values sufficient to fund the desired level of retirement benefits. While a $200,000 per year pension is not an uncommon retirement plan objective for a highly paid employee, a $7,500,000 life insurance benefit may appear to be excessive.

Early termination.   As noted earlier, the financial analysis should measure the potential after-tax financial results of early termination of an insurance program—at the end of the 1st, 5th, 10th, 15th, and 20th years, for example.

A program terminated after only a few years will often produce minimal returns and even losses. If the policies are surrendered, any investment gain (gross cash values, without regard to loans that have been made, less premiums paid) will be taxable as income. Further, early year cash values will not reflect significant investment gains because the insurance policy is front-loaded to recover acquisition expenses. In fact, some policies will impose a surrender charge if the policy is terminated within a certain number of years after it has been issued. Long-term investment projections also rely on the payment of significant tax-free life insurance proceeds; these anticipated death claims may not have materialized in the early years of the program's operation.

Assumed interest.   Insurance proposals project financial results that are premised on assumptions as to dividend payments by the insurer; conclusions or opinions as to financial results are not guaranteed but are based on best estimates as to the insurer's future financial performance. Thus, proposals should be analyzed under several different future dividend scenarios. In selecting these scenarios, it is helpful to look at the historical investment performance of the insurer's total asset portfolio, as well as the insurer's dividend history with respect to the specific type of policy being contemplated, and how well it performed in the past compared with the dividend projections it made.

Other factors.   The following points are also important in analyzing insurance proposals:

- All costs and cost summaries should be shown on an after-tax basis—both for the employer and the executive.
- Costs to the executive, including direct contributions, taxes, or the time value of any money he or she has advanced, should be taken into account in looking at the total cost implications.
- Possible changes in anticipated financial results that could occur if the employer has tax losses or becomes an alternative minimum tax-payer should be determined.
- Financial results should be projected over the life expectancies of insured individuals.
- Any additional costs for executives who are not insurable at standard rates should be established.
- Because the purchase of permanent insurance is a long-term investment, the creditworthiness of the insurer should be carefully investigated.

Other matters may warrant scrutiny in specific proposals. And every analysis of permanent life insurance should include consideration of alternative ways of achieving employer objectives.

NOTES

1. For a discussion of the use of group universal life insurance (GULP) in executive benefit programs, see Chapters 7 and 10.
2. In general, a corporation will be allowed a deduction for interest paid on loans on policies covering individuals who are officers of the employer or who are financially interested in the employer's business, but only if at least four of the first seven annual premiums are paid other than by policy loan. See IRC Section 264(c)(1).
3. This $50,000 limit does not apply to policies that were purchased on or before June 20, 1986. See IRC Section 264(a)(4).
4. The amount taxable to the executive is determined under rates published by the Internal Revenue Service (often called PS 58 rates) or under the insurer's published term insurance rates, if lower.
5. These changes include a limit on the deductibility of policy loan interest to a maximum loan, per life, of $50,000, and the inclusion of life insurance proceeds and the inside buildup of cash values in determining whether the company is subject to the corporate alternative minimum tax.

6. Taxing this buildup for all individuals would be controversial, but has been recognized by the Congressional Budget Office as a potential source of major tax revenues—an important consideration if Congress seeks to gain additional tax revenues without raising tax rates.

7. This interpretation is consistent with the language of IRC Section 264(a)(4), which allows the interest deduction with respect to policies "covering the life of any individual who (A) *is* an officer or employee of, or (B) *is* financially interested in any trade or business carried on by the taxpayer . . . " (Emphasis added)

8. See Chapters 10 and 11.

9. Not surprisingly, the cost and pricing of insurance works the same way from the insurer's viewpoint. The insurer must collect enough money from premiums and investment income to cover its expenses, profit, and the amount of benefits it pays; in other words, the price of insurance is equal to the sum of the claims paid plus expenses (and profit), less income received on investments.

Chapter Thirteen

Securities Law Issues

The federal securities laws intersect with executive benefit plans, especially those sponsored by publicly held companies, at several points. All public companies are required to disclose specified information about the compensation they pay their executives, including benefits. Stock-based plans may bring additional rules into play, including registration and reporting requirements and insider trading restrictions. These requirements are the subject of this chapter.

PROXY DISCLOSURE RULES

By and large, a publicly traded company must disclose specified information about the compensation awarded to, paid to, or earned by the CEO and the company's four most highly paid officers in the proxy material distributed to shareholders and in the company's annual report on Form 10-K. (Disclosure of CEO compensation is always required. The pay disclosure threshold for the other executives is $100,000.) These proxy disclosure rules are issued by the Securities and Exchange Commission (SEC) under the Securities Exchange Act of 1934 (Exchange Act).

Under the rules, a CEO who departs before year-end would have to be named in the proxy, along with the new CEO and the four other highest-paid executive officers on the payroll as of year-end. In addition, a company must disclose pay for up to two other departed executives, assuming their actual salary plus bonus (not an annualized rate) would have been sufficient to place them among the top four highest paid had they been executive officers at year-end.

The information must be provided in a prescribed format, as described below. While a lengthy discussion of executive pay (salary, bonuses, stock options) is beyond the scope of this book,[1] it is important to weigh benefit programs in a total compensation context, which is what shareholders do when they read proxy disclosures. Thus, we will describe all required disclosures, not just those that apply to pensions and other executive benefits.

Summary Compensation Table

The proxy disclosure rules require employers to provide a Summary Compensation Table setting forth annual, long-term, and other compensation of the CEO and four other executive officers (determined as noted in previous paragraphs) for each of the last three years.

Annual Compensation.   The dollar amount of salary, bonus, and other annual compensation must be set forth in separate columns. Both cash and noncash amounts must be included.

- *Base salary and annual bonus.* Base salary and annual bonus must be stated separately. Amounts of base salary and annual bonus deferred at the election of the executive (including amounts contributed to a 401(k) plan) are included in the table as salary or bonus, as the case may be, in the year earned. As indicated above, these amounts also include salary and annual bonuses paid in the form of stock or other property.

  An election to receive options or restricted stock in lieu of salary or bonus must be footnoted. The dollar amount of the foregone salary or bonus need not be disclosed, but is taken into account for purposes of the $100,000 threshold and determining the most highly paid other executive officers. Any options or restricted stock received pursuant to such an election are reported in the appropriate column(s) for such compensation. If the form of the "in lieu of" grant is reportable in a table other than the Summary Compensation Table (e.g., a performance unit award), that fact must be disclosed in a footnote.

- *Other annual compensation.* The following items are disclosed in the aggregate, except for certain perquisites.

  Perquisites or personal benefits. Disclosure is required if the aggregate amount of such benefits equals or exceeds the lesser of $50,000 or 10 percent of total annual salary and bonus reported in the Summary Compensation Table. The type and amount of each perquisite or other personal benefit that exceeds 25 percent of the total amount of such benefits reported for a named executive must be footnoted.

Above-market or preferential earnings. Only above-market or preferential earnings on deferred compensation must be disclosed.[2] Such earnings on deferred compensation or on restricted stock, options, or stock appreciation rights (SARs) must be disclosed as "Other Annual Compensation" if paid or payable but deferred at the election of the executive. Thus, only earnings that the executive actually receives or could have received are reported here (e.g., preferential dividends actually paid to the executive on a restricted stock award). Where the plan or arrangement automatically defers and accumulates earnings, any above-market or preferential earnings are reported in the "All Other Compensation" column, as described below. This is the case even where the salary or bonus itself was electively deferred.

Generally, interest on deferred compensation is above-market if the rate exceeds 120 percent of the applicable federal long-term rate (the AFR) at the time the interest rate or formula is set under the plan. Only the above-market portion of the interest must be disclosed since it is only this portion that represents compensation as opposed to a payment by the company for the use of the executive's money. Dividends or dividend equivalents on restricted stock, options, SARs, or deferred compensation denominated in stock are preferential only if earned at a higher rate than dividends on the company's common stock. Again, only the preferential portion of the dividend must be disclosed.

Long-term earnings. Earnings on long-term incentive plan compensation are included if, prior to the payout or maturation of the award, such earnings are paid or payable but deferred at the election of the executive. Unlike the rule described above applicable to deferred compensation, all earnings, not just above-market earnings, are reportable since such earnings do not represent payments for the company's use of the executive's money. (Any earnings disclosed pursuant to this item would not be included in the amount received upon payout of the award.)

An example of the type of plan that could result in disclosure here is a restricted stock plan that includes performance-based conditions that the company has elected to treat as long-term incentive plan compensation. Any dividends paid (or payable but deferred by the executive) on such stock prior to vesting would be included in this column, even where such dividends are not preferential.

Tax gross-ups. Amounts reimbursed during the year for the payment of taxes are reported in this column. This includes, for example, tax gross-ups in connection with option exercises.

Discount stock purchases. This includes the dollar value of the difference between the price paid by the executive for any employer security and its fair market value on the date of purchase. Purchases made through salary or bonus deferrals would be included. Discounts available generally, either to all stockholders or all salaried employees, need not be disclosed. Thus, for example, discounts available under a qualified stock purchase plan would not be disclosed.[3] The reporting requirements for stock options are discussed in the paragraphs that follow.

Long-term compensation. The dollar amounts of restricted stock awards, long-term incentive plan payouts, and the number of stock options and SARs granted must be set forth in separate columns.

- *Restricted stock.* The dollar value of any restricted stock award (i.e., the closing price on the day of grant times the number of shares) must be shown, and the following additional information must be footnoted:

    The number and value of the executive's restricted stock holdings as of the end of the preceding year.

    If any part of the award will vest in under three years, the vesting schedule and the total number of shares awarded.

    Whether dividends are paid on the award, but not the amount. (As noted, dividends need only be disclosed to the extent they are preferential. Preferential dividends paid or payable but deferred at the executive's election are reported as Other Annual Compensation, or, if automatically deferred, as All Other Compensation.

Note that all aggregate year-end restricted stock holdings would have to be disclosed in the footnote, whether or not the new grants were disclosed.

A restricted stock award that includes performance-based conditions may alternatively be reported as a long-term incentive plan award in the separate table for such awards. When an award vests, however, the full value of the shares at that time is reported as a long-term incentive plan payout in the Summary Compensation Table. Note that in this case dividends on such shares would be reportable in full, whether or not preferential (see previous discussion).

Restricted stock units receive the same treatment as actual shares of restricted stock.

* *Long-term payouts.* The dollar value of all long-term incentive plan payouts must be disclosed. Amounts payable (because the award has matured or the performance cycle has ended) but deferred at the executive's election must also be disclosed. Long-term incentive plans are plans providing incentives for performance, however measured, over more than one year, other than restricted stock, stock option, or SAR plans. If any performance condition has been waived, that fact must be footnoted. Also, restricted stock that a company elected not to report in the Summary Compensation Table when awarded because it was subject to performance conditions must be reported here when such stock vests, based on the fair market value of the stock at vesting. Note that where the payout of the long-term award has been deferred at the executive's election, only above-market or preferential earnings thereon would be disclosed thereafter. A separate table, described in a later section, requires detailed disclosure of long-term awards.

* *Stock option and SAR grants.* The aggregate number of stock options (with or without tandem SARs) and freestanding SARs granted must be disclosed. No distinction is made between cash and stock SARs. Any options and SARs that have been repriced are included here. (See discussion under "Compensation Committee Report" for additional required disclosures in the case of repricings.) More detailed option and SAR disclosures are required in separate tables.

All other compensation.   Compensation not properly reportable under any of the columns described above is set forth in a separate column in the Summary Compensation Table. Amounts reported for the most recent year must be identified and quantified in a footnote. The items enumerated do not constitute an exclusive list.

* *Termination and change in control.* Amounts paid, payable, or accrued in connection with a termination of employment or change in control must be disclosed. Unlike the requirements regarding the narrative disclosure of employment contracts, termination arrangements, and golden parachutes, this requirement is not subject to any dollar threshold. Payouts under employee benefit plans, whether defined benefit or defined contribution, are *not* reportable under this item. Because executive officer status is determined as of the end of the preceding year, many such payments will apparently not be reportable.

- *Above-market or preferential earnings.* All above-market or preferential earnings on restricted stock, options, SARs, or deferred compensation must be reported here, *other than* those above-market or
  preferential earnings that have been paid to the executive or that
  were payable but were deferred at the executive's election. (As discussed previously, such earnings are reported in the Other Annual
  Compensation column.) Thus, in the typical deferred compensation
  arrangement where a percentage of salary or bonus is deferred either
  automatically or at the executive's election, and earnings on such
  deferred compensation are not payable until the end of the deferral
  period, any above-market or preferential earnings must be reported
  here. Again, only the above-market or preferential portion need be
  reported.

  As noted, no earnings need be reported where amounts have actually been invested. Presumably it is not necessary to actually "fund"
  this obligation or use a trust (rabbi or secular).

- *Long-term plan earnings.* Unlike the above-market rule applicable
  to deferred compensation, the full amount of earnings on long-term
  incentive plans is treated as compensation. Earnings prior to maturation or payment are reportable in this column unless such earnings
  have actually been paid or were payable but were deferred at the
  election of the executive (in which case such earnings would be
  reportable as Other Annual Compensation.) Note that if earnings
  under long-term incentive plans have been previously reported in
  the Summary Compensation Table, either as Other Annual
  Compensation or as All Other Compensation, such amounts would
  not be included in the amount reported at payout or maturation
  under Long-Term Incentive Plan Payouts. Finally, long-term incentive awards and amounts received upon exercise of stock options or
  SARs are not reportable as All Other Compensation.

- *Contributions to defined contribution plans.* Annual contributions or
  other allocations by the company on behalf of the executive to
  defined contribution plans must be reported. All defined contribution plans are subject to this requirement, whether qualified or nonqualified, and regardless of whether the executive's benefits are
  vested or not. Salary, bonus, or other amounts deferred pursuant to a
  mandatory or involuntary program would be disclosed here. (A plan
  may cover one person.)

  Earnings on defined contribution plan contributions are not
  reportable. It is clear that qualified plan earnings are not disclosed.
  The same rule apparently applies to earnings on supplemental or
  nonqualified plans, regardless of whether the contributions have

actually been invested with a third party or whether the earnings would otherwise be considered to be above-market.

Defined benefit and actuarial plans are not covered in the Summary Compensation Table; information regarding these plans is provided in the pension table, as discussed later in this chapter.

- *Split-dollar life insurance.*[4] The portion of the premium paid by the company that is attributable to term life insurance coverage must be reported. Additional disclosure is required if the executive has or will have an interest in the policy's cash value. The company can report either (1) the full dollar value of the remainder of the premium paid by it or (2) if the premiums will be refunded to the company, the current dollar value of the benefit to the executive of the remainder of such premium. The benefit is determined actuarially for the period between the payment of the premium and the earliest possible time, under the terms of the policy, that the company can recoup the premium. While not entirely clear, a footnote to the preamble indicates that the benefit to the executive is akin to an interest-free loan.

Option/SAR Tables

Information regarding the grant and exercise of options and SARs and unexercised options and SARs held by each executive are provided in two tables: One table sets forth each grant and its related value, and a second table includes aggregate exercises and the value of year-end holdings.

Grants and their values. For the CEO and each of the other named executive officers, the Option/SAR Grant Table includes: the number of options and SARs granted; the percent the grant represents of the total options and SARs granted to all employees during the year; the per share exercise or base price (and if such price is below market on the date of grant, a separate column indicating market price on the date of grant); the expiration date and either the potential realizable value of each grant or its present value. Potential realizable value is determined assuming that the market price of the underlying securities appreciates from grant to the end of the term at 5 percent and 10 percent. The present value of the grant at grant date may be determined under an option pricing model.

Exercises and year-end values. Information regarding exercises is presented on an aggregate basis for each named executive. The table must indicate the number of shares received and the aggregate dollar value realized. If no shares were received, the number of securities with respect to which options or SARs were exercised would be indicated. The value realized is calculated by subtracting the exercise price from the fair market value of the underlying securities as of the date of exercise. Thus, the withholding of shares to pay the exercise price or taxes will not affect the calculation. Similarly, tax reimbursements or gross-ups would not be reflected in this column but would be reported in the Other Annual Compensation column of the Summary Compensation Table, as discussed previously.

This table would also show the total number of options and SARs held at year-end (distinguishing between exercisable and nonexercisable) and the aggregate amount by which the market value of the underlying stock exceeds the exercise price of in-the-money options and SARs. Underwater options are disregarded in calculating this aggregate amount since such options do not affect the amount that could be realized from other options.[5]

Repricings

If at any time during the last year the company has adjusted or amended the exercise price of options or SARs previously awarded to an executive officer (whether through amendment, cancellation, or replacement grants, or by any other means), the company must make certain disclosures.

First, the compensation committee must explain in reasonable detail any such repricing, as well as the basis thereof. Second, a table must set forth information concerning all repricings of any options or SARs held by any executive officer during the last 10 years, the name and position of the executive, the date of the repricing, and the number of replacement or amended options or SARs.

No disclosure is required for repricings occurring through the operation of the plan formula in existence at the time of the original grant (as in the case of some indexed and premium options), the operation of a plan antidilution provision or a recapitalization or similar transaction affecting all shareholders equally.

Long-Term Incentive Plan Awards

The information required in the long-term incentive plan table includes the number of shares, units, or other rights awarded under the plan; the performance period; and, for plans not based on stock price, the dollar value of the range of estimated payouts under the award (i.e., threshold, target, and maximum amounts), regardless of whether the award itself is denominated in cash or stock. Estimated payout information is not required for plans based solely on stock price. There is also no requirement that the company attribute a grant date value to any award.

In a footnote, the material terms of the award, including a general description of the formula or criteria to be applied, must be disclosed. However, no disclosure is required of any factor or condition that involves confidential business information.

A restricted stock award whose vesting is performance-based may be reported in this table if not reported as an award of restricted stock in the Summary Compensation Table.

The term *long-term incentive plan* is defined in the discussion of earnings on long-term incentive plans as Other Annual Compensation. Thus, the term excludes restricted stock, stock option, and SAR plans.

Pension and Other Defined Benefit Plan Disclosures

The proxy disclosure rules require only that estimated benefits under defined benefit or actuarial plans be disclosed. No information regarding these plans is required to be included in the Summary Compensation Table, and annual accruals need not be disclosed, either pursuant to this or any other disclosure item (e.g., as part of a long-term incentive plan or deferred compensation plan).

A pension table showing benefits by compensation and years of service classifications must be used for defined benefit and actuarial plans that base benefits primarily on final (or final average) compensation and years of service. Amounts attributable to supplementary or excess plans will be reflected in the table on an aggregate basis with qualified plan benefits. Narrative disclosure of the estimated years of service for each executive and the basis on which benefits are shown (e.g., life annuity with no Social Security offset) is required. Note that the pension table should show benefits payable under both qualified and nonqualified plans in the aggregate.

Disclosure must include a comparison of pension compensation to the compensation reflected in the Summary Compensation Table. Pension compensation must be disclosed if it differs substantially (by more than 10 percent) from that set forth in the Summary Compensation Table. Since all items reported in the Summary Compensation Table must be taken into account for this purpose, not merely those reported as annual compensation, many companies may be required to disclose pension compensation.

Defined benefit plans that determine benefits other than by reference to final (or final average) compensation and years of service will continue to be subject to the alternative disclosure rule. This rule requires disclosure of the formula by which benefits are determined and an estimate of the annual benefits payable at normal retirement age to each executive.

Finally, no disclosures are required pursuant to this item with respect to defined contribution plans. Accordingly, the only information required for defined contribution plans will be amounts reported in the All Other Compensation column of the Summary Compensation Table.

Stock-Based SERPs

Proxy disclosure is a relatively straightforward matter for the stock-based target benefit SERP described in Chapter 11. Grants of stock in lieu of normal SERP benefits will be disclosed in the same manner as other awards of such stock under a company's long-term incentive plans; in most cases, the dollar value of a grant of shares will be disclosed in the Summary Compensation Table under the column Restricted Stock Awards. A company will probably want to include a footnote disclosure explaining that the shares granted are designed to provide a source of income at retirement and are in lieu of normal SERP benefits.

Similar proxy disclosure is required for the elective approach; grants of options in lieu of normal SERP benefits will be disclosed in the Summary Compensation Table under the column Options/SARs. Footnote disclosure of the fact that the options have been granted in lieu of SERP benefits is probably warranted. Additional disclosures respecting the options will be required in the table on Option/SAR Grants In The Last Fiscal Year, including the potential realizable value of the options or a Black-Scholes type value.

The appropriate way to illustrate a floor-offset SERP is less clear. As noted, the proxy rules indicate that disclosure for pension and other defined benefit or actuarial plans is limited to the pension table, and that nothing about these plans need be disclosed in the Summary Compensation Table. As explained previously, however, grants of restricted stock must be disclosed in the Summary Compensation Table. Because the amount of SERP benefits an individual receives will be contingent on share price performance, while the value of the shares will not be affected by the SERP benefits, it is probably appropriate to disclose the restricted stock in the normal way in the Summary Table, accompanied by footnote disclosure explaining the offset of SERP benefits by the value of the shares granted. In calculating estimated SERP benefits for purposes of the pension table, it is probably reasonable to calculate an offset for assumed future share price performance, which means that no SERP benefit, or only a small one, will have to be disclosed. Footnote disclosure of the use of this approach is probably also advisable.

Employment Contracts and Severance and Change of Control Agreements

A company must also disclose, in narrative form, all employment contracts with the CEO and other named executives, as well as termination of employment and change of control arrangements, where the amount involved is $100,000 or more. Note that this dollar threshold is inapplicable to payments actually made pursuant to these arrangements. See the discussion regarding All Other Compensation.

Compensation Committee Report

The rules require the compensation committee (or in its absence, the board of directors) to provide a report disclosing the compensation policies applicable to the company's executive officers, including the specific relationship of corporate performance to executive compensation with respect to compensation reported for the last year. There need not be a discussion of each individual committee member's reasoning, nor any discussion of the relationship between the compensation of each individual executive and company performance other than as to the CEO. However, the report must identify performance measures that were considered by the committee, such as sales, earnings, return on assets or equity, or market share. Disclosure of specific target levels or any factors involving confidential information is not required.

In the case of the CEO, more detail is required. The report must discuss the relationship of the company's performance to the CEO's compensation for the last year, including a description of each measure of company performance, both qualitative and quantitative, on which compensation was based.

Performance Graph

To complement the compensation committee's report, the proxy statement must include a performance graph comparing the yearly percentage change in a company's cumulative total shareholder return on its common stock with the cumulative total return of a broad equity market index and a more selective group of peer companies. In all cases, cumulative shareholder return is measured assuming dividend reinvestment. The returns must be shown for a five-year period.

REGISTRATION AND REPORTING REQUIREMENTS

The principal purpose of the Securities Act of 1933 (the Securities Act) is to ensure that prospective shareholders have access to relevant information before they buy securities. To that end companies must file a registration statement with the SEC before they can offer or sell shares of stock unless an exemption from registration is available.[6]

Section 11 of the Securities Act imposes civil liability in connection with a registration statement. Liability may be imposed if the registration statement contains an untrue statement of a material fact, or omits a material fact required to be included in the registration statement or necessary to make the statements made not misleading. Under Section 11, a purchaser of the securities may sue every person who signed the registration statement (e.g., the company's principal executive officer, principal financial officer, and controller or principal accounting officer), every director, certain professionals (such as an accountant who has, with his consent, been named as certifying or preparing the financial statements used in the registration statement), and every underwriter of the securities.

The term *security* may include interests in voluntary, contributory employee benefit plans, such as thrift, savings, 401(k), and similar plans. These interests are exempt from the registration requirements, however, except where employees may invest their own contributions, including salary reduction contributions, in employer stock.[7]

The cost of Securities Act registration can be a significant burden to an employer, largely because of the extensive financial disclosure required. If the employer is subject to the reporting requirements of the Exchange Act,[8] however, registration can be accomplished with relative ease using Form S-8, which is specifically designed for employee benefit plans.

A company may use Form S-8 if, immediately prior to the time of filing the registration statement, it is subject to the reporting requirements of Section 13 or 15(d) of the Exchange Act and has filed all reports and other materials required to be filed during the preceding 12 months (or for such shorter period that the company was required to file such reports and materials).[9]

As a registration statement, Form S-8 is relatively simple. Each participant in an executive benefit arrangement must receive material information regarding the plan and its operations to enable the participant to make an informed decision regarding investment in the plan. Participants must also be given a written statement advising them of the availability on request of the Exchange Act reports and other documents incorporated by reference into the Form S-8 registration statement. The plan information and written statement do not have to be in the form of a customary prospectus.[10] A registration statement filed on Form S-8 is effective immediately upon filing with the SEC.[11]

Reoffers and resales of certain securities may also be made pursuant to a registration statement on Form S-8 by means of a separate prospectus (a reoffer prospectus).[12]

Generally, the amount of securities reoffered and resold by means of the reoffer prospectus by each person cannot exceed the volume limitations of Rule 144 during any three-month period. Note that the limitation is not an aggregate limit but is applied separately to each person.

SEC Rule 701 provides an exemption from the registration requirements of the Securities Act for offers and sales of securities pursuant to compensatory benefit plans or written contracts by companies that are not subject to the reporting requirements of the Exchange Act and are not investment companies.[13] The amount of securities that may be subject to outstanding offers plus the amount sold in the preceding 12 months cannot exceed the greater of $500,000 or amounts determined under two different formulas. One formula limits the amount to 15 percent of the company's total assets and the second to 15 percent of the outstanding securities of the same class. In no event can this amount exceed $5 million. In calculating this amount, bonus or restricted stock may be excluded.[14] The exemption is not exclusive; that is, a company can also claim the availability of any other applicable Securities Act exemption. There is no exemption from the antifraud provisions of the federal securities laws nor from the provisions of any applicable state securities laws.[15]

INSIDER TRADING

Section 16 of the Exchange Act is designed to provide the public with information on the securities transactions and holdings of insiders[16] of publicly held companies and to deter them from engaging in transactions while in possession of material nonpublic information. This provision prohibits insiders from purchasing and selling stock of the company within a six-month period, and requires those who violate this trading restriction to turn over all profits made on the transaction (known as short-swing profits) to the company. Because Section 16 is a strict liability provision, an insider's short-swing profits can be recovered regardless of whether the insider is actually in possession of material nonpublic information.

Stock Award Plans

The grant or award of a derivative security—including stock options, SARs, convertible debentures and, in general, any similar security with a value derived from an equity security—is deemed a purchase of the underlying securities for purposes of Section 16.[17]

Most stock option and similar stock-based plans are designed to satisfy the requirements of SEC Rule 16b-3 and thus exempt shares granted to an insider executive under the plan from being treated as a purchase. The conditions for the exemption are as follows:

Six-month holding period: The exemption for grants or awards of new bonus stock, stock options, and other derivative securities is conditioned on a six-month holding period. A total of six months must elapse between grant and sale; the timing of the exercise does not affect the six-month period. If the insider sells the securities within the six-month period, the exemption for the grant or award is lost, and the sale is matchable with the grant or award transaction or any other nonexempt acquisitions for purposes of short-swing profit liability. However, the insider is free to sell other securities during this six-month period.

Written plan: The plan must be in writing and must set forth the means or basis for determining eligibility to participate and either the price at which the securities may be offered and the amount of securities to be awarded or the method by which the price and the amount of the award are to be determined. The plan or a written agreement also must provide that derivative securities (e.g., options) are not transferable other than by will or by the laws of descent and distribution. However, the rule makes it clear that a beneficiary designation is not a transfer and also permits transfers pursuant to qualified domestic relations orders (QDROs) under the Internal Revenue Code or ERISA.[18]

Shareholder approval: The plan must have been approved by the holders of a majority of the shares of voting securities of the corporation represented at a shareholders meeting.

Disinterested administration: If the plan provides for discretionary awards, award decisions must be made by a committee of two or more directors who are disinterested. (Award decisions can no longer be made by nondirectors.) A director is disinterested if he or she has not during the immediately preceding one year been granted or awarded equity securities pursuant to the plan or any other company plan. Certain awards made automatically to directors pursuant to a formula plan are ignored for this purpose.

Benefit Plans

An allocation of company stock to an insider under a broad-based employee benefit plan, such as a 401(k) plan, is also considered a purchase by the insider absent an exemption. In the past, broad exemptions were available for many transactions involving company stock in qualified plans; for example, an insider's election to switch into or out of a company stock fund within the plan was generally not considered a purchase or sale, and the transaction was not required to be reported to the SEC. In 1991, the SEC issued final regulations that would have dramatically changed the requirements that apply to broad-based savings, stock purchase, and other qualified plans. In response to employer objections, however, the SEC reconsidered its position. On August 10, 1994, the SEC released proposed amendments to the 1991 regulations and delayed the compliance deadline (originally set for September 1, 1994) until September 1, 1995.

Under the proposed amendments to the final regulations issued in 1991, the insider trading rules would continue to exempt certain purchases and sales under a written employer plan that is approved by shareholders or qualifies for an exemption from this requirement.

Many broad-based plans allow participants to direct transactions under the plan, including transactions that result in the purchase or sale of employer stock. In a 401(k) plan, for example, a participant may be able to elect the level of contributions (some or all of which may be invested in the employer stock fund) and elect to move his or her account balance into or out of the plan's employer stock fund. Purchases or sales of employer stock at the direction of a participant may be matched with other purchases or sales within the prior or succeeding six months to create liability under Section 16(b) unless an exemption is available.

Some broad-based plans, employee stock ownership plans (ESOPs), for example, may simply allocate stock to participants with no direction on their part. Although insider-participants cannot control their receipt of such shares, allocations to their accounts would also be treated as purchases potentially matchable with recent sales absent an exemption.

Qualified plan transactions.   The proposed rules would exempt all purchase transactions (other than intra-plan transfers) resulting from employee pretax or after-tax contributions or employer contributions (including matching contributions and nonelective employer contributions) under a broad-based plan. Both initial purchases as well as ongoing purchases would be entitled to the exemption. The exemption applies to plans qualified under Section 401(a), as well as employee stock purchase plans under Section 423, that do not discriminate in favor of highly paid employees. Thus, the stock acquired with pretax contributions made by an insider participating in a Section 401(k) plan would not be considered a purchase and would not be matched with sales within the prior or succeeding six months. In addition, the insider could change the level of his or her contributions or stop making contributions to the plan at any time without triggering insider trading liability. The theory behind the exemption is that significant Internal Revenue Code and ERISA restrictions make it unlikely that insiders will use these plans in the manner that Section 16(b) is designed to prevent.

Nonqualified plans.   Many employers sponsor nonqualified plans that mirror the qualified plan. For example, a nonqualified 401(k) plan might allow participants to defer additional amounts in excess of the $7,000 (indexed) limit on elective deferrals, measuring investment returns under the nonqualified mirror according to the participant's investment elections under the qualified plan. If one of the investment options under the qualified plan is an employer stock fund, the nonqualified mirror plan might provide for distributions to participants in the form of employer stock to the extent of the insider's "investment" in the employer stock fund. But the ability to have compensation rights under the nonqualified plan determined by the employer's stock price would generally be a derivative security and subject to Section 16(b).

The proposed amendments would exempt purchase transactions under such nonqualified mirror plans, defined as those providing benefits that would be provided by the qualified plan except for the $150,000 pay limit under Section 401(a)(17), the limit on contributions and benefits under Section 415, and any other limit on contributions or benefits under the IRC, i.e., the $7,000 (indexed) limit on elective deferrals under Section 402(g) and the ADP/ACP tests. The rationale for the exemption is that such plans, though not subject to ERISA or the IRC, are so closely tied to the qualified plan that insiders are not able to use them for speculation in employer securities.

Because of the narrow definition of a mirror plan for this purpose, it appears that a nonqualified plan that provides benefits in excess of those that can be provided under the qualified plan for reasons other than the tax law limits—such as a plan that provided a higher rate of matching contribution than that provided under the qualified plan—would not be entitled to the exemption. Thus, purchase transactions under such a plan would be subject to insider trading liability. If a nonqualified plan that does not otherwise qualify for an exemption as a mirror plan pays benefits in cash only, the plan may be completely exempt from the insider trading rules (including the reporting rules).

Fund switches. As under the 1991 final regulations, purchases and sales of stock caused by a participant's election to transfer investments in or out of an employer stock fund under a plan are exempt if certain conditions are met. Basically, an insider may use either of two alternative definitions to exempt a fund switch: a window period election or a six-month advance election.

The insider's election to transfer into or out of the employer stock fund must be made during one of the quarterly ten-day window periods relating to the release by the employer of its financial information to the public. The period begins on the third business day after the release of such information and ends on the twelfth business day after release. The primary change in the proposals would allow participants to make such elections *every* quarter instead of waiting a minimum of six months from the last such election, as required by the 1991 rules. This would still require plans to change the election period for insiders to move some or all of their account balances into or out of the employer stock funds to coincide with the quarterly ten-day window period. The exemption would apply to both qualified and nonqualified plans.

As an alternative, a plan could require an insider to elect to switch into or out of the employer stock fund under the regular provisions of the plan—but the election would not be effective for six months. Although the election must be "irrevocable," the proposed amendments would clarify that the election could be revoked or changed by a subsequent election that does not take effect for six months.

The proposed amendments also would exempt fund switches made by an insider because of the diversification requirements under Section 401(a)(28) that apply in the case of ESOPs. Those rules generally allow an insider who is age 55 with 10 years of participation under an ESOP to make an election to transfer out of the stock fund within 90 days after the end of the plan year.

Plan distributions.   Under the 1991 regulations, distributions of securities that were acquired in an exempt manner were exempt. Under the proposed amendment, the exemption for distributions of stock to insiders would be broadened to apply to all distributions of employer stock regardless of whether the stock was acquired in an exempt transaction. The theory behind this rule is that stock is considered to have been purchased by the insider when it was allocated to his or her account under the plan; the distribution of the stock is therefore simply a change in the form of ownership.

In general, if a plan distributes the cash value of the employer stock in an insider's account, the distribution would not be exempt and would be viewed as a sale. This would be the case in a plan that allows an insider to convert employer stock held under the plan into cash before it is distributed. However, distributions of stock and cash, or the deferral of such a distribution, would be exempt if made on account of death, retirement, disability or termination of employment. The exemption would be available whether or not the distribution is made pursuant to the insider's election. Also, an exemption would apply to distributions of cash and stock from an ESOP pursuant to a diversification election under Section 401(a)(28), as well as involuntary distributions of stock or cash (including cash in lieu of fractional shares) for the purposes of satisfying the ADP and ACP tests under Section 401(k). To be eligible for both of these exemptions, the plan would have to be in writing and meet the shareholder approval requirements mentioned earlier. The plan would not have to be a Section 401(a) or Section 423 plan, however.

An in-service distribution made to an insider of all or a portion of the value of his employer stock fund account in cash would not be exempt and would be considered a sale. Such an in-service distribution would nonetheless be exempt if made pursuant to a six-month irrevocable election by the insider to take the distribution. This is impractical for a hardship distribution from a Section 401(k) plan, however, and none of the other expanded exemptions seem to apply. It may be possible, although it is doubtful, to exempt the transaction as the economic equivalent of a fund switch permitting the election to be made during a window period.

Stock-Based SERPs

As noted, the insider trading rules restrict an insider's ability to acquire or dispose of derivative securities—options, warrants, stock appreciation rights, or other similar rights with an exercise or conversion privilege at a price related to stock or other equity securities of the issuer or similar securities with a value derived from the value of such stock or other securities. Derivative securities are either call equivalents such as an option entitling the holder to purchase stock at a certain price, or put equivalents, such as an option entitling the holder to sell stock at a certain price. An insider who acquires a put equivalent derivative security is treated as having sold the underlying stock at the time the put is acquired.

It is possible that an accrual under a floor-offset stock-based SERP[19] could be treated as a grant of put equivalent derivative securities for purposes of these rules, since a put equivalent position is broadly defined as any derivative security that increases in value as the value of the underlying securities decreases. This is precisely what happens to a SERP accrual that is offset by the value of company stock.

If a stock SERP accrual is treated as the grant of a put equivalent security, an insider receiving such an accrual would be treated as having sold employer stock equal to the value of the benefit accrued and would be liable to return short-swing profits to the company resulting from any nonexempt purchase of stock that occurred within six months before or after the date on which the SERP benefit accrued. (Note that other sales of employer stock by an insider in this case will not create any problems.)

It is not clear whether a floor-offset stock-based SERP will be entangled in this rule, however. Arguably, SERP accruals do not constitute derivative securities because they are not similar to an option, warrant, or stock appreciation right in that they provide no explicit exercise or conversion price.[20] Until the SEC offers formal guidance, employers considering the use of a floor-offset stock-based SERP should seek the advice of legal counsel on this issue. A cautious employer might consider modifying its SERP to meet the requirements of SEC Rule 16b-3, in which case grants of put equivalent derivative securities in the form of SERP accruals will be exempt from triggering short-swing profit liability.

Reporting and Disclosure

The following reporting requirements govern insider stock transactions:

- *Form 3:* Initial statements of beneficial ownership of equity securities must be filed on Form 3. This form is required to be filed within 10 days after the event by which the person becomes an insider.

- *Form 4:* An insider must report all purchases and sales after becoming an insider on Form 4, as well as all other changes in beneficial ownership, except those transactions reportable on Form 5. Form 4 must be filed on or before the 10th day after the end of the month in which the change in beneficial ownership occurred. In general, transactions reportable on Form 4 are those that are not exempt from short-swing liability.

- *Form 5:* Form 5 must be used by insiders to report transactions exempt from short-swing profit liability (e.g., grants and awards under a 16b-3 plan and previously unreported exercises of stock options and SARs) and certain other types of transactions. Form 5 must be filed within 45 days of the company's fiscal year-end. Every person who was an insider at any time during the year must report all transactions during that period that were not previously reported on a Form 4 either because of deferred reporting or failure to file required reports. No Form 5 filing is required if the insider had no reportable transactions.

Although insiders are solely responsible for their reports, companies will get involved in the process through changes made to the disclosure rules. The SEC has adopted new Item 405 of Regulation S-K, which requires a company to disclose in its proxy statement and Form 10-K information regarding delinquent Section 16 filings by insiders, including the names of the insiders and the number of delinquent filings and transactions. The SEC is also considering certain changes to the reporting requirements.

A company will not be liable for incorrect disclosures if the information reported is consistent with the information disclosed on the Forms 3, 4, and 5 sent to the company by the insider. A company will have no obligation to research or make any inquiries regarding delinquent filings.

OTHER REQUIREMENTS

If the shares of stock to be offered under an executive arrangement are listed on a stock exchange, the employer must comply with the requirements of the exchange. State corporation law may also have an impact on executive programs.

Stock Exchange Rules

Both the New York Stock Exchange and the American Stock Exchange generally require that an employer disclose all the essential elements of a stock option, stock purchase, or other stock-based compensation plan to be offered to executives and obtain shareholder approval of the arrangement. Both exchanges also require that shareholders be informed of any changes that the employer may make to the plans without seeking shareholder approval. The American Stock Exchange does not require approval by a specified percentage of voting stock; the New York Stock Exchange requires approval by the majority of votes cast, and total votes cast must represent over 50 percent of the shares entitled to vote. Note that these requirements may not apply if the executive benefit arrangement uses treasury shares only (i.e., shares that have already been listed on the exchange in question).

Both exchanges also require the employer to disclose the issuance of options in its annual report. The information that must be disclosed includes, for example, the number of shares issuable under options outstanding at the beginning of the year; changes in the total resulting from issuance, exercise, cancellation, or expiration of options; and changes in the exercise price and the number of shares available for option grant at the beginning and close of the year.

State Law

State corporate law will govern the employer's ability to adopt stock option plans and other executive benefit arrangements, such as loan programs. State corporate law will also determine whether shareholders must approve of a stock-based compensation plan as well as any amendments to the plan. For example, a company incorporated in Delaware does not need shareholder approval to adopt a stock-based compensation arrangement, whereas a company incorporated in New York would if it is also listed on a national stock exchange. Thus, every company must ascertain the law in the state in which it was incorporated to determine whether shareholder approval is required. Even if a company is incorporated in a state that does not expressly require shareholder approval for stock-based incentive plans, this does not insure that no approval is required; a corporation's charter or bylaws might require such approval. Employers should consult with legal counsel as to whether shareholder approval is required with respect to a particular plan.

NOTES

1. See Chapter 2 for a brief discussion of stock options and other elements of executive pay.

2. Issues involved in determining the interest to be credited to deferred amounts are discussed in Chapter 6.

3. A stock purchase plan is qualified under Section 423 of the IRC if, among other things, it covers all employees, with certain exclusions for part-time and seasonal employees, individuals employed less than two years, and highly compensated employees. A Section 423 plan can provide discounts of up to 15 percent.

4. See Chapter 12 for a discussion of split-dollar insurance.

5. Options and SARs are in the money if the value of the underlying securities exceeds the exercise or base price of the options or SARs. All other options or SARS are underwater.

6. Section 5 of the Securities Act of 1933. Under Sec. 12(1) of the Securities Act, a person who offers or sells a security in violation of the registration requirements is liable to the purchaser (i) where the purchaser still owns the security, for the amount of the consideration paid for such security, plus interest but less the amount of any income received on the security and (ii) where the purchaser no longer owns the security, for damages.

7. See, generally, SEC Release No. 33-6188, February 1, 1980, and Release No. 33-6281, January 15, 1981. Note that stock bonus plans may not be subject to the registration requirements on the theory that there is no sale within the meaning of the Securities Act.

8. The reporting requirements of the Securities Exchange Act of 1934 apply to companies whose securities are registered under the Exchange Act. In general, such registration is required for securities listed on a stock exchange registered under the Exchange Act, such as the New York, American, Boston, Midwest, Pacific, and Philadelphia Stock Exchanges, and for securities with 500 or more record holders of a class of equity securities where the company has total assets of more than $5 million (typically, companies whose securities are traded in the over-the-counter market). Exchange Act reporting requirements also apply to companies whose securities are registered under the Securities Act.

9. In general, a company satisfies its Exchange Act reporting requirements by filing annual reports on Form 10-K and quarterly reports on Form 10-Q. Form 10-K calls for (among other things): a description of the company's business, including a discussion of recent developments; financial information about industry segments and foreign and domestic operations; audited

financial statements and supplementary data, and management's discussion and analysis of financial condition and results of operation. Form 10-Q calls for less extensive financial disclosure and for other information. When certain significant events occur, such as a change in control or the acquisition or disposition of a significant amount of assets, the company must file a current report on Form 8-K.

10. SEC Release No. 33-6867.

11. SEC Rule 462; SEC Release No. 33-6867.

12. While the reoffer prospectus is filed under cover of Form S-8, it contains the disclosure required by Part I of Form S-3. The offer prospectus is filed with the registration statement or, in the case of control securities, a posteffective amendment thereto.

13. Offers and sales that are exempt from the registration requirements of the Securities Act are still subject to the antifraud provisions of both the Securities Act and the Exchange Act (Sections 12 and 17 of the Securities Act and Section 10(b) of the Exchange Act).

14. Rule 701 et seq.; SEC Release No. 33-6768, April 14, 1988.

15. See, generally, the Preliminary Notes to Rule 701.

16. Insiders include every person who is directly or indirectly the beneficial owner of more than 10 percent of any class of equity securities registered pursuant to Section 12 of the Exchange Act, and every director and officer of the company issuing a class of equity securities so registered.

17. The SEC has proposed to exempt from insider trading liability (and reporting) all "cash only" rights issued in the context of a compensation arrangements between an employer and its employees. To be entitled to the exemption, the insider must not have the option to take, or the employer must not have the discretion to pay, the benefit in stock. Thus, SARs that can be settled only in cash would be exempt. The exemption is controversial and may not be adopted by the SEC.

18. The SEC has proposed to eliminate the restriction on transferability.

19. See Chapter 11 for a discussion of stock-based SERPs.

20. If the SERP benefit is payable in cash only, the SERP accrual would not constitute a derivative security under the proposed "cash-only" rights exemption discussed in footnote 17.

Chapter Fourteen

The Special Problems of Tax-Exempt Employers

The wants and needs of executives do not differ greatly based simply on the taxable or tax-exempt status of their employers. Nonetheless, the benefits that tax-exempt organizations may offer their executives differ considerably from those available to their for-profit counterparts, especially in the area of retirement plans and deferred compensation arrangements—the focus of this chapter.

BACKGROUND

Internal Revenue Code Section 501, entitled "Exemption from tax on corporations, certain trusts, etc.," sets forth more than 20 different categories of organizations and entities that are exempted from tax. These are in addition to the single largest group of tax-exempt organizations, namely governmental units. Even if the government sector is disregarded, the overall significance of tax-exempt organizations in the U.S. economy is enormous.

The following are just some of the categories of organizations exempt from tax under IRC Section 501(c):

- Organizations operated exclusively for religious, charitable, educational, or scientific purposes; for public safety testing; to foster national or international amateur sports competition; or for the prevention of cruelty to children or animals. These are known as 501(c)(3) organizations; non-profit hospitals fall within this category of tax-exempt organizations.
- Civic leagues operated exclusively for the promotion of social welfare; labor, agricultural, or horticultural organizations; business

leagues, chambers of commerce, real estate boards, boards of trade; clubs organized for pleasure, recreation, and other nonprofit purposes; and fraternal beneficiary societies, orders, or associations. These organizations, exempted under IRC Section 501(c)(4) through (c)(8), include professional football leagues.

- Voluntary employees' beneficiary associations providing for the payment of life, sick, accident, or other benefits to members. Known as VEBAs or 501(c)(9) trusts, these funding vehicles, established by employees but funded by the employer, allow for the tax-free accumulation of assets to pay death benefits, benefits due to illness or personal injury, and other benefits intended to safeguard or improve health or protect against contingencies that impair earnings.
- Teachers' retirement fund associations of a local nature.
- Credit unions.
- Certain mutual insurance companies.
- War veterans' posts or organizations.

Many people equate *tax-exempt organization* with *charitable organization,* or at the very least, with *not-for-profit organization.* And while it is certainly the case that many tax-exempt organizations do provide extensive charitable services and many are run on tight budgets, other tax-exempt entities provide little or no charitable work and operate on huge budgets. Thus, for many tax-exempt organizations, the environment into which executives must be recruited and will hopefully be retained is identical to the for-profit environment in several ways: it is complex, highly competitive, and involves significant amounts of capital and large numbers of employees. And just as in the for-profit world, tax-exempt organizations must draw their executives from a relatively limited pool of individuals. If there is a difference in environments, it is that compensation programs in tax-exempt organizations tend to be subject to a level of public scrutiny usually reserved for the largest for-profit companies.

Tax-exempt organizations face a number of obstacles in providing retirement benefits for their executives. In 1978, the IRS released proposed regulations calling for employees to be taxed on amounts deferred pursuant to a salary reduction agreement at the time of deferral. Shortly thereafter, Congress decided to give *taxable* organizations relief from those regulations via the Revenue Act of 1978, which states that employees of such employers will be taxed only when they actually receive compensation. But it decided not to extend the same tax relief to state and local governments. Instead, it imposed some special restrictions, codified in Section 457 of the IRC, on the deferred compensation plans of these employers.[1] Section 457 was extended to *other* tax-exempt employers in the Tax Reform Act of 1986.[2] As a result, nongovernmental tax-exempt employers now have limited options in assembling deferred compensation packages for their higher-paid executives.

RETIREMENT PLANS

A brief overview of the various retirement vehicles available to nongovernmental tax-exempt employers and how they interact is essential to an understanding of the special situation executives of these organizations face relative to their for-profit peers. These vehicles include:

- 401(a) plans: Defined benefit pension plans, money purchase pension plans, profit-sharing plans, and stock bonus plans qualified under IRC Section 401(a), other than plans with a 401(k) elective deferral feature.
- Grandfathered 401(k) plans: As a general rule, only those nongovernmental tax-exempt organizations that had 401(k) plans in place before July 2, 1986, may continue to maintain these grandfathered plans. State and local government employers must have had plans in effect before May 6, 1986, for them to be grandfathered.[3]
- 403(b) plans: These plans, described in detail later in this chapter, are similar to 401(a) plans insofar as the employer's contributions made on behalf of the employees (and earnings thereon) are not considered to be owned by the employer and, therefore, are beyond the reach of the employer and its creditors; amounts contributed (and earnings thereon) are not subject to tax until distributed; and amounts contributed are not included in current income of the employees on whose behalf the contributions are made.

  These plans are also similar to 401(k) plans because they can be structured to allow participants to electively defer (or, as with 401(k) plans, authorize the employer to electively defer on their behalf) amounts that otherwise would be paid to them as salary.
- 457 plans: Nonqualified plans that allow for deferral of current income under IRC Section 457. These, too, will be described in detail later in this chapter.

Table 14–1 indicates what types of entities can maintain which of the previously described plans.

TABLE 14–1
Retirement Plans of Tax-Exempt Employers

	401(a)	403(b)	457	Grandfathered 401(k)
Governmental entities	X		X	X
Nongovernmental tax-exempt entities	X		X	X
Educational institutions established by state or local government or agency	X	X	X	X
Organizations exempt under IRC Section 501(c)(3)	X	X	X	X

As Table 14–1 shows, all governmental entities and all other tax-exempt organizations are eligible to sponsor 401(a) plans, 457 plans, and grandfathered 401(k) plans, and organizations exempt from tax under IRC Section 501(c)(3) and educational institutions established by governmental entities are allowed to establish 403(b) plans (in addition to 401(a) plans, 457 plans, and grandfathered 401(k) plans).

Thus, for secured retirement accumulations (amounts that are not considered assets of the employer and are, therefore, beyond the reach of the employer and its creditors) executives of tax-exempt organizations and governmental entities can look to a 401(a) plan like their counterparts in for-profit companies.

By contrast, while executives of for-profit companies might find themselves enjoying deferrals and secured accumulations under a 401(k) plan, executives of tax-exempt organizations and governmental entities may do so only if the 401(k) was in existence as of a given date and therefore is grandfathered; if no plan existed at that time, none can be established currently. The executives of at least some of these entities—organizations exempt under IRC Section 501(c)(3) and educational institutions established by governmental entities—might find themselves able to make up for the lack of a 401(k) plan by participating in a 403(b) plan.

In any case, the only means of nonqualified deferred compensation for executives of tax-exempt organizations and governmental entities is through 457 plans. This contrasts sharply with the full array of nonqualified deferred compensation arrangements allowed executives in for-profit companies.

The remainder of this chapter will focus on secured retirement accumulations under 403(b) plans, nonqualified deferred compensation under 457 plans and their areas of interaction, as well as ineligible plans under Section 457(f).

403(b) Plans

The IRC sets forth two types of 403(b) plans:

1. The first provides for the employer's purchase of, and payment of premiums for, an annuity contract under favorable tax circumstances. This type of 403(b) plan is often referred to as a tax sheltered annuity or TSA. Contributions, which are made directly to an insurance company's annuity contract, can be nonelective, matching, salary reduction, and/or made on an after-tax basis. Earnings grow tax-free and taxable distributions are made as payments from the annuity contract.

2. The second type of plan is sometimes referred to as a 403(b)(7) plan, since it is allowed under IRC Section 403(b)(7). Such a plan requires a custodial account invested in regulated investment company stock. As is the case in a TSA, contributions are made to the account (nonelective, matching, salary reduction, and/or after-tax), earnings grow tax-free, and taxable distributions are made from the account.

A 403(b) plan can be used only for employees; independent contractors cannot be covered under such plans.

These plans are used in two ways: as broad-based employee retirement plans with employer contributions, and as supplemental plans (usually without employer contributions) that allow employees to defer compensation.

A 403(b) plan is considered a pension plan and is generally subject to ERISA. Note, however, that government plans (in the 403(b) context this means plans maintained by public schools and universities) and church plans are exempt from ERISA. Plans maintained by organizations exempt from tax under IRC Section 501(c)(3) will also be exempt from ERISA if:

- Participation is completely voluntary for employees.
- All rights are enforceable solely by the employee and his/her beneficiary.
- The employer's involvement is limited to certain functions, including but not limited to: holding the annuity contract in its name, permitting agents to publicize their products, and collecting and remitting salary reduction contributions.

Further, the employer must receive no consideration or compensation (other than for direct and necessary expenses related to salary reduction contributions).

If a 501(c)(3) tax-exempt organization makes matching or nonelective contributions to a 403(b) plan, the plan would not fall within the exemption (salary reduction contributions made by the employer would *not* be considered to be employer contributions that would cause an otherwise exempt plan to become subject to ERISA).

If the 403(b) plan is covered by ERISA, all of ERISA's requirements must be met, including participation, vesting, joint and survivor annuities (to the extent applicable), reporting and disclosure, and so forth.

If employee contributions are made through salary reductions, they must be made pursuant to a binding agreement that may be changed only once annually (although it can be terminated at any time by the employee with regard to monies not yet earned). The employee's rights under the annuity contract must be nonforfeitable and the contract must be nontransferable.

The Tax Reform Act of 1986 subjected 403(b) plans (other than church plans) to nondiscrimination rules. Different nondiscrimination rules apply to nonsalary reduction or salary reduction contributions to a 403(b) plan.

Nonsalary reduction contributions (such as nonelective contributions, matching contributions and employee after-tax contributions) are subject to:

- The nondiscriminatory contributions/benefits rules of IRC Section 401(a)(4).
- The permitted disparity rules of IRC Section 401(a)(5) and 401(l).
- The $150,000 cap on compensation of IRC Section 401(a)(17).
- The minimum participation rules of IRC Section 401(a)(26).
- The ACP test of IRC Section 401(m) for after-tax and matching contributions.
- The coverage test of IRC Section 410(b).

Salary reduction contributions are *not* subject to the ADP test that applies to elective deferrals to a 401(k) plan. Instead, they must be made available to virtually all employees, provided they contribute at least $200 per year. The employees who can be excluded for these purposes include employees who participate in a 457 plan, a 401(k) plan, or another 403(b) plan of the employer, and certain nonresident aliens.

Installment distributions from 403(b) plans are taxed in the same manner as qualified plan distributions under the annuity rules of IRC Section 72. Lump sum distributions are *not* treated the same as distributions from

401(a) plans: they are not eligible for special 5-year/10-year averaging. Thus, the executive whose primary retirement accumulation occurs in a 403(b) plan is at a disadvantage when compared to his counterpart in a for-profit company in terms of available tax-planning opportunities.

Most distributions may be rolled over tax-free to another 403(b) or an IRA (but not to a 401(a) qualified plan). Loans from 403(b) plans, like loans from 401(a) plans, will be treated as taxable distributions unless the requirements of IRC Section 72(p) are met regarding the amount of the loan, the length of the repayment period, and the amortization of principal and interest.

Distributions from 403(b) plans are subject to the 10 percent early distribution tax and the 15 percent excess distribution tax that apply to distributions from 401(a) plans. Lump sum distributions from a 403(b) plan do not qualify for the $750,000 threshold for the 15 percent tax because they are not eligible for income averaging. Instead, the $150,000 threshold applies. Minimum distributions, similar to the requirements of IRC Section 401(a)(9), must be made with respect to benefits accrued after 1986. Thus, in the case of a 403(b) plan sponsored by a nongovernmental, nonchurch employer, distributions must commence by April 1 of the year following the year in which an individual attains age 70½. (In the case of governmental and church plans, the required beginning date is the April 1 of the later of the year following the year in which an individual retires or the year in which the individual attains age 70½.)

Restrictions on in-service distributions apply depending on how the plan is structured and the kinds of contributions made. If the plan is a custodial account invested in mutual funds (a 403(b)(7) plan), distributions cannot be made until death, disability, age 59½, financial hardship, or termination of employment. For annuity contracts, these restrictions apply only to salary reduction contributions. Amounts held under an annuity contract as of December 31, 1988, are grandfathered and may continue to be withdrawn at any time.

The rollover rules, the direct rollover requirements and the withholding rules instituted by the Unemployment Compensation Amendments of 1992 and applicable to 401(a) plans also apply to distributions from 403(b) plans.

One of the most problematic sets of rules applicable to 403(b) plans concerns the limitation on the amount that may be contributed to the plan by the employer and excluded from the current income of the employee on whose behalf the contribution is made. These rules are fraught with complications and exceptions. A brief summary of this complex area follows.

In a plan that does not allow for salary reductions, the maximum amount that may be excluded from an employee's current income is the lesser of two amounts: the employee's exclusion allowance or the employee's 415 limit.

In a plan that allows for salary reductions only, the maximum amount that may be excluded from an employee's current income is the smallest of three amounts: the employee's exclusion allowance, the employee's 415 limit, or the combined annual elective deferral cap.

In a plan that allows for salary reduction and nonsalary reduction contributions, the salary reduction contributions are limited by the combined annual elective deferral cap, while both the salary reduction and the nonsalary reduction contributions are subject to the lesser of the exclusion allowance or the 415 limits.

An employee's exclusion allowance is determined by subtracting (b) from (a), where: (a) is the product of 20 percent of the employee's includable compensation with the employer for the year of calculation times the employee's years of service with the employer, and (b) is the amount previously excluded from the employee's gross income.

Each of the terms in this formula, includable compensation, years of service and amounts previously excluded, is specifically defined. A brief description follows.

- *Includable compensation* is compensation received from the employer for the most recent period that can be counted as a year of service (this generally means the current taxable year). It generally includes only compensation that is currently includable in income. Thus, salary reduction contributions to the 403(b) plan are subtracted out to determine includable compensation. There is a special rule regarding certain foreign income paid to U.S. citizens.

- *Years of service* are credited on the basis of one year for each full year of employment with the employer.

- The term *amounts previously excluded* is defined as "amounts that have been contributed by the employer for annuity contracts for such employee and that were excludable from the gross income of the employee for any taxable year prior to the taxable year for which the exclusion allowance is being determined."

  These amounts include, among other things, any prior years' employer contributions (both salary reduction and nonsalary reduction) to 403(b) and 401(a) plans that were excluded from income. They also include contributions that were not excluded from income if the reason they were not was because they violated the 415 limitations.

If an individual has two or more employers during the same taxable year and more than one employer makes 403(b) contributions for the individual, separate exclusion allowances are computed for each employer's plan. The exclusion allowance calculation for one employer will *not* reflect includable compensation from the other employer, years of service with the other employer, or amounts previously excluded through contributions by the other employer.

An employee's 415 limits are the lesser of $30,000 or 25 percent of compensation.[4]

An employee's combined annual elective deferral cap depends on the plans in which the employee participates. If the only plan in which he participates is the 403(b) plan, the cap is currently $9,500. (The $9,500 limit applies until the $7,000 indexed limit that applies to 401(k) plans—$9,240 for 1994—exceeds $9,500, at which time the limit on elective deferrals to a 403(b) plan will be the same as the 401(k) limit.) Note that the $9,500 limit can be increased for an employee with at least 15 years of service with certain types of organizations.

These rules are summarized in Table 14–2 (where "NECs" means non-elective deferral contributions, *ELDs* means elective deferral contributions, and *MEA* means maximum exclusion allowance).

There are three elections an employee may consider making to cause a larger amount to be excludable from current income than would otherwise be the case under the regular rules discussed above. To be eligible to make any of these elections, the individual must be an employee of an educational organization, a hospital, a home health service agency, a health and welfare service agency, or certain churches.

1. One of these elections, the so-called A Election, is available only in the employee's year of separation. It allows the excludable amount to be determined without regard to the 25 percent-of-compensation limit of IRC Section 415. Instead, a modified exclusion allowance is constructed, using only 10 years of service in the formula (rather than the larger number that might actually apply) and limiting the amount previously excluded to those amounts excluded during the immediately preceding 10 years. Thus, if the A Election is made, the maximum excludable amount for the employee in the year of separation is the greater of (i) or (ii), where:

   • (i) is the amount determined without regard to the election (the lesser of the regular exclusion allowance or the 415 limit), and

   • (ii) is the amount determined by the modified exclusion allowance up to $30,000.

TABLE 14–2
Limits and Exclusions

	MEA	$9,500	415 Limits $30,000 or 25% of Comp
NECs only	X		X
ELDs only	X	X	X
Both: ELDs		X	
Total	X		X

2. Another election, the B Election, can be made any year. It too eliminates the 25 percent-of-compensation limit of Section 415 (and
effectively eliminates the $30,000 limit as well) by substituting
another limit in its place: the smallest of $15,000, the exclusion
allowance, or the sum of $4,000 plus 25 percent of includable com-
pensation. Thus, if the B Election is made, the maximum excludable amount for the employee for the year is the greater of (i) or
(ii), where:

- (i) is the amount determined without regard to the election (the
lesser of the exclusion allowance or the 415 limit), and
- (ii) is the smallest of (A), (B) or (C), where:
(A) is the exclusion allowance
(B) is $15,000
(C) is the sum of $4,000 plus 25 percent of includable
compensation.

3. The final election, the C Election, can also be made at any time and
is sometimes called the overall limit. Here the exclusion allowance
is eliminated and the limit is based on the 415 limits (the lesser of
$30,000 or 25 percent of compensation).

Whether or not a special election is made, the amount excluded from
compensation by virtue of salary reduction contributions cannot exceed
the combined annual elective deferral cap.

These special elections should be made carefully, since they are irrevocable and may eliminate the opportunity to make other elections in the
future, even if the individual changes employers. Making the A Election
eliminates the opportunity to make any other elections in the future.

Making the B Election eliminates the opportunity to make either the A or C Elections in the future (but the B Election may be made again in future years). Similarly, making the C Election eliminates the opportunity to make either the A or B Elections in the future (but the C Election may be made again in future years).

457 Plans

As noted earlier, a Section 457 plan is a nonqualified deferred compensation plan governed by IRC Section 457. These plans can either be eligible plans or ineligible plans.

- An eligible plan generates certain tax advantages—namely, amounts deferred are not considered current income to the employee until actually received, but must meet certain rules, including a limitation on the amount that may be deferred under the plan.
- An ineligible plan does not automatically generate exclusion of deferrals from current income (the plan must be specifically structured in order to achieve this result) but is not subject to the limitations on deferrals that apply to eligible plans.

In addition, 457 plan deferrals can result from either salary reduction elections by employees or from nonsalary reduction contributions made by the employer (although contributions to ineligible plans typically are not made through salary reductions).

An eligible plan is a 457 plan that is maintained by an eligible employer and meets certain other rules. (An ineligible plan, while also maintained by an eligible employer, does not have to meet the additional rules.) The term *eligible employer* for 457 plan purposes encompasses a broader group of employers than are eligible to establish 403(b) plans, as follows:

- A governmental unit (a state, political subdivision of a state, and any agency or instrumentality of a state or political subdivision of a state), not just an educational institution of such an entity, as is the case with 403(b) plans.
- Any organization exempt from tax under Subtitle A of the IRC, not just organizations exempt under IRC Section 501(c)(3), as is the case with 403(b) plan. Churches and qualified church-controlled organizations are not considered to be qualified employers for 457 purposes. (Churches, however, are allowed to establish 403(b) plans and can have nonqualified deferred compensation arrangements outside the parameters of IRC Section 457.)

Among the rules that an eligible 457 plan must meet in order to provide for tax deferral of income are the following:

- Only individuals who perform services for the employer may participate. These individuals are not limited to employees; employers may also establish 457 plans for independent contractors.

- The maximum amount that may be deferred for any one year is the lesser of $7,500 or 33⅓ percent of the participant's includable compensation (although this limit may be increased during any of the final three years before normal retirement age). This limit, which, prior to the Tax Reform Act of 1986 applied only to governmental units, not to nongovernmental tax-exempt organizations, may prove particularly unattractive to nongovernmental tax-exempt organizations, which thus might opt to maintain ineligible plans that are not subject to this limit.

  There are special grandfathering rules that allow deferred compensation arrangements of nongovernmental tax exempt organizations to be exempt from 457, and this limit on excludable compensation, if certain conditions are met. Specifically, IRC Section 457 does not apply to amounts deferred after January 1, 1987, under an agreement in writing on August 16, 1986, that provided for deferral of a fixed amount or an amount determined under a fixed formula.

- Deferrals for any given month can be made only if a written agreement providing for the deferrals is in effect prior to the beginning of the month. Deferrals may be made by a new employee for his first month of employment if an agreement regarding such deferrals is in effect before he becomes an employee.

- Distributions from the plan cannot be made until the year the participant attains age 70½, separates from service, or is faced with an unforeseeable emergency, whichever occurs first. The term *unforeseeable emergency* is strictly defined and is much more limited than the definition of *hardship* for 401(k) plans.

- The plan must meet the minimum distribution rules of IRC Section 401(a)(9) and certain additional rules. If the plan is maintained by a governmental unit, it is subject to a somewhat more lenient version of the 401(a)(9) rules: distributions may be delayed beyond age 70½ until the date of retirement, if later.

- Amounts deferred (and income thereon) are considered to be owned by the employer, subject to the claims of the employer's general creditors. In this respect, 457 plans are quite different from 401(a),

401(k) and 403(b) plans, under which amounts intended to provide benefits are not considered to be owned by the employer and are thus beyond the reach of creditors. Some employers attempt to ameliorate participants' insecurity (though it cannot be eliminated altogether) by constructing various funding arrangements, including, for example, rabbi trusts, to meet the employer's promise to provide deferred compensation. These arrangements are discussed in detail in Chapter 10.

Unlike 403(b) and 401(a)/(k) plans, 457 plans are *not* subject to nondiscrimination rules. In fact, 457 plans maintained by nongovernmental tax-exempt organizations should only be offered to a select group of management and highly compensated employees, thereby avoiding the general ERISA rule that pension plans (which a 457 plan is, since it provides for the deferral of income to a date beyond employment) must maintain plan assets in a trust. This is not necessary in 457 plans maintained by governmental units and churches—that is, they can be offered to a broad-based group of employees—because they are already exempt from ERISA and its trust requirements.

As noted earlier, eligible plans automatically allow for deferred amounts to be excluded from current income, but this comes at a price: an eligible plan must meet certain rules, including a limit on the amount that may be deferred. An eligible employer (especially a nongovernmental tax-exempt organization) might find this limit too restrictive and choose instead to offer an ineligible plan. This would allow for deferral of amounts in excess of the $7,500-or-33⅓ percent limit, but exclusion from current income of the amounts deferred would not be automatic; instead, it would depend on the plan's being structured so as to meet another standard, the substantial risk of forfeiture. This standard is discussed in detail later in this chapter.

Plan Interaction

As noted previously, a tax-exempt organization may maintain more than one type of plan. Accordingly, it is important to see where and how 401(a) plans, 401(k) plans (including grandfathered 401(k) plans), 403(b) plans, and 457 plans interact. The four most critical areas of interaction are in determining:

1. Maximum annual aggregate salary reductions (amounts that may be electively deferred at the employee's election in a given year).

2. The 415 limits that apply to individuals participating in more than one type of plan.
3. Includable income under a 403(b) plan and a 457 plan.
4. Amounts previously excluded under a 403(b) plan.

The IRC limits the annual amount of salary reduction contributions that may be made on an individual's behalf to each of these plans. The limits are relatively simple when an individual participates in only one plan at a time:

- Salary reduction contributions to a 401(k) plan are limited to $7,000, as adjusted ($9,240 in 1994).
- Salary reduction contributions to a 403(b) plan are limited to $9,500 (or the limit that applies to salary reduction contributions to a 401(k) plan, if greater).
- Salary reduction contributions to an eligible 457 plan are limited to the lesser of $7,500 or 33⅓ percent of includable compensation. This limit may be increased in certain circumstances.
- Salary reduction contributions to an ineligible 457 plan are not subject to specific limits.

The limits become more complex when an individual participates in more than one plan in a given year. The salary reduction contribution limits that apply to possible combinations of plans are as follows:

- 401(k) plan and 403(b) plan: $9,500, but in no event may the elective deferrals to the 401(k) plan exceed $7,000, as adjusted ($9,240 for 1994). For example, if in 1994 an individual defers $9,240 to the 401(k) plan, he may defer an additional $260 to the 403(b) plan, for a total of $9,500. If, instead, he had deferred $100 to the 403(b) plan, he may *not* defer $9,400 to the 401(k) plan and can defer only $9,240. This will no longer be an issue when the same limit becomes applicable to both types of plans.
- 401(k) plan and eligible 457 plan: $7,500. The IRC states that amounts deferred under a 401(k) plan count against the $7,500 cap of IRC Section 457. If an individual deferred $6,000 to a 401(k) plan, he could defer an additional $1,500 to the eligible 457 plan. Note that the aggregate limit here is $7,500, not the greater amount of $7,000 as adjusted. A 1991 IRS Private Letter Ruling (9152026) states that "even though an employee may otherwise defer under a 401(k) plan a greater amount of gross income . . . if the same

employee also participates in a 457 plan . . . such employee would be limited to the $7,500 limit."[5]

- 401(k) plan, eligible 457 plan, and 403(b) plan: $7,500. Because IRC Section 457(c)(2) states that deferrals to a 403(b) plan count against the 457 limit (just as contributions to a 401(k) plan do), the rationale in the IRS's 1991 Private Letter Ruling, which only addresses a 401(k)/457 combination, would presumably also apply here: namely, any contribution to the 457 plan causes the aggregate limit for all plans to be $7,500.

  For example, if in 1993 an individual defers $1,500 to the 457 plan and $1,000 to the 403(b) plan, he may defer an additional $5,000 to the 401(k) plan. If, instead, he made no deferral to the 457 plan, the $9,500 limit described under the first bullet would apply to the contributions to the 401(k) plan and 403(b) plan.

- 403(b) plan and eligible 457 plan: $7,500. As noted, amounts deferred under a 403(b) plan count against the $7,500 cap of IRC Section 457. If the rationale of the IRS's 1991 Private Letter Ruling 9152026 were applied here, any deferral to the 457 plan would presumably cause the $7,500 limit to apply to the aggregate contributions instead of the 403(b)'s $9,500 limit.

Two points should be noted regarding the above limitations. First, when reference is made to being able to defer $7,500 to a 403(b) plan, this assumes that such amount is less than 33⅓ percent of the individual's includable compensation. Thus, in the case of executives, the limit will generally be $7,500. Second, the above limits refer to an eligible type of 457 plan. In the event an individual participates in an ineligible 457 plan, deferrals thereunder are not subject to limits and do not impact the limits otherwise applicable.

IRC Section 415(c) limits the amount of annual additions to an individual's defined contribution plan account balance for any one year to the lesser of $30,000 or 25 percent of compensation. These limits apply directly to account allocations in defined contribution 401(a) plans and in 401(k) plans. They also apply to 403(b) plans: 415 represents one of the possible caps that determine the maximum amount that may be excluded from an employee's current income for a given year under a 403(b) plan (the general rule is that the excludable amount cannot exceed the lesser of the 415 limits or the employee's exclusion allowance).

There are two aspects of the 415 limits that are affected by the interaction of these plans. The first is the limitation itself, specifically the 25 percent-of-compensation limitation. The issue here is whether compensation is determined before or after reduction for deferrals to any, some, or all of these plans.

The regulations under Section 415 state that the term *compensation*, for purposes of determining the 25 percent-of-compensation limit, is compensation after it has been reduced for any and all pretax elective deferrals to 401(k) plans, 403(b) plans, and 457 plans. (In fact, it is also reduced for pretax contributions under IRC Section 125, such as deferrals to a health care spending account.)

The second aspect of Section 415 that is affected by these limits is how annual additions are determined. As a general rule, an individual's annual additions under all defined contribution plans maintained by the employer are aggregated to determine if the limit is exceeded. Thus, for example, if an employee participates in the employer's profit-sharing plan and money purchase pension plan, annual additions under both plans for the year are aggregated and compared to the lesser-of-25 percent-of-compensation-or-$30,000 limit of Section 415.

The only interaction among these combinations of plans in this respect, other than participation in more than one defined contribution 401(a) plan and/or 401(k) plan, is when an employee participates in a 403(b) plan and in a 401(a) or grandfathered 401(k) plan. Contributions to the 403(b) plan count as annual additions and are aggregated with annual additions in the 401(a) plan or the 401(k) plan in two circumstances: (1) if the individual has more than a 50 percent ownership interest in the entity that maintains the 401(a)/401(k) plan, or (2) if the individual has made the C Election by which the amount excludable from income under the 403(b) plan is increased beyond its regular limits.

Note that in no event will amounts deferred to a 457 plan count as annual additions.

Another area of interaction among these plans is in the determination of *includable compensation,* a term that is used in two places:

1. When determining the exclusion allowance for 403(b) plans (where the exclusion allowance is the product of 20 percent of includable compensation times years of service, less amounts previously excluded from income).

2. When determining the maximum amount that may deferred under an eligible 457 plan (the lesser of $7,500 or 33⅓ percent of includable compensation).

The term *includable compensation* when defined for 403(b) plan purposes is to be taken literally: it is limited to that compensation that is actually included in the individual's currently taxable income. Since pretax elective deferrals to 401(k) plans, 403(b) plans, and 457 plans are *not* included in current income, includable compensation is determined *after* reduction for these deferrals.

The final area of interaction is in determining amounts previously excluded when calculating the exclusion allowance for a 403(b) plan. The term includes the employer's contributions, whether nonsalary reduction or salary reduction contributions, made to any of the plans being examined here: 401(a) plans (including defined benefit plans), 401(k) plans, 457 plans, as well as contributions to the 403(b) plan itself. Note that while the term *employer* generally is limited only to the employer who maintains the 403(b) plan, it encompasses *any* employer when applied to contributions to 457 plans.

Ineligible Plans under 457(f)

Because of the $7,500 limit on the amount of deferrals under an eligible 457 plan, most tax-exempt employers and their executives are interested in an ineligible plan under Section 457(f).

Under Section 457(f), a participant in a plan that does not meet the requirements of an eligible plan discussed above will be taxed on amounts deferred in the first taxable year in which there is no substantial risk of forfeiture of the rights to the compensation. Note that the following plans are not subject to the rules of Section 457(f):

- Qualified plans under Section 401(a), including Section 401(k) arrangements.
- Tax-sheltered annuities and nonqualified annuities under Section 403.
- The portion of a plan consisting of a transfer of property under Section 83.
- The portion of a plan consisting of a trust to which Section 402(b) (i.e, the taxation of nonexempt trusts), applies.

Substantial risk of forfeiture.   Generally, a substantial risk of forfeiture exists if the rights to the compensation are conditioned on the future performance of substantial services by an individual.

The IRS is expected to apply the standards of IRC Section 83 to determine whether a substantial risk of forfeiture exists. Under IRS regulations, a facts and circumstances test is generally used to determine whether a substantial risk of forfeiture exists. Each arrangement must be looked at individually. Generally, a substantial risk of forfeiture will exist if an employee must work for a stated number of years or until a specified event or both in order to get the benefit. Thus, a deferral until age 65 or for 10 years would be considered a substantial risk of forfeiture. This appears to be the case even if the benefit is payable because of death or disability during the vesting period. However, forfeiting benefits only upon death or discharge for cause would not give rise to a substantial risk of forfeiture.

Under the Section 83 regulations, conditioning benefits on postretirement consulting services or noncompetition may or may not be a substantial risk of forfeiture depending upon the facts and circumstances. Whether a postretirement consulting arrangement will be considered a substantial risk of forfeiture depends upon whether the executive is expected to render such services. The factors that must be considered in the case of a noncompetition clause are the age of the employee, the availability of alternate employment opportunities, the likelihood that the employee could obtain other employment, the employee's health, the degree of skill of the employee, and the employer's practice in enforcing such a covenant. (Presumably, a noncompetition clause may constitute a substantial risk of forfeiture even in the case of a tax-exempt employer as well, based on the fact that such organizations must compete for revenue.)

Rolling vesting date. It appears that, at a minimum, the IRS requires at least a two-year vesting period for a substantial risk of forfeiture to exist. Arguably, the longer the vesting period, the greater the likelihood that the IRS will find a substantial risk of forfeiture. Many executives do not want their deferred compensation to be at risk for long periods of time.

One approach that has been suggested is the idea of the rolling vesting date. That is, an employee would elect an initial employment condition (e.g., three years), and before the three-year period expires, may elect to extend the period for another three years. The IRS and some courts have permitted the deferral of the *receipt* of benefits under deferred compensation arrangements before the date of payment specified in the initial agreement; in that case, the executive will not be in *constructive receipt* of the deferred compensation. However, the IRS has never addressed the deferral of a vesting date and whether a deferred compensation arrangement will be considered subject to a substantial risk of forfeiture if an executive may delay vesting; in fact, the IRS has indicated orally that it is concerned about such arrangements. Thus, any employer considering implementing such an arrangement should consult legal counsel.

Taxation upon vesting.   When there is no substantial risk of forfeiture of the deferred amounts, the participant is taxed on the value of the promised deferrals. In the case of a defined contribution type of arrangement, the executive would be taxed on the allocations (including interest) at the date of vesting. Thereafter, the executive would be taxed on the additional allocation each year. It appears that taxation on earnings on the vested (and previously taxed) deferred compensation is delayed until the earnings are paid. A similar result should occur in the case of a defined benefit type of arrangement. In this case, the present value of the promised benefit would be taxed at the point of vesting. Arguably, the executive would be taxed on the present value of the additional accruals each year thereafter. Because the IRS has not issued any guidance on the calculation of the present value for this purpose, presumably any reasonable method may be used.

Alternatives to Section 457(f)

Because many executives do not want their deferred compensation subject to forfeiture, tax-exempt employers are exploring other mechanisms to provide either delayed taxation or greater security. These methods are discussed below.

Split-dollar life insurance.   One approach that a tax-exempt employer may wish to consider is split-dollar life insurance, covered in Chapter 12. It operates in the same manner in the case of a tax-exempt employer. One of the drawbacks of split-dollar life insurance in the profit-making sector is that the employer is not entitled to deduct premium payments made to purchase the split-dollar life insurance. (As an insurance policy, split-dollar appears to be a "property interest" subject to Section 83 rather than being characterized as deferred compensation.) This should not be an issue in the case of a tax-exempt employer, who would not be concerned with the deductibility of premiums in any event.

Severance pay.   Because bona fide severance pay plans are exempt under Section 457, bona fide severance pay is not subject to tax when no longer subject to a substantial risk of forfeiture, but rather as payments are received by the executive. Thus, severance pay has been another approach that has been suggested to provide deferred compensation to executives outside the scope of Section 457.

As previously discussed in Chapter 4, under Department of Labor (DOL) safe harbor regulations, a severance pay plan will be considered a welfare plan under ERISA if the following conditions are met: The plan may not pay more than two times the employee's compensation, payments may not be made over more than a 24-month period, and the payments may not be conditioned, directly or indirectly, on retirement. In the absence of any other guidance on the definition of severance pay under Section 457, some tax-exempt employers have structured a severance pay program for their executives within the DOL's parameters. IRS officials have stated informally that the definition of severance pay for ERISA purposes is not necessarily the one it will use for purposes of Section 457 and that such arrangements cause them some concern.

However, the IRS has adopted the DOL definition of severance pay for purposes of voluntary employees' beneficiary associations (VEBAs) under Section 501(c)(9). The IRS VEBA regulation excludes as a permissible benefit under a VEBA any benefit that is similar to a benefit provided under a pension or profit-sharing plan, as well as those that are payable by reason of the passage of time, rather than the result of an unanticipated event. This suggests that a VEBA may not provide severance pay based on years of service, although this type of severance pay arrangement appears permissible under the DOL regulation.

Another issue with respect to severance pay plans is whether the payments under such a plan may be paid on account of voluntary, as well as involuntary, termination of employment. IRS officials have expressed some concern in the case of severance pay arrangements that are paid in all cases. However, there is some authority in support of paying severance even in the case of voluntary termination of employment. The DOL has held that a plan that paid benefits upon termination of employment for any reason (other than death and dishonesty) is a severance pay plan under ERISA.[6] The IRS took a similar position in two General Counsel Memorandums, stating that payments made on voluntary as well as involuntary termination constituted severance pay permissible under a VEBA.[7] Certain court cases support this position as well.[8]

It is also unclear when a severance pay arrangement will be considered bona fide for purposes of Section 457. The exemption for bona fide severance arrangements was added to the code by the Technical and

Miscellaneous Revenue Act of 1988. The legislative history on this change is silent on this issue. However, prior to the legislative change, the IRS issued Notice 88-68, in which it stated that a major factor in determining whether a severance pay plan will be considered bona fide is whether it is a mere device to provide deferred compensation. This suggests that, although a severance pay plan may provide some deferred compensation, it must have some other purpose for it to be considered bona fide.

Because of the uncertainty surrounding what constitutes an exempt bona fide severance pay arrangement under Section 457, a tax-exempt employer should consult with legal counsel before establishing such an arrangement.

Nonqualified secular trust. Because a nonqualified secular trust is taxable under Section 402(b), it is also exempt under Section 457(f). This type of trust, which is a separate taxable entity, is discussed in detail in Chapter 10. Such a trust would operate in the same manner in the tax-exempt environment with one notable exception: a tax-exempt employer would not be able to deduct the contributions it makes to the trust when the amounts are includable in the gross income of the executive.

Annuities. Because annuities are taxed under Section 403, a tax-exempt employer may also consider purchasing such annuities for its executives in order to provide them with deferred compensation. Of course, if the annuity contract is purchased and distributed to the executive, the executive would be subject to tax on the amounts used to purchase the annuity. Although the executive would be currently taxed, he would be relatively secure that he would receive the benefits. The investment buildup in the annuity would be tax-free until payments commenced, when the executive would be taxed under Section 72.

NOTES

1. Deferred compensation is typically paid out of a corporation's general assets, so amounts deferred in a taxable organization do not really result in lost tax revenues for the government. When deferred compensation is included in the general assets of a tax-exempt organization, however, it does result in a current loss of tax revenue.

2. In 1988, Congress exempted church organizations from Section 457, reinstituting prior law (i.e., the law as it applies to taxable employers). Repeated attempts to extend relief to other tax-exempts such as hospitals, fraternal organizations, trade organizations, and secular charities have met with defeat.

3. Pension reform legislation (H.R. 3419) that is pending as this text goes to press would extend 401(k) plans to tax-exempt organizations.

4. The dollar limit is indexed and will start to increase when the defined benefit limit reaches $120,000.

5. An interesting result of this position is that an individual who elects to defer $1 to an eligible 457 plan may defer only $7,499 to a 401(k) plan (since, by virtue of the 457 deferral, he participates in the 457 plan). If the individual had chosen not to defer at all to the 457 plan (and, thus, not participate in the plan), he would have been able to contribute a full $7,000, as adjusted, to the 401(k) plan. In 1994 with the 401(k) plan limit at $9,240, the individual would lose a 401(k) deferral opportunity of $1,741 (the difference between $9,240 and $7,499) as a result of making the $1 deferral to the eligible 457 plan.

6. Advisory Opinion 84-15A.

7. GCMs 39300 and 39818.

8. See *Petrella* v. *NL Industries, Inc.*, 529 F. Supp. 1357 (D.N.O. 1982) and *Donnelly* v. *Aetna Life Ins. Co.*, 465 F. Supp. 696 (E.D. Pa. 1979).

Chapter Fifteen

Golden Parachutes

The term *golden parachute* really refers to the circumstances surrounding the payment of executive compensation or benefits rather than to a unique form of compensation or benefit. It encompasses various payments to which an executive may become entitled if corporate control changes as a result of a takeover or similar event, as described in this chapter.

WHY PARACHUTES?

Golden parachutes have become a necessary part of a compensation and benefits package designed to attract and retain senior executives. For one thing, senior executives have come to expect them to provide protection against the financial dislocation of an unanticipated termination. For another, a golden parachute arrangement can help retain key executives and motivate them to act in the best interests of shareholders in the event of a potential control change. Given a measure of financial security, executives at a company that is a potential takeover target will be less likely to seek employment elsewhere as a preemptive move. In the event that a company does become a takeover target, a golden parachute allows an executive to focus on the merits of the proposal with some degree of detachment.

In Towers Perrin's analysis of the 1994 proxy statements of the S&P 500, 53 percent of these companies disclosed some form of change-in-control protection for executives.

Shareholder Interests

Whether golden parachutes are in the best interests of shareholders depends in large part on whether these arrangements are an appropriate way to attract and retain management and are reasonable in amount in view of the unique circumstances involved in a change in control.

As noted, a golden parachute can conceivably help shareholders by enabling management to weigh takeover proposals with some detachment. Nonetheless, shareholders do not always like parachutes, and some of them have asked corporate boards to revoke any such arrangements triggered by a change in control. In 1990, the Securities and Exchange Commission (SEC) changed its longstanding position that a company could exclude shareholder proposals on golden parachutes from being submitted to shareholders for a vote. To date, however, no individual shareholders have managed to convince sufficient numbers of their fellow shareholders to vote to revoke parachute arrangements triggered by changes in control.

In some cases, shareholders have also initiated litigation challenging the validity of golden parachute arrangements. These suits have generally not been successful. See, for example, *Orin* v. *Huntington Bancshares, Inc.* (Ohio Court of Common Pleas, decided September 30, 1986 [not officially reported]), which upheld the validity of golden parachutes because they served shareholders' interests insofar as they encouraged management to remain with the company during a potential change in control.

PARACHUTE PROVISIONS

Employers may include golden parachute provisions in each of the many separate documents governing different executive compensation and benefit programs. For example, a SERP document or a stock option plan might include a special provision for the payment of supplemental pensions in the event of a change in control as will a separate stock option plan.

In other cases, employers include parachute provisions in individual employment contracts. A CEO's employment agreement might specify that he is entitled to a lump sum equal to three times pay in the event his employment is terminated through a change in control, for example, while an executive vice president's contract might provide for a parachute equal to two and a half times pay.

In still other cases, golden parachute arrangements are covered by a separate document that describes the compensation and benefits payable in the event of a control change. Such a document will, of necessity, cross-reference other documents governing executive compensation and benefits, providing, for example, that supplemental pensions usually payable only as a life annuity pursuant to the terms of a separate SERP document will be accelerated and paid as an immediate lump sum to a covered executive who is terminated in connection with a change in control.

Common Elements

Types of benefits. It is difficult to generalize about the types of benefits that might inure to an executive pursuant to a change in control agreement. This really depends upon the types of underlying compensation and benefit programs that an employer maintains. A well-designed parachute arrangement should have considered whether special provisions are needed for each of these underlying programs. Nevertheless, certain types of benefits are frequently included in parachute arrangements, and each is summarized in the following paragraphs.

Severance pay. This may be either an explicit provision of a specified amount of severance pay in lieu of future salary, bonuses, and so forth, or it may be a provision for the continued payment of salary and bonuses for a specified period. Where the amount to be paid is determined with reference to an element of compensation that varies in amount, such as an annual bonus, the amount used is often the highest such amount that has been paid within a specified number of prior years.

This type of parachute benefit is generally intended to replace future salary and short-term incentive pay. Where the amount to be paid is explicitly determined with reference to such elements of pay, it is usually a multiple of these items. Typical multiples range from one to three times the referenced items. Where the parachute amount is not explicitly based on salary and bonus, as in the case of a stated dollar amount of severance pay, it is often still determined implicitly with reference to the approximate dollar amount of the items that it is intended to replace.

Deferred compensation. Deferred compensation payable to executives comes in a variety of forms and, likewise, parachute provisions with respect to these deferrals vary. The primary focus of special parachute provisions on deferred compensation relates to unfunded arrangements. Funded arrangements such as qualified pension and 401(k) plans are not usually addressed. The reasons for this are twofold. First, executives generally are not concerned about the security of benefits under a tax-qualified plan. Second, special treatment of executives with respect to qualified plan benefits generally will be barred by the requirement that such plans not discriminate in favor of highly compensated employees.[1]

Deferred compensation that is not normally paid as a lump sum when an executive terminates employment might be paid in this form in the event of a control change. For example, SERPs often delay the start of benefits until an executive has met certain age and service conditions (in addition to having terminated employment). SERPs also sometimes only make benefit payments in the form of an annuity for the life of an executive. In these cases, the normal age and service conditions to payment might be waived and payments commuted to an immediate lump sum in the event of a change in control.

In some cases, SERP or other deferred compensation benefits are not vested for a prolonged period. For example, a SERP might provide that an executive who terminates employment before attaining age 55 with at least 15 years of service will forfeit his right to receive payments under the plan. In the event of a change in control, such benefits might be vested without regard to the executive's age or years of service. Sometimes such accelerated vesting is the only special event under the deferred compensation plan triggered by a change in control, and benefits payments are not accelerated in the manner described in the previous paragraph. Instead, they will be paid under the normal provisions of the plan. In the previous example, this might mean that benefit payments will not commence until the executive has terminated employment and attained age 55.

Sometimes a change in control will not change the substantive provisions of a SERP or other deferred compensation plan as to the amount of benefits or time or manner of payment. The only event that will occur is that assets may be placed in a trust to secure the future payment of such benefits. Usually, the trust used is a rabbi trust.[2] When funding of the trust only occurs upon a change in control, such a trust is sometimes referred to as a springing rabbi trust. The intention in designing a trust in this way is to avoid diverting assets from the employer to the trust until it is necessary to do so.

Stock options and SARs.   Stock options and stock appreciation rights (SARs) often are not immediately exercisable when they are granted. Rather, they become exercisable only after the passage of time (e.g., one or two years) or upon the occurrence of some other event usually tied to the financial performance of the employer. In the event of a change in control, these options and SARs often become immediately exercisable.

In some cases, executives are granted limited stock appreciation rights. The limitation on these SARs is that they are *only* exercisable in the event of a change in control. Due to this limit, the employer can avoid the adverse accounting treatment normally associated with SARs until it becomes likely that the SARs will become exercisable (i.e., a change in control is likely).

Restricted stock.   Restricted stock, by definition, only vests after a specified period of time or after the occurrence of some other event usually related to the financial performance of the employer. In the event of a change in control, shares of restricted stock often will become immediately vested.

Long-term incentive awards.   A common element of many long-term incentive plans is that the amounts to be paid thereunder are based upon corporate and/or individual performance measured over a period of several years. The main issue sometimes addressed with respect to such plans in the event of a change in control is determining an amount payable based on performance prior to the end of the performance cycle. Where median awards are specified, this is sometimes accomplished by paying a proportionate amount of a median award.

Welfare benefits.   Executives are sometimes also provided with continued life insurance, medical benefits, and long-term disability benefits in the event their employment is terminated in connection with a change in control. Such continued coverage will usually last for a period ranging from one to three years.

Triggering event.   The other key element in a golden parachute arrangement is the description of the event or events that will make a covered executive entitled to benefits. The triggering event is often composed of two items: (1) a change in control and (2) a termination of the executive's employment. This is a so-called double trigger because the entitlement to golden parachute benefits does not arise unless both events occur. In some instances, golden parachute benefits are subject to a single trigger (i.e., they will be paid in the event of a change in control without regard to whether the executive's employment has been terminated).

Change in control.   The definition of a change in control varies among golden parachute arrangements. As a design matter, a proper balance must be struck between a definition that is too narrow and will not provide adequate protection and one that is too broad and will pay unintended benefits.

In particular, employers may be concerned about parachute provisions that will be triggered in the event of a "friendly" change in control. Sometimes this is addressed directly in the definition of a change in control. For example, the parachute arrangement will expressly provide that an event that would otherwise fit within the definition of a change in control will be excluded if it is approved by the company's incumbent board of directors. Sometimes, this situation is handled on an ad hoc basis. For example, if a transaction would otherwise constitute a change in control, the board of directors will amend the definition (prior to the occurrence of the event) to exclude the particular transaction.

Following are some events typically found in a definition of a change in control:

- An entity or group acquires beneficial ownership of a stated percentage (ranging from 20 percent to 50 percent) of the voting stock of the employer.
- Shareholders approve an agreement to merge or consolidate the employer with or into another corporation.
- Shareholders approve an agreement to sell or otherwise dispose of substantially all of the assets of the employer.
- The composition of a majority of the board of directors changes within a prescribed period (generally a year or two), ignoring for this purpose any new board members who were approved by a specified portion of the existing members of the board. This definition protects against changes in control that occur through successful proxy battles.

Sometimes the definition of a change in control involves a cross-reference to certain events that are required to be reported under the securities laws. For example, a change in control might be defined to include a transaction with respect to a company "that is of a nature that would be required to be reported in response to item 1(a) of the Current Report on Form 8-K, pursuant to section 13 or 15(d) of the Securities Exchange Act of 1934." Definitions like this generally include the same types of transactions described previously, since these are the referenced reportable transactions. Whether one or the other approach is used generally depends on the preference of the company's legal counsel. However, one potential defect with a definition that incorporates events solely by reference to securities laws is that those laws may change over time, through legislative, judicial, or administrative action rendering the definition contained in the document inaccurate.

Termination of employment. Most parachute benefits are only triggered if an executive's employment also terminates in connection with a change in control. The connection is usually defined in a chronological sense. That is, if employment terminates within a specified number of years after a change in control (e.g., one or two), it is deemed to be connected with the control change.

Most parachute arrangements provide that any termination of employment is sufficient to create a benefit obligation unless it is one of several specifically enumerated exceptions. Common exceptions are for death, disability, or retirement. Where retirement is excepted, care should be taken to define it in such a way as to preclude post-takeover management from adopting a special retirement program for executives covered by the parachute arrangement in order to avoid triggering parachute benefits in connection with their ouster. Another common exception is a termination for cause. Cause is usually narrowly defined to encompass only egregious conduct by an executive, such as theft of company property.

Some parachute arrangements allow an executive to receive benefits even if the executive voluntarily terminates employment. However, the more common practice is to exclude such voluntary terminations from giving rise to benefits unless the termination is triggered by a constructive discharge by the employer. The events constituting constructive discharge are often defined in parachute agreements as terminations for "good cause" or for "good reason." If and only if these events occur, the executive may initiate his termination and still be entitled to parachute payments. Examples of the events that might constitute a constructive discharge allowing an executive to terminate employment are: (1) a significant reduction in responsibilities coupled with any reduction in pay or any demotion from any office or titled position (2) a significant reduction in pay, or (3) a requirement that the employee relocate more than a specified number of miles (e.g., 30) from his principal place of business.

SPECIAL TAX RULES

In an attempt by Congress to indirectly regulate social policy through the tax code, golden parachute payments that exceed a certain limit are subject to some tax sanctions. Specifically, parachute payments to which these sanctions apply are not deductible by the paying employer. Also, an executive receiving such payments is subject to a 20 percent excise tax in addition to regular income tax. With the top individual income tax rate now set at 39.6 percent, excess parachute payments could therefore be subject to tax at a rate of just under 60 percent.

The existence of these tax sanctions is relevant for two reasons. Obviously, they should be considered in determining the overall cost to the employer of any golden parachute program that it may provide and of the after-tax benefits of the program to covered executives. They should also be considered in designing a parachute program. Specifically, some companies cap the amount of parachute benefits payable to an executive so as not to exceed the IRS limit and trigger the tax sanctions. Other companies include in their programs a tax gross-up payment to executives who are subject to the 20 percent excise tax. Such a tax gross-up is intended to place the executive in the same after-tax position as if the excise tax did not apply. A third group of companies do neither of these (i.e., a cap or a gross-up).

While these golden parachute tax rules seem to be rather straightforward, their application in many situations can be quite complex. Further, the rules' operation depends on a number of key definitions. Basically, the tax sanctions do not apply in respect of all employees, just to certain disqualified individuals. They only apply in the event of a change in control and they only apply to payments that are contingent on this control change (i.e, these payments are defined as parachute payments). Finally, they only apply if the total of all parachute payments made to an individual exceeds 2.99 times that individual's average compensation over the five years preceding the control change. This five-year average is known as an individual's base amount. Where parachute payments are made over a number of years after a change in control, it is necessary to calculate the present value of these payments and compare this value to the 2.99 limit. Once this threshold has been exceeded, however, the tax sanctions apply to all parachute payments that exceed one times the individual's base amount.

Disqualified Individuals

The golden parachute rules only apply to disqualified individuals. These are defined as certain shareholders, officers, and highly compensated individuals of the corporation undergoing a change in control. As a practical matter, few individuals become subject to the tax sanctions due solely to their status as shareholders. Proposed IRS regulations apply the rules only to shareholders whose stock has a value exceeding $1 million (or, if less, 1 percent of the total fair market value of the outstanding shares of all classes of stock).[3]

Whether an individual is an officer is determined on the basis of all the facts and not just by examining a person's title. This can cut both ways. A person with an officer's title who lacks the authority of an officer is ignored. The maximum number of individuals who will be treated as disqualified due to their status as officers is 50 (although a smaller limit applies to corporations with fewer than 500 employees).[4]

An individual must earn more than $75,000 per year to be considered a highly compensated individual. And the total number of employees so included is limited to the 250 with the highest pay (or, if less, the highest paid 1 percent of employees).

The period for determining who is a disqualified individual is determined with reference to the date on which a change in control occurs. It is the portion of the taxable year of the corporation preceding the change in control date plus the entire preceding year. For example, if a corporation with a calendar year tax year has a change in control on September 17, 1994, the reference period will be all of 1993 and the period in 1994 preceding September 17. Where business is conducted through an affiliated group of corporations, all employers who are members of the same affiliated group (under IRC Section 1504) are treated as a single employer. Thus, when a parent corporation experiences a change in control, it is possible that highly compensated individuals and officers of subsidiary corporations who receive parachute payments also may be treated as disqualified individuals.

Change in Control

A change in control may occur in any one of three ways: (1) a change in ownership of a corporation, (2) a change in effective control of a corporation, or (3) a change in ownership of a substantial portion of the assets of a corporation. A change in ownership occurs when an entity or a group acting in concert acquires stock that increases its interest from 50 percent or less to more than 50 percent of the total voting power or value of a corporation's stock.

A change in effective control of a corporation is presumed to occur whenever an entity or a group acting in concert acquires, within a 12-month period, voting stock that increases its interest in the corporation by 20 percent or more. It is also presumed to occur whenever a majority of the board of directors is replaced during a 12-month period by members not endorsed by a majority of the incumbent board.

A change in the ownership of a substantial portion of the assets of a corporation occurs whenever an entity or a group acting in concert acquires, within a 12-month period, assets at least equal to one-third of the total value of all assets of the corporation. This could occur if a corporation sold assets or if a parent corporation sold its stock of a subsidiary that possessed one-third or more of the total assets of the combined corporations. In this respect, all members of an affiliated group of corporations are treated as a single corporation.

While not entirely free from doubt, most tax advisers believe that the sale by a parent corporation of stock in a subsidiary will only cause a change in control if the value of the subsidiary's assets equals or exceeds one-third the total value of all assets of the parent and all subsidiaries that are members of the same affiliated group. The percentage change in the stock ownership of the subsidiary or the change in composition of the subsidiary's board are irrelevant. This is because the statute and the proposed regulations appear to ignore the separate corporate status of subsidiaries and treat all members of an affiliated group as if they were a single corporation.[5]

PARACHUTE PAYMENTS

Any payment of cash, stock, or other property to a disqualified individual that is in the nature of compensation is potentially treated as a parachute payment.

However, to be a parachute, such payments must be contingent on a change in control. A payment will be treated as having been made because of a change in control unless it was substantially certain to have been paid even if the change in control had not occurred.

Example: An executive exercises a limited stock appreciation right. This right became exercisable only because of the occurrence of a change in control. The payment is a parachute payment. It was not substantially certain that it would have been paid had the control change not occurred.

So-called double trigger payments that are expressly conditioned on the occurrence of a change in control and some other event like employment termination are parachute payments under this definition since they were not going to be paid unless a change in control occurred.

Moreover, payments that are not expressly conditioned on the occurrence of a change in control at all may still be considered parachute payments if they are contingent on certain events that are closely associated with a change in control. Examples of closely associated events include: (a) the onset of a tender offer, (b) a substantial increase in the price of a company's shares, (c) delisting of a company's stock, (d) the acquisition of more than 5 percent of a company's stock by an entity or a group not already in control, and (e) the voluntary or involuntary termination of employment.

Payments contingent on one of these events will be presumed to be parachute payments provided that a change in control actually occurs within one year before or after the event. The event of termination of employment is particularly important to note. Many payments not expressly conditioned on a change in control will be treated as parachute payments because they are conditioned on termination of employment and the termination occurs within one year after (or even before) an actual change in control.

Example: A company maintains a severance pay plan for executives providing them with three times their regular salary in the event of their involuntary termination for any reason. This program is not conditioned in any way on the occurrence of a change in control. A change in control occurs and an executive is fired by the new management three months after the change. His severance pay is presumed to be a parachute payment since it was conditioned on a closely associated event that occurred within one year following a change in control. And it was not substantially certain that the payment would have been made if this termination had not occurred.

Some payments that are not conditioned on either a change in control or on a closely associated event will still be treated as parachute payments if a change in control or a closely associated event accelerates the time at which the payment would have been made.[6] In this case, only a portion of the payment will be treated as a parachute. The portion so treated is the excess of the actual payment over the discounted present value of the payment that would have been made absent the acceleration. This rule can apply to cause payments of vested deferred compensation to be treated as parachutes.

Example: An executive was entitled to receive a vested SERP benefit in a lump sum at retirement. A change in control occurs; the executive is terminated and receives a payment of his lump sum. It was substantially certain that the SERP benefit would have been paid whether or not the control change occurred. However, the change in control caused the payment to be accelerated. The executive actually receives a payment of $500,000. The proposed regulations provide little detailed guidance on how to determine the present value of the SERP benefit that would have been paid had the change not occurred. The only exception is the interest rate to be used. However, it is also necessary to make an assumption about when the executive would have retired if the change had not occurred. In this regard, the regulations suggest that estimates based on accepted actuarial principles may be used.[7] Assume that the employer determines the present value to be $400,000. In this case only $100,000 is treated as a parachute payment.[8]

If a change in control accelerates the time for payment of vested deferred compensation that is being credited with a variable rate of interest or with other phantom gains and losses, the regulations suggest that no part of the payment should be treated as a parachute.[9] Thus, in contrast to defined benefit SERP payments, accelerated payments of unfunded deferred compensation held in the individual account of an executive generally will not be treated as parachute payments where these payments were certain to be made at some point without regard to the change in control.

In some instances, an event will be treated as a parachute payment although no payment has occurred in the normal sense of the word. This is particularly relevant with respect to stock and stock options. The proposed regulations treat the vesting of shares of stock as a payment. If vesting is contingent on a change in control or on a closely associated event, the payment will be treated as a parachute payment. The amount so treated is based upon the value of the shares at the time they vest. If the stock would have vested over time in any event and the change in control only accelerated vesting, a portion of the full value of the stock is treated as a parachute. That portion is composed of two parts:

1. The excess of the current value of the stock at vesting over the discounted present value of that same amount payable at the future date when the stock normally would have vested.

2. An amount to reflect the value of the lapse of an obligation to continue performing services, which cannot be less than 1 percent multiplied by the current value of the shares and the number of full months of accelerated vesting.[10]

Example: An executive receives 1,000 shares of stock that will vest in three years if he continues working. One year after grant, a change in control occurs and the shares immediately vest. At the time of vesting, the shares are worth $50,000. The present value of $50,000 payable in two years (i.e., when the shares otherwise would have vested) is $48,050. The excess of $50,000 over this present value, or $1,950, is one part of the parachute payment with respect to these shares. The minimum value of the other part is determined by multiplying $50,000 by 1 percent by 24 (the number of full months remaining before the shares normally would have vested). This value is $12,000. Thus, of the $50,000, at least $13,950 is treated as a parachute payment.

The foregoing calculation may at times result in a value that exceeds the full value of the shares. In this case, the amount treated as a parachute is simply the full value of the shares. Note also that this special rule does not apply where shares would have normally vested based on an event other than the mere passage of time (e.g., vesting based on company financial performance). In such cases, unless it is substantially certain that the performance targets would have been fulfilled absent the change in control, the full value of shares that become vested due to the control change should be included as a parachute payment.

Stock options are treated in a similar fashion to shares of stock. However, in contrast to the normal income tax treatment of options, a parachute payment is not delayed until the option is exercised. Instead, if a change in control causes an option to become vested, this vesting is treated as a parachute payment. The proposed regulations are ambiguous about the meaning of vesting in the context of stock options. Many tax advisers consider an option to be vested for this purpose if a change in control causes the option to become exercisable.[11]

Unlike shares of stock, the value of stock options is not obvious. The regulations indicate that an option's value should be derived from factors such as, but not limited to: the option spread at the time of vesting (i.e., the excess of the value of the shares subject to the option over the option price); the price volatility of the optioned stock; and the duration of the option.

It is interesting to note that these are some, but not all, of the factors used to determine the Black-Scholes value of a stock option. This value is used by some companies as the basis of their annual proxy disclosure concerning options granted to the top five executives. Using this approach, the value of an option may be more or less than its spread alone.

Once the value of an option is determined, the portion of this value that is treated as a parachute payment is identical to that used for shares of stock. That is, the portion is generally determined on the basis of two values, the time value of the accelerated payment and the value of the lapse of the obligation to continue performing services.

Excluded Payments

Certain corporations are not subject to the parachute tax sanctions. These are S corporations and other corporations with no stock that is traded on a securities exchange. However, this exception only applies to a non-S corporation if 75 percent of the voting shares of the corporation have approved the parachute payments.

Payments to or from a tax-qualified retirement plan are excluded from treatment as parachute payments. However, other welfare-type benefits, such as post-termination medical benefits or life insurance, may be treated as parachute payments in appropriate circumstances.[12]

Also excluded are payments of reasonable compensation for services rendered after a change in control. Payments will generally be considered as reasonable if they satisfy two conditions: They relate only to the period during which services are actually performed; and the annualized rate of these payments is not significantly greater than the executive's annual compensation prior to the change in control or the annual compensation customarily paid by the employer or comparable employers for comparable work.[13]

This exception is sometimes used by an acquiring corporation and executives of the acquired corporation entitled to parachutes to try to avoid the tax burdens on both parties. That is, the acquiring corporation will agree to consider employing these individuals after the change in control if they renounce their rights to parachute payments from the acquired corporation in excess of the 2.99 times limit. Such a gambit is based on the assumption that payments after the change in control will be reasonable compensation for post-change services and, hence, not parachutes. It is also based on a provision in the proposed regulations that any payments made under an agreement entered into after a change in control are not parachute payments unless they are made pursuant to a legally enforceable agreement entered into before the change.[14] Whether this approach will work is a factual matter.[15]

The proposed regulations provide that damages paid to an executive for breach of an employment contract will be treated as reasonable compensation for services rendered after a change in control if certain conditions are met.[16] Damages that meet these conditions are not considered to be parachute payments. While not discussed in the regulations, this favorable treatment may apply to liquidated damages as well as damages recovered through a law suit. Thus, an executive with an employment contract providing for liquidated damages that is prematurely terminated after a change in control could receive a lump sum payment that would not be subject to the parachute tax sanctions. To qualify for this treatment, the following conditions must be satisfied:

- The contract was not entered into, amended, or renewed in contemplation of the change in control. At a minimum, this means the employment contract should not have been entered into within one year of the change in control.
- The salary and other compensation provided for under the contract was itself reasonable.
- The damages do not exceed the present value of the payments that otherwise would have been made under the contract had employment continued. For example, a lump sum payment of liquidated damages must not exceed the discounted present value of the future compensation that it is designed to replace.
- The executive is willing to continue working under the contract, but the employer refuses.
- The damages are reduced by mitigation. That is, the amount payable as damages is reduced by the executive's earnings from another employer during the contract period. It is unclear whether the executive must actively seek employment or whether the employment sought may be limited to a comparable job. Also, if damages are paid as an up-front sum, mitigation would require the executive to return a portion of this payment to the extent of the executive's earnings.

The proposed regulations provide that reasonable compensation for the performance of services includes compensation for refraining from performing services, such as under a covenant not to compete or a similar arrangement.[17] In a 1993 ruling, the IRS indicated that amounts paid to executives upon termination of employment following a change in control would thus not be parachute payments if they were reasonable compensation for not competing with the acquiring company for a specified period of time after the change in control.[18] Payments that are reasonable compensation for services rendered *before* a change in control are not subject to the golden parachute tax sanctions. However, this may have little practical significance to the tax liability created by the parachute arrangement. Such payments nevertheless count in determining whether the present value of all parachute payments equals or exceeds three times an individual's base amount. Also, such payments only reduce tax liability if they exceed the portion of the individual's base amount allocated to them. This is because the tax sanctions do not apply in any event to the portion of a parachute payment that is equal to the allocated base amount.

Base Amount

An executive's base amount determines the level of parachute payments he may receive without generating tax sanctions. Specifically, if the present value of all parachute payments equals or exceeds three times the base amount, the tax sanctions will apply.

The base amount is the average annual taxable compensation paid to a disqualified individual during the five calendar years preceding the year in which the change in control occurs. Thus, the base amount will vary from one individual to another. Also, since the base amount is an average of compensation received over a five-year period, it will often be significantly lower than the compensation currently paid to an executive due to the effect of pay raises.

The base amount includes those items of compensation that are includable in gross income. In addition to salary, bonuses, and other incentive pay, it would also include the ordinary income attributable to the exercise of nonqualified stock options. Excluded from the base amount are those items not includable in an executive's gross income. For example, 401(k) deferrals and deferrals to nonqualified unfunded plans serve to reduce the base amount of participating individuals. The proposed regulations specifically provide that items excluded from gross income are excluded from the base amount determination even if they are considered parachute payments. The best example of this is a nonqualified stock option that becomes vested upon a change in control, but is not exercised. [19]

Because the base amount is determined with reference to the five calendar years ending before a change in control, it is difficult for executives to manipulate their base amount by manipulating the amount included in their gross income (e.g., by exercising stock options). For example, if a change in control occurs in June of 1994, the last year used in calculating the base amount for individuals is the 1993 calendar year.

The period for determining the base amount of an individual who was hired within five years of a change in control is the entire period of the individual's employment with the corporation. If the person was hired on a day other than the first day of a year, compensation for the year is annualized. The only exception to this is for payments that are made no more frequently than once a year, such as an annual bonus; this amount is not annualized.

Determining Present Value

Parachute payments may be made over a single year (e.g., severance pay in a lump sum). Parachute payments may also be paid over a number of years (e.g., annual SERP payments to an executive). In determining whether these payments exceed the golden parachute limit of 2.99 times the base amount, the *present value* of each parachute payment must be calculated.

Some guidance is provided on the manner in which the present value of parachute payments is to be determined. The present value of parachute payments is generally determined on the change in control date. The interest rate to be used is 120 percent of the applicable federal rate. In this regard, the proposed regulations indicate that the interest rate used may be either the rate in effect as of the change in control date or, by prior election, the rate in effect when the parachute agreement was entered into.

If, at the time of the change in control, uncertainties exist as to the amount or timing of parachute payments, the proposed regulations indicate that estimates must be used. For example, if payments will not start until an employee terminates employment, the timing of these payments must be estimated as of the change in control date to determine their present value. In making these estimates, the regulations provide that uncertainties that reduce value must be ignored unless the chance of occurrence can be determined on the basis of generally accepted actuarial principles or otherwise with reasonable accuracy.[20] Where such estimates are used, the regulations seem to contemplate that when actual payments are made of amounts previously estimated, the parachute tax calculations must be redone and, if necessary, amended returns must be filed.[21]

Tax Sanctions

If the present value of all parachute payments exceeds 2.99 times the base amount for a disqualified individual, the excise tax and nondeductibility apply to any excess parachute payments made to that individual. In a simple case where an executive receives just one parachute payment, the portion of this payment subject to the tax sanctions is the excess of the entire payment over the individual's base amount.

Example: An executive receives a severance pay parachute in a single sum six months after a change in control. The amount of the severance pay is $800,000. The executive's base amount (i.e., his five-year average compensation) is $250,000. The present value of the parachute is $777,028. This present value exceeds 2.99 times his base amount (i.e., $777,028 exceeds $749,999). The portion of the severance pay treated as an excess parachute payment to which the tax sanctions apply is $550,000 (i.e., $800,000 less $250,000).

If an executive receives several parachute payments at different times, the calculation of the portion of each such payment that is treated as an excess parachute payment is somewhat more complicated. In this case, it is necessary to allocate the base amount to each parachute payment. The base amount is allocated to the parachute payments in the same proportion that the present value of each parachute payment bears to the present value of all parachute payments. This is generally favorable, since more of the base amount is allocated to earlier parachute payments, thereby delaying the time for payment of the excise tax and the loss of a deduction.

Assume, for example, that a change in control entitles an executive to an immediate parachute payment of $400,000 and a second parachute payment of $400,000 to be made in two years. The first payment has a present value of $400,000 and the second payment has a present value of $355,998. The total of these present values exceeds 2.99 times the executive's base amount of $250,000 (i.e., $755,998 exceeds $749,999). Of the entire base amount, $132,275 is allocated to the first $400,000 and the remainder, $117,725, is allocated to the second parachute payment. Therefore, $267,725 of the first parachute is an excess parachute payment (i.e., $400,000 less $132,275), and $282,275 of the second parachute payment is an excess parachute payment (i.e., $400,000 less $117,725).

PROXY DISCLOSURE

A separate narrative disclosure is required of any plan or arrangement providing payments to executive officers of the reporting company contingent on a change in control. The disclosure required is a description of the plan or other arrangement. That is, disclosure is not delayed until the change in control occurs. An exception from such disclosure is provided when the total amount involved is $100,000 or less.

In addition, the proxy rules require disclosure of amounts paid, payable, or accrued in connection with a change of control, regardless of any dollar threshold. Disclosure is required for those who are elective officers at the fiscal year-end of the reporting company and also for any individual who acted as CEO for any part of a year and for up to two other former executive officers who would be among the highest paid executives (ignoring CEOs) based on their actual salary and bonus for the year they departed.

ELEVENTH HOUR PARACHUTES

If a golden parachute arrangement is adopted as a defensive reaction to a potential change in control, the arrangement may be subject to a higher standard of review than would otherwise apply. A parachute arrangement that does not meet this standard could be voided. Due to this, it is preferable to adopt parachute arrangements before there is any evidence that a change in control might occur.

Normally, the propriety of actions of a board of directors as to compensation or other matters is tested under the so-called business judgment rule. According to one court, this rule is essentially designed to prevent a board's business decisions from being "fodder for in-depth ex post legal scrutiny," absent any wrongdoing.[22]

However, many courts apply a different standard to actions of a board of directors that may be characterized as defenses to a potential takeover. In this case, courts fear that incumbent boards have a natural desire to remain entrenched, even to the detriment of shareholders. Hence, courts apply a so-called modified business judgment rule to determine whether a board has acted properly in this context.[23]

The modified business judgment rule requires a parachute arrangement to meet a two-part standard. First, the directors must be able to demonstrate their good faith belief, after reasonable investigation, that the potential change in control posed a danger to corporate policy and effectiveness. This standard is often met through a showing that the board believed the potential change in control might cause the corporation to lose key executives. Second, the board must show that the parachute arrangement was a reasonable reaction to the threat posed.[24]

In this regard, there is some evidence that parachute benefits triggered by a change in control alone that do not also require an executive's employment to be terminated are more likely to fail this second part of the modified business judgment rule. Such single trigger parachutes include new option awards or the vesting of outstanding options upon the occurrence of a change in control. Another example is the extension of an employment contract.[25]

NOTES

1. Occasionally, companies would adopt provisions known as pension parachutes with respect to their tax-qualified defined benefit plans. These provided extra retirement benefits to all plan participants (not just senior executives) in the event of a change in control. However, the primary motivation for such provisions was not to protect dislocated employees, but to exhaust any surplus assets in the plan by increasing plan liabilities. These surplus assets would then be unavailable to a potential acquirer willing to terminate the plan to recover them. With the advent of a 50 percent excise tax on recoveries of surplus pension assets in 1990 (along with regular income tax at a 35 percent rate), the continued need for pension parachutes is questionable since most of a plan's surplus assets will be paid to the IRS.
2. See Chapter 10.
3. IRS Prop. Reg. 1.280G-1, Q/A-17.
4. IRS Prop. Reg. 1.280G-1, Q/A-18(c).
5. IRC Section 280G(d)(5) and IRS Prop. Reg. 1.280G-1, Q/A-46.
6. IRS Prop. Reg. 1.280G-1, Q/A-22(c).
7. See IRS Prop. Reg. 1.280G-1, Q/A-24(b), Q/A-32 and Q/A-33.
8. See IRS Prop. Reg. 1.280G-1, Q/A-24(e) example (4) for a similar example concerning a SERP.
9. IRS Prop. Reg. 1.280G-1, Q/A-24(e) example (3).
10. IRS Prop. Reg. 1.280G-1, Q/A-24(c).
11. It is common for stock options to be first exercisable only after a specified period of time following their grant. The waiting period commonly is from

six months to two years. Thereafter, the option may be exercised at any time until it expires (usually 10 years after grant). Many options will become immediately exercisable in the event of a change in control.

12. In some cases, benefits under the following plans may be treated as reasonable compensation for services rendered before a change in control: group term life insurance, medical benefit, group legal services, cafeteria, educational assistance, and dependent care plans. IRS Prop. Reg. 1.280G-1, Q/A-41. The plans must be nondiscriminatory. However, the extended post-termination welfare benefits provided to executives as part of a parachute arrangement rarely fulfill the requirements for such treatment since they are not provided to all employees.

13. IRS Prop. Reg. 1.280G-1, Q/A-42(a).

14. IRS Prop. Reg. 1.280G-1, Q/A-23.

15. In *Balch* v. *Comr.,* 100 T.C. No. 21 (1993), the Tax Court indicated that a willingness by an acquiring corporation to use its best efforts to employ executives after the control change in exchange for their renunciation of excess parachute payments was a sufficient prechange agreement to cause the exception for payments made under an agreement executed after a change in control to be inapplicable in this case. Thus the court examined whether the compensation paid to the executives after the control change was reasonable in light of the amount of services provided to the acquiring corporation. Using this analysis, the court held that most of the payments were unreasonable in amount and should be treated as parachutes.

16. IRS Prop. Reg. 1.280G-1, Q/A-42(b).

17. IRS Prop. Reg. 1.280G-1, Q/A-11.

18. PLR 9314034.

19. IRS Prop. Reg. 1.280G-1, Q/A-34(c).

20. IRS Prop. Reg. 1.280G-1, Q/A-33(a).

21. IRS Prop. Reg. 1.280G-1, Q/A-33(b) and (c), examples (2) and (3).

22. *International Insurance Co.* v. *Johns,* 874 F. 2d 1447 (CA 11 1989).

23. *Buckhorn, Inc.* v. *Ropak Corp.,* 656 F. Supp 209 (S.D. Ohio 1987) and *Johns, supra.* The courts are not consistent on when the modified business judgment rule applies. Some courts, such as in *Buckhorn,* apply the rule only if an offer has actually been made. Other courts, such as in *Johns,* look to whether the board intended the parachute to be a takeover device and not whether an offer has been made. However, if an offer has been made, this is obviously strong evidence that the board may have intended a subsequently adopted parachute arrangement as a reaction to the offer.

24. Ibid.

25. *Buckhorn, supra.*

Chapter Sixteen

Perquisites

Webster's New Collegiate Dictionary defines a perquisite as "a privilege, gain, or profit incidental to regular salary or wages," as well as "something held or claimed as an exclusive right or possession."[1] This definition certainly holds true when it comes to executive benefits. None of the items described in this chapter represents significant elements of an executive's overall package in monetary terms. Nonetheless, company cars and aircraft, club memberships, and other perquisites are often highly valued as symbols of executive status. In addition to conferring status, employers may provide perquisites to enhance the executive's safety or convenience (such as company cars, aircraft), assist the executive in generating business (such as club memberships), or achieve tax efficiencies (such as executive physicals).

Common perquisites are described in the following pages.

COMPANY CARS

Employers have a number of options for providing cars for executives. One is simply to provide an automobile for the executive's discretionary use for both business and nonbusiness travel. Another is to provide a car and driver, typically for business-related travel only. The company generally leases or owns the car, though it may let the executive choose the model; ownership is typically not transferred to the executive.

The executive will have taxable income to the extent he or she uses the car for nonbusiness travel but does not reimburse the company for this use. For tax purposes, use of a car to commute to and from work is not considered a business use. Absent reimbursement by the executive, the amount of taxable income attributable to nonbusiness use of a company car should be determined on the basis of business versus nonbusiness mileage. The

IRS will treat the full value of the use of the car as taxable income if adequate records as to business and nonbusiness use are not maintained. While the IRS does not require the maintenance of a contemporaneous log, it will give little credence to records that were not created at or near the time of use.[2] As a practical matter, an employer should obtain periodic reports from its executives as to business travel mileage. The company will also need these records to claim tax deductions for company cars.[3]

An employer can report the entire use value of an automobile as taxable income each year without regard to relative amounts of business and non-business use. In such cases, it will be up to the employee to claim a deduction for business use mileage for which he or she has maintained adequate records. Because this approach essentially shifts tax recordkeeping burdens to the executive, it is not particularly attractive to companies interested in rewarding their senior people.

When a company car is made available for personal use, the value of that use must be determined each year to calculate how much taxable income to report for the executive. In general, value is determined with reference to the cost to the executive to lease the car in a normal market transaction. The IRS has also provided a number of special valuation rules. By following these rules, employers should be able to avoid subsequent disagreements with the IRS over the use value of a vehicle.

The principal special valuation method is known as the annual lease value method. This approach uses an IRS table to determine the annual lease value for four years based on the purchase price of the car. The value is approximately 25 percent of the car's price;[4] a car with an initial value of $40,000 would have an annual lease value of $10,750. If the car is still in use after four years, the annual lease value is recalculated for another four-year period based on the value of the car at the start of year five.

The cents-per-mile special valuation method is based on the standard mileage allowance determined by the IRS each year. Because it is not available for cars with an initial value of more than $12,800 (adjusted for inflation each year since 1989), it generally is not helpful for executive vehicles. Another alternative, the commuting value method, is very favorable, but is available only if a number of very restrictive conditions are satisfied: the individual using the vehicle cannot be an officer paid at least $50,000 a year, a director, an employee paid at least $100,000 per year, or a 1 percent or more owner of the employer. Hence, this special rule is also of little use in the context of executive autos.

Special rules applicable to so-called luxury automobiles complicate the employer's tax situation. The term *luxury automobile* is not defined in the statute.[5] Instead, the rules operate indirectly to limit the maximum depreciation allowable with respect to any automobile used in business in any year. This limit essentially applies to any automobile with an initial cost of more than $12,800, as adjusted for inflation. The details of these special rules are well beyond the scope of this book and do not affect the tax treatment of the executive.

Although personal use of a company car generates taxable income for the executive, special withholding rules allow an employer to elect no withholding with respect to this income.[6] To avail itself of this election, the employer must notify the employee that it is not withholding. Thus, an employee concerned about being underwithheld may adjust his or her other withholdings accordingly.

If a company provides one or more of its executives with a chauffeured limousine as opposed to an auto operated by the executive, the basic tax rules described previously apply: the executive will be treated as having received taxable income for any personal use of the limousine, including its use to commute to and from work. If the executive uses the limousine only for business travel, no part of the value of this travel will be taxable to the executive. But some special rules also apply when the company car is a chauffeured limousine.

First, the executive's taxable income for personal use of the limousine will reflect not only the value of the car, but also a portion of the value of the chauffeur's services. IRS regulations specify two ways to value these services: on the basis of what the company pays the chauffeur, or on the basis of what it would cost to obtain such services in an independent, arm's-length transaction.[7] The portion of this value that is taxable to an executive is the same as the portion of the chauffeur's total hours that are spent on the executive's personal transportation needs. These hours include on-call time. Any time a chauffeur is on-call outside of the executive's normal business hours is presumed to be personal on-call time.

When a company provides a chauffeur-driven limousine because of concerns about an executive's security, it is possible to exclude from income a portion of the value of the car and driver that would otherwise be taxable due to personal use (e.g., commuting). The excludable portion of the total value is that which is attributable to special security features, including bulletproof glass, armor plating, and the extra value of the services of a chauffeur trained in personal security.[8] Note, however, that even this partial exclusion is not available unless the security measures are in response to a specific security concern (such as death or kidnapping threats) and are part of an overall security program.[9]

COMPANY AIRCRAFT

Executives and their guests are sometimes permitted to use company aircraft for personal travel. Company policies differ as to when aircraft will be available for personal use. Many employers permit personal travelers to ride along with other executives who are traveling on business. Letting executives make personal use of company aircraft that would not otherwise have been flying is less common. Policies also differ as to whether and in what circumstances an executive would be required to reimburse the company for personal use of a company plane. Absent such reimbursement, the value of any personal (as opposed to business) travel is treated as additional taxable income to the executive.

Elaborate IRS regulations govern how to determine the value of noncommercial flights used by employees for personal purposes. In many cases, the value of personal travel on company aircraft is determined according to a special aircraft valuation formula that encompasses (1) miles traveled, (2) a cents-per-mile rate established and periodically adjusted by the Department of Transportation (the so-called SIFL rate), (3) the size of the aircraft by weight (used to adjust the otherwise applicable SIFL rate), and (4) a terminal charge, also established and periodically adjusted by the Department of Transportation. The rate is higher for executives who are control employees, defined for this purpose as the 10 board-appointed officers with the highest compensation, the top 1 percent paid employees (up to 50), all directors, and any 5 percent owners.[10]

In applying the special aircraft valuation formula, the miles traveled are determined on the basis of the statute miles between the place the executive boards and the place where he deplanes; the actual travel route is irrelevant. Departure and arrival locations used to determine the value of the flight could vary depending upon whether the executive's travel was primarily for business or personal reasons. The regulations do not provide objective standards for determining whether travel is primarily business or personal.

An executive flying primarily for business reasons must include in income the excess of the value of all flights taken over the value of the flights that would have been taken had there been no personal flights. Assume, for example, that an executive flies from Chicago to Miami on business, flies on to Orlando for personal travel, and returns from Orlando to Chicago. The amount included in income is the excess of three flights (Chicago to Miami, Miami to Orlando, Orlando to Chicago) over the flights that would have occurred without personal travel (Chicago to Miami and Miami to Chicago).

If the trip is primarily personal, the executive must include in income the value of the personal flights he or she would have taken had there been no business travel. If the flights had been primarily personal, for example, the executive would have been taxed on the value of the personal flights that would have occurred without the business travel (Chicago to Orlando and Orlando to Chicago).

Another special rule may be used in some cases in lieu of the special aircraft valuation formula. Where it applies, the seating capacity rule is quite favorable: nonbusiness travelers will not recognize any taxable income for the value of the flight. The rule is available only if at least half of the regular seating capacity of the aircraft is occupied by individuals traveling on company business.[11] In addition, it is available only to current employees, retired or disabled former employees, widows of individuals who died while active, and spouses and dependent children of any of the foregoing. Directors may not use this rule unless they also come within one of the other categories. The requirement that at least half the seats must be occupied by business travelers is determined with reference to each nonbusiness traveler and must be satisfied from the time that person embarks until he or she disembarks.

Senior executives of one company often serve as directors of other unrelated companies. If an executive uses his employer's plane to travel to a board meeting of an unrelated company, this is normally considered a use of the plane other than for company business. Thus, the employer must include the value of the flight on the executive's W-2 as additional taxable compensation. The executive may be entitled to an offsetting deduction for this business expense since he is considered to be self-employed in his capacity as a director and may deduct ordinary and necessary expenses incurred in connection with this business.[12]

WORKING CONDITION FRINGE BENEFITS

Employers provide a variety of things to help executives better perform their duties—subscriptions to professional publications, expenses for attending professional meetings, expense reimbursements for business-related travel and entertainment, and use of company cars or aircraft for business-related travel. The value of any such working condition fringe benefit is not includable in the taxable income of the recipient so long as there is sufficient connection with the executive's performance of services as an employee of the providing organization.

The standard for determining whether a particular perquisite is a working condition fringe benefit is whether its cost would have been deductible by the executive if he or she had paid for it. The 2 percent floor on miscellaneous itemized deductions that normally applies to employee business expenses does not apply here.[13] Thus, an executive is often better off with a tax-free working condition fringe benefit than if he had paid for the item himself with extra salary, since the 2 percent floor will often prevent him from claiming a deduction.[14] A working condition fringe benefit is excludable from an executive's income without regard to whether its availability is limited to one or more executives.

For some items such as travel and entertainment expenses, the working condition fringe benefit exclusion is expressly conditioned on satisfaction of specific IRS recordkeeping requirements.

The IRS has indicated that outplacement services generally qualify as a tax-free working condition fringe benefit (Rev. Rul. 92-69). According to the ruling, this treatment does not depend upon whether the outplacement program covers a nondiscriminatory group. In fact, an example in the ruling suggests that a higher level of outplacement services may be provided to executives than to other employees so long as services are related to the needs of individual employees. IRS officials have made informal comments suggesting that a program limited to just a few select executives may not qualify, however.

Outplacement will only qualify for tax-favored treatment if the employer can demonstrate that it derives a substantial business benefit from the provision of the services that is distinct from the benefit it would derive from paying additional compensation—for example, to promote a positive corporate image, maintain morale among remaining employees, avoid wrongful termination lawsuits, or attract quality employees. While employers must normally provide working condition fringe benefits to employees, the ruling indicates that outplacement services will not fail to qualify simply because a recipient is not currently employed.

Finally, the ruling indicates that tax-favored treatment of outplacement services will be forfeited where participating individuals can choose between outplacement services and additional severance pay. In this situation, employees that choose outplacement services may be able to claim an offsetting deduction for the income reported, but only after reducing the deduction by the 2 percent floor on miscellaneous itemized deductions.

CLUB MEMBERSHIPS

Companies sometimes pay for the costs of social club memberships for their executives. In cases where an executive mixes business and personal activities at the club, dues are apportioned on the basis of each such use, and the portion of the dues attributable to personal use represents taxable compensation to the executive. Individual expenses that the employer reimburses will be taxable or not depending upon whether they relate to a business activity.

Starting in 1994, an employer is no longer allowed a deduction for any club dues, including dues for airline and hotel clubs.[15]

EXECUTIVE PHYSICALS

In general, a company may provide medical benefits to its employees tax-free; the employee will recognize no taxable income as a result of the coverage or of any benefits actually received. This favorable tax treatment does not depend on whether the benefits are available on a nondiscriminatory basis to all employees unless the arrangement constitutes a self-insured medical reimbursement plan.[16]

IRS regulations specifically indicate that reimbursements for medical diagnostic procedures for an employee are not treated as a self-insured arrangement. Hence, these procedures (i.e., physicals) may be offered exclusively to executives and nevertheless are not taxable to the recipients.

The types of procedures covered by this special rule include routine medical examinations, blood tests, and X rays. The exclusion is not available for procedures relating to a known illness, disability, or physical injury, nor does it include any activity undertaken for exercise, fitness, nutrition, recreation, or general improvement of health. Finally, this tax-favored treatment is only available for physicals for employees, not their dependents.[17]

COMPANY PARKING

Employers often provide parking spaces for executives, either on company or leased premises, or by reimbursing the executives for parking fees.

Company-provided parking is tax-free to the recipient with limited exceptions. To qualify for the exclusion, the space must be on or near the business premises of the employer or a location from which the employee commutes to work by mass transit. In no event may the value of the space exceed $155 per month. If the value exceeds this figure (which is adjusted in $5 increments to reflect inflation), the excess is includable in the executive's income.[18]

COMPANY LOANS

While executives are likely to appreciate a company loan program, employers need to consider whether they want to enter into transactions that may someday necessitate collecting money from individuals who are unable or unwilling to pay. In many cases, loan programs exist only to enable and encourage executives to purchase company stock.

The tax consequences of a loan to an executive are governed by a rather elaborate set of rules.[19] Basically, the loan will have no individual tax consequences (beyond those associated with any borrowing) if the executive pays interest at a rate that meets certain market-based standards. If the company charges no interest or a below-market rate, the value of interest that the executive avoids paying will be treated as additional taxable income.

Whether a loan generates taxable income is determined by comparing the interest rate with a schedule of applicable federal rates published by the IRS. This schedule, which is updated monthly, provides short-term, mid-term, and long-term rates. The rate used for comparison depends on the duration of the loan. Demand loans are compared with the applicable short-term rate in effect for the month in which the loan is initiated.

Some loans are excepted from this tax treatment. De minimis loans (those for less than $10,000) are not subject to the imputed interest rules unless one of the principal purposes of the loan is the avoidance of federal income tax. Certain loans incurred in relocating an executive may also be exempt.

EXECUTIVE-DESIGNATED GIFTS

Executives may be permitted to designate charities to which their employer will make charitable donations, either while the executive is employed or as postmortem gifts (often funded through the purchase of life insurance on the life of the executive). Companies typically set a maximum amount that they are willing to contribute on behalf of any executive.

As long as the executive does not derive any personal benefit from such a charitable contribution, the executive will not be treated as having received any taxable compensation as a result of the arrangement.

In designing a charitable gift program, the company should bear in mind that it, and not the executives, can deduct the donations. In general, charitable deductions are limited to 10 percent of the corporation's taxable income. While contributions in excess of this limit may be carried forward, the delay will dilute the value of the deduction.

PROXY DISCLOSURE

Securities and Exchange Commission proxy disclosure rules require disclosure of perquisites in certain instances.[20] The value of a perquisite provided to an individual must be disclosed if it exceeds $50,000 or, if less, 10 percent of the executive's total annual salary and bonus. Perquisites and other personal benefits are to be valued on the basis of the aggregate incremental cost to the company. This is a relatively favorable method. For example, if an executive makes personal use of a company plane that was also taking another executive on a business trip, the IRS would require that substantial value be imputed to the executive for tax purposes in most cases, while the incremental cost approach of the proxy rules might require little or no disclosure.

Any loans from the company to an executive must be separately disclosed in the proxy materials. Any loan to an executive officer or director with a balance of $60,000 or more at any time during the company's fiscal year triggers this disclosure. The company must disclose the name of the borrower, the largest outstanding balance during the year, the nature of the loan and of the transaction in which it was incurred, and the rate of interest charged.[21]

NOTES

1. *Webster's Ninth New Collegiate Dictionary.*
2. IRS Reg. Section 1.274-5T.
3. IRS Reg. Section 1.274-5T

4. IRS Reg. Section 1.61-21(d)(2).

5. See IRC Section 280F.

6. IRC Section 3402(s).

7. IRS Reg. 1.61-21(b)(5).

8. See IRS Reg. Section 1.132-5(m)(8), example (1).

9. IRS Reg. Section 1.132-5(m)(2).

10. IRS Reg. Section 1.61-21(g)(8).

11. IRS Reg. Section 1.61-21(g)(12).

12. IRS Reg. Section 1.132-5(a)(2).

13. Under IRC Section 67, certain miscellaneous itemized deductions, including unreimbursed employee business expenses, cannot be claimed as a deduction except to the extent that the total of all such deductions exceeds 2 percent multiplied by the employee's adjusted gross income for federal income tax purposes.

14. Note that if the employer reimburses the executive for any business-related expenses initially paid by the executive, the same tax result is achieved as if the employer provided the working condition fringe benefit directly to the executive.

15. IRC Section 274(a).

16. Health and welfare benefits are discussed in more detail in Chapter 7.

17. IRS Reg. Section 1.105-11(g).

18. IRC Section 132(f).

19. IRC Section 7872.

20. See Chapter 13.

21. SEC Reg. S-K, item 404.

Chapter Seventeen

International Issues

As organizations expand beyond domestic borders, they encounter many new challenges in compensating their executives. U.S. pay and benefit programs may not travel well; what is tax-efficient in this country may be very inefficient in another, and what is common practice here may be rare elsewhere, or vice versa. Currency fluctuations and inflation only serve to complicate matters further.

While multinational organizations can look to local practice for guidance in compensating their local nationals (such as a French citizen who spends his entire career in a U.S. company's Paris office), international mobility adds further challenges. What is the most effective compensation package for an expatriate—for example, a U.S. citizen who works in the company's London office and will probably move along to Paris and then Buenos Aires? What about a third-country national (TCN)—for example, a Japanese citizen who runs the same company's Canadian operations?

Comprehensive treatment of international executive compensation and benefit issues would require a separate text. Thus, this chapter will simply highlight some of the key issues U.S.–based multinational employers face in creating and maintaining programs for their executives around the world.

OVERVIEW

An organization that must pay many thousands of dollars per month to house an executive in Hong Kong obviously needs to factor in this expense when it weighs the relative merits of hiring a local national against bringing in a manager from overseas. Thus, the phrase *total compensation* is particularly meaningful in the international arena. In fact, at least at the highest executive levels, the line between compensation, benefits, and perquisites blurs considerably and may be almost irrelevant.

The exact mix of salary, incentives, benefits, and perquisites payable to an individual executive will reflect a number of factors. Income tax levels, mandated contributions to social programs, and the rules governing the tax treatment of benefits and perquisites vary widely from country to country, making tax considerations very important. But quality of life elements such as climate, geographic location, living costs, schooling and education, cultural facilities, and personal security can affect the pay package. Status also plays a role. While it might not be tax-effective to provide an executive with an expensive car and a driver in Country X, for example, custom might dictate otherwise.

Other noneconomic elements that may be important components of total compensation are often overlooked. For example, a benefit such as a training course in another country might have a higher perceived value than a salary increase.

Internal factors, including the way an organization views its international operations, will also shape the development of executive compensation programs. Some organizations maintain a largely domestic orientation, treating their overseas operations as investments or outposts. These organizations tend to leave their local operations in the hands of local management and to let local pay and benefit practices prevail there. Other organizations have now moved further along the continuum to what is often termed the multinational stage of development. Multinationals view their foreign operations as key components of their business, but tend to manage them as miniature versions of the home country operation. At the far end of the continuum are organizations with a global orientation. These companies tend to focus on lines of businesses rather than geographic borders.

The external influences and internal considerations outlined above can combine in myriad ways and are subject to continual change. Thus, we will not attempt to catalog practices in individual countries. Instead, we will briefly touch on salary and incentives and then summarize the options available to employers with respect to retirement and health and welfare benefits for their international executives.

SALARY AND INCENTIVES

Base salaries for executives, whether they are local nationals, expatriates, or TCNs, tend to reflect local practice. The more global an organization's orientation, however, the less likely it is to make local practice the dominant consideration. Global companies that rely on an internationally mobile group of executives often stress consistency in pay practices across the organization (or line of business) to facilitate the frequent redeployment of staff. U.S. multinational companies have frequently kept short-term expatriates on a United States base salary scale while adding various allowances for cost-of-living differences, hardship, schooling and the like. This approach (called the balance sheet) is still widespread, though there is some evidence that companies are beginning to streamline programs for their short-term expatriates.

Practices with respect to annual bonuses will also reflect a company's international orientation. A company that is largely domestic will often cover all executives under the corporate plan, with both eligibility and performance criteria set at headquarters; performance criteria are typically based on worldwide results, and performance is measured at headquarters. A multinational organization is more likely to let its local operations set eligibility and performance criteria in line with local practice and measure performance. As with base salary, the global organization is more likely to strive for consistency across the company or by line of business, with performance measured at the line-of-business level against line-of-business results. Because developing an internationally mobile talent pool is important to these organizations, they aim for a degree of global consistency in their compensation and benefit programs, paying their mobile executives to reflect their worth to the corporation on an any-country basis. Some companies maintain tax equalization programs, paying an executive on a location-neutral scale and reducing his or her take-home pay by the amount of U.S. taxes that would be paid if the executive were a domestic resident. The company then pays the executive's actual foreign and domestic income taxes, making any adjustments necessary to the actual returns. If actual taxes are less than the executive would have paid had he or she been a United States resident, the company keeps the difference. If actual taxes are higher, the company grosses up the executive's pay to reflect the difference. As a result of tax equalization, tax rates in the foreign country where the executive is working are not an issue for the executive.

Local practice is obviously important, however, since it is in local markets that executives actually work. Thus, pay for individual executives will take local parity issues into account as well.

When it comes to long-term incentives, both domestically oriented and multinational organizations tend to extend the U.S. plan to their top-level executives around the world, making adjustments only as necessary to conform with local laws.[1] Global organizations are more likely to use multiple plans for divisional executives, structured by line of business, and a companywide holding company plan for the most senior executives. These organizations also tend to emphasize performance plans tied to line-of-business results rather than stock plans; such a plan might be tied to return on equity or assets over a specified period, for example, with a pay-out in the form of parent company shares.

In linking pay to performance, international employers must grapple with critical issues. Should goals for executives be set and measured in one currency—U.S. dollars, for example—or in local currencies? What weight should be given to corporate performance versus local performance? Should results be measured on a pretax or after-tax basis? Failure to focus on these questions can seriously undermine the overall effectiveness of the executive compensation program.

RETIREMENT BENEFITS

Employers that operate in more than one country face both technical and practical problems in providing retirement income for their executives. The questions that arise at home—the appropriate level of retirement income, the taxation and deductibility of contributions, methods and forms of payment, benefit security, and the like—now arise in multiple locations where they may have very different answers. There are new questions as well, including the country and currency in which retirement income is to be paid, and how best to coordinate or offset benefits payable from multiple sources (e.g., social security benefits from more than one country).

Retirement benefits for local nationals, including executives, almost always reflect the local marketplace. While many organizations strive to maintain a consistent philosophy worldwide (e.g., to use a nonqualified plan where necessary to supplement benefits payable under broad-based programs) the *level* of benefits under both plans will be driven by local practice.[2] Retirement benefits for expatriates and TCNs are another matter, as discussed in more detail in this chapter.

Expatriate Issues

If a U.S. employer sends an executive who is a U.S. citizen to work in Country X, it can either continue covering the executive under the U.S. retirement plans, or it can move the executive into the Country X plans. If the overseas assignment is to be relatively brief,[3] it usually makes sense to continue coverage under the U.S. plans. If an assignment extends over a longer period, coverage under local plans will usually be more tax-efficient.[4]

Unfortunately, moving from plan to plan can create problems comparable to moving from job to job. When an executive leaves the U.S. plan, his or her benefit will be frozen at his or her then-current salary, and any benefit accrued in another country's plan will be similarly frozen when the executive moves on, unless the country in question requires that benefits be indexed. Added together, the benefits payable from the plans in which the executive has participated over the course of his or her career are likely to fall short of what the executive would have been entitled to had he or she stayed in one place. Some companies make up such shortfalls with additional cash or deferred compensation amounts. Others use the TCN plan to make up shortfalls. TCN plans are described following a discussion of expatriate participation in U.S. plans.

Participation in U.S. Plans

A U.S. corporation may choose one of two routes to provide retirement benefits to its employees in overseas service through its tax-qualified pension or profit-sharing plans: (1) coverage of the whole group of U.S. citizens working in a foreign affiliate, permitted under IRC Sections 406 and 407 or (2) coverage of selected U.S. citizens or non-U.S.citizens under Section 414. Executives who continue coverage under broad-based U.S. plans would presumably also participate in any supplemental retirement benefit programs offered by the employer.

When a U.S. citizen is transferred to a company's overseas branch operation, the Internal Revenue Code (IRC) poses no impediments to continuing coverage under the U.S. qualified plan, since a branch office is merely an extension of the company. Such an employee is also automatically covered under U.S. Social Security. If the employee is transferred to an overseas subsidiary, however, there is a potential problem with continuing qualified plan coverage.

Qualified plans must be maintained for the exclusive benefit of the employer's employees. Before 1964, this meant that an employee transferred to an overseas subsidiary could not be covered under the parent company's domestic plan because the transferred employee was no longer directly employed by the parent. In 1964, Congress enacted IRC Sections 406 and 407, which permit U.S. companies to treat employees of foreign affiliates as employees of the parent for purposes of qualified plan coverage. Thus, the exclusive benefit issue was resolved. Note, however, that under IRC Section 406(d), the parent will lose a deduction under IRC Section 404 for any contribution on behalf of an employee of another corporation, even if that other corporation is an affiliate. The deduction is granted only to the foreign affiliate.

Many employers adopted provisions in their qualified plans to grant coverage to expatriates under Sections 406 and 407, but some problems remained, including the following:

- Coverage was limited to U.S. citizens.
- If one U.S. citizen in an affiliate was included in the parent company's plan, all other U.S. citizens in the affiliate had to be covered as well.
- If plan coverage was extended, the parent company would also have to extend Social Security coverage to all U.S. citizens in the affiliate.

Most of these problems were solved in 1974, when Section 414 was added to the IRC with the passage of ERISA. Under Section 414, an employer may continue qualified plan coverage for one transferred employee without having to extend coverage to all other U.S. citizens in the foreign affiliate. As under Section 406(d), however, the tax deduction for contributions is allowed only to the foreign affiliate. Social Security coverage can also be continued if the employer executes an agreement to do so under Section 3121(l) of the IRC, but such coverage is optional (though irrevocable once extended) and need not be extended to other expatriates.[5] In addition, non-U.S. citizens or residents covered under a U.S. plan while working in the U.S. may remain in the U.S. plan when they are transferred elsewhere.[6]

Third-Country National Plans

As noted earlier, a third-country national is an employee who is a citizen of a country other than the country where he is employed or the home country of his employer—for example, a Canadian citizen who manages the Swiss operation of a U.S. corporation. Many U.S. multinational employers maintain special pension plans, called TCN plans, designed to meet the needs of these individuals.[7]

Some organizations provide all retirement benefits for their TCNs through these special plans. Others let their TCNs participate in local plans whenever possible, and use TCN plans to make up for any shortfalls, either offsetting local plan benefits against wrap-around TCN plan benefits at retirement or by designing the TCN plan to anticipate needs. While it is simpler to structure the TCN plan as the only source of benefits, participation in local plans where possible is generally more tax-efficient.

Before discussing various approaches to TCN plans, it is important to remember that the cost of such a plan will be deductible in the United States only if that cost is borne by the taxable entity that is the common law employer of the TCNs. Thus, while XYZ Company, a U.S. multinational, will be able to deduct the pension costs associated with TCN employees working for overseas branches of XYZ, it will not be able to deduct contributions it makes on behalf of TCN employees of its overseas subsidiaries. Instead, these contributions would be considered nondeductible contributions to capital of the subsidiary.

Unfunded nonqualified plans. The most common type of TCN plan is a nonqualified, unfunded arrangement, typically structured as a defined benefit plan. The plan may be designed to be a top hat plan for a select group of management or highly compensated employees, as discussed in Chapter 4, and thus be exempt from most ERISA requirements. Alternatively, the TCN plan may be exempt from all ERISA requirements as a plan "maintained outside of the United States primarily for the benefit of persons substantially all of whom are primarily nonresident aliens."[8] A plan is maintained outside the United States if it covers all or primarily nonresident aliens, the work location is outside the United States and plan records and documentation are located outside the United States.[9]

Thus, a plan sponsor is free to maintain the plan on an unfunded basis—that is, not accumulating assets for future benefit obligations, but instead paying benefits out of corporate assets as the benefits become payable. Such a plan offers maximum flexibility of design and, in its early years, requires minimal cash flow. Employers with a high rate of return on corporate assets may prefer this approach. Its principal disadvantages are that it requires some cash-flow planning, which makes it difficult to allocate costs equitably, and it offers participants little security.

It should be noted that TCNs receive their plan benefits free of U.S. tax, because all services are presumably rendered outside the United States by nonresident aliens. This is not true if they become U.S. residents at the time of receipt. In such a case, they will be taxable if the plan is unfunded.

Qualified plans.   Another option often overlooked is to offer TCNs a qualified plan of their own. While TCNs are typically higher-paid employees, nonresident aliens are ignored for purposes of determining whether a plan is discriminatory. Moreover, a TCN plan may be treated as part of a U.S. multinational's home plan for testing overall coverage under the nondiscrimination rules if the TCN plan provides benefits comparable to those provided by the U.S. plan, including U.S. employer-paid Social Security benefits. Accordingly, qualification is often available to TCN plans.

Another alternative is simply to include TCNs in the U.S. home plan, as employees of an affiliate of the U.S. plan sponsor.

Under IRC Section 871(f), a U.S. nonresident alien who receives benefits from a qualified plan for services performed outside the United States will pay no U.S. taxes on those benefits so long as 90 percent or more of plan participants are U.S. citizens or residents. Otherwise, the employee will be taxed on the portion of contributions attributable to U.S. service, plus the portion of the distribution that represents earnings on the trust. If the recipient becomes a U.S. citizen or resident while receiving benefits, all such benefits will of course be taxable.

Funded nonqualified plans.   One seldom used but interesting alternative is to fund a nonqualified TCN plan on a tax-exempt basis through an offshore tax haven. Under this approach, the benefits are secure and completely free of U.S. tax to nonresident aliens, and the design is totally flexible.

Even with an employer-employee relationship, however, contributions for such a program will be deductible only if separate accounts are maintained for each participant. This is usually difficult in the case of defined benefit plans.

Section 404A.   If a foreign deferred compensation plan of a U.S. multinational employer meets certain requirements, the employer can make an election under Section 404A of the IRC that enables it to claim U.S. tax deductions for contributions to a foreign branch plan or to increase deemed foreign tax credits for contributions to a foreign subsidiary plan.[10] Section 404A is extremely complicated, but it is possible to use a 404A plan to cover TCNs. If the plan is funded outside the United States, the benefits will be nontaxable to nonresident alien TCNs who do not render service in the United States.

Phantom qualification. A nonqualified, nonfunded TCN plan can be funded on a qualified basis if the U.S. multinational is not making the maximum tax-deductible contribution to its qualified plan for home country employees. Under this approach, the multinational contributes an amount to the U.S. qualified plan (which would not cover the TCNs) equal to the actuarial liability associated with the TCN plan. The company pays TCN benefits directly (i.e., not from the qualified plan), at which point it reduces its contribution to the U.S. qualified plan by an equivalent amount.[11] The cost of the TCN plan will, in effect, be covered by the extra contributions, with tax-exempt interest, made to the U.S. qualified plan. The TCN plan's actual direct costs will be deductible, assuming an employer-employee relationship.

This approach is known as phantom qualification because the TCN plan is not really funded and offers no real security. But TCN participants also have no real U.S. source income, so the nonqualified benefits are nontaxable to TCNs who render no service in the United States.

WORKING ABROAD: SPECIAL TAX RULES

When executives who are U.S. citizens work outside the United States, they become subject to special U.S. tax rules as well as to the tax rules of the countries in which they work. Certain U.S. citizens and residents working outside the United States are eligible to exclude from their U.S. taxable income up to $70,000 of compensation annually, for example, but excludable compensation does not include amounts received as a pension or annuity, amounts included in income under the rules for taxing nonqualified trusts and annuities, or amounts received after the close of the tax year following the tax year in which the compensation was earned.

Thus, many items of income generated by participation in a foreign pension plan will not qualify for the exclusion. For example, payments under an unfunded pension will not qualify because they are generally received after the close of the tax year following the tax year in which earned.[12] Similarly, taxable contributions to a nonqualified trust will not qualify.

If a U.S. citizen or resident who is subject to U.S. tax with respect to a foreign pension is also subject to foreign country taxation with respect to the same pension, the U.S. foreign tax credit may alleviate double taxation. The credit operates to reduce, on a dollar for dollar basis, U.S. tax on income that also generates a foreign tax.

The precise application of the tax credit is subject to a number of elaborate rules. For example, there is an annual limit on the amount of foreign tax creditable that depends on the relative proportions of foreign source taxable income to total taxable income for the year. Also, the tax credit only arises when the foreign tax is paid. In a funded pension arrangement, an individual will be subject to U.S. tax as benefits are earned, but may only pay foreign taxes years later when benefits are distributed. If, in those later years, the individual has little or no foreign source income that is taxed in the United States (because it was already subject to U.S. tax in an earlier year), the credit for the foreign taxes paid in respect of the pension will be severely limited or may be completely unavailable.

The foreign tax credit does not apply on an item-by-item basis, however. And an individual who is covered by a foreign pension arrangement will typically also receive substantial current compensation for his services that gives rise to foreign taxes. Due to the relatively low rate of tax in the United States compared to rates in some other nations, the foreign taxes in respect of this current compensation may well be generating excess credits. In this case, additional foreign source income that is subject to current U.S. tax but not current foreign tax (e.g., the foreign pension) may actually be welcome because the U.S. tax on the pension may be completely offset by the excess credits generated in respect of the current items of compensation.

Most tax treaties between the United States and other countries have special provisions concerning the coordinated taxation of pensions. Unfortunately, most of these provisions only address the taxation of pension distributions and do not address the taxation of contributions (e.g., such as those made by an employer under a funded arrangement). For example, the U.S./Canada tax treaty contains provisions on pensions, but defines a pension as simply "any *payment* under a superannuation, pension, or retirement plan. . ." [emphasis added]. Thus, tax treaties typically offer little assistance in avoiding the normal tax rules applicable to funded, nonqualified arrangements.[13]

HEALTH AND WELFARE BENEFITS

Whether medical benefits for an executive who is working abroad will be provided under the home country plan or the local plan depends on several factors. Home country coverage generally makes sense for short foreign assignments. In theory, there is no problem in maintaining such coverage for long assignments as well, but it is not easy to check claims, enforce reasonable limits, and deal with other logistical issues when care is delivered locally.

The merits of a local coverage approach will obviously depend on the availability and quality of local services. Some foreign operations may not provide medical benefits if coverage is provided through the social security system, for example. In such cases, employers sometimes supplement that coverage with locally purchased insurance. It is also fairly common for employers to purchase insurance offshore to cover serious medical problems or medical evacuations.

Similarly, many employers want to ensure that their executives have specified minimum levels of life insurance coverage at all times—something that may not be common practice at the local level. Some insurers (or insurance networks in the case of multinational pooling) provide products that will cover people no matter where they are. While coverage of this type is generally expensive, it may be a convenient approach to providing insurance protection to a group of mobile executives.

NOTES

1. Stock-based compensation is not common outside the United States, though its prevalence is growing in some countries. It is important to recognize that tax and securities laws relating to these plans can vary widely. Currency issues and cultural considerations (e.g., no tradition of share ownership or the concept of pay at risk, low perceived value, etc.) are also important.
2. The U.S. rules prohibiting discrimination in benefits on the basis of pay are the most rigorous in the world, and many countries impose no such constraints.
3. In general, brief means five years or less, though different tax treaties will produce different results.
4. U.S. tax law issues raised by participation in foreign plans are discussed later in this chapter.

5. U.S. citizens who work abroad are covered by social security programs in the countries where they are employed, resulting in duplicate coverage (and additional employer/employee contributions) for those who continue to be covered under U.S. Social Security. To address this issue, the United States has entered into totalization agreements with a number of countries to permit coverage under a single system (in general, under the U.S. system if foreign employment will be for less than five years, and under the local system if more than five years), and to adjust amounts payable from the systems of the treaty partners where necessary.

6. Qualified plan coverage for foreign citizens is not mandatory and may be prohibited by the terms of the plan document.

7. As noted earlier in this chapter, TCN plans can also be used to provide benefits to expatriates who are likely to experience shortfalls as a result of transferring from one retirement plan to another.

8. ERISA Section 4(b)(4).

9. DOL Opinion Letter 83-27A, June 8, 1983.

10. Key requirements are that 90 percent of amounts claimed must be in connection with employees who are not U.S. taxpayers, and that the U.S. company can claim amounts only if they are deductible in the local jurisdiction.

11. The reduced qualified plan contributions must still meet the required minimum funding levels for the U.S. plan.

12. Rev. Rul. 72-279.

13. Moreover, tax treaties may not help minimize the taxes of U.S. citizens in any event due to the savings clause found in many U.S. treaties. For example, Article I(3) of the Treasury Department's model treaty provides that the United States may tax its residents and citizens as if the treaty did not exist (with a limited exception relating to social security and other public pensions).

Chapter Eighteen

Issues for Executives at Retirement

Most of this text relates to the design, funding, and administration of executive benefits from the employer's perspective. This chapter focuses on issues an executive often faces at retirement, including:

- The taxation of benefits paid from tax-qualified defined contribution and defined benefit plans.[1]
- Different ways to use employer-provided benefits and considerations that may influence the choice of available options.
- Social Security (both taxes and benefits) and such matters as stock options, insider trading issues, and state taxation of benefits.

TAXATION OF QUALIFIED PLAN ASSETS AND DISTRIBUTIONS

At retirement, an executive has a number of choices to make with respect to benefits payable under defined benefit and defined contribution plans. Knowledge of the tax implications of each choice is essential to making an informed decision. This is particularly true with respect to defined contribution plans, where the before-tax compound rate of return on plan assets can lead to the accumulation of significant sums. Key issues are summarized in the paragraphs that follow.

Minimum Distribution Requirements

The tax law requires that a terminating individual with at least $3,500 in vested benefit values must be given the right to defer distribution of the benefit until normal retirement age, usually age 65.[2] While plans may allow distributions to be deferred beyond this time, payments *must* begin

TABLE 18–1

Annual Minimum Distribution (Account Balance $1 Million at Age 62;
10 Percent Interest Assumption; Single Life Expectancy)

Age	Annual Distribution	Age	Annual Distribution
62	$ 0	79	$263,648
63	0	80	277,524
64	0	81	294,676
65	0	82	308,356
66	0	83	321,628
67	0	84	334,232
68	0	85	345,858
69	0	86	350,646
70	133,974*	87	353,520
71	145,358	88	354,140
72	157,842	89	352,136
73	171,014	90	340,164
74	185,136	91	325,688
75	200,242	92	308,664
76	214,546	93	289,090
77	231,594	94	260,180
78	247,326	95	231,350

*Amount paid out in following year—first payment due April 1 after age 70½.

by April 1 of the year following the year the individual turns age 70½. At that time, distributions must be made at least as rapidly as dictated under the minimum distribution rules.

In general, these rules require that payments be made over the individual's life expectancy or the joint life expectancy of the individual and his or her beneficiary. If distributions fall short of this minimum, the individual is subject to an excise tax equal to 50 percent of the amount of the shortfall.

By deferring payments from a defined contribution plan until age 70½ and taking the minimum allowable payments thereafter, an executive can continue to accumulate substantial amounts of capital,[3] as Tables 18–1 and 18–2 illustrate. Thus, if this payment option is available to an executive under the terms of a plan, it should be carefully weighed against the other alternatives.

TABLE 18–2

Account Balances under Minimum Distribution (Account Balance $1 Million at Age 62; 10 Percent Interest Assumption; Single Life Expectancy)

Age	Beginning of Year Balance	Age	Beginning of Year Balance
62	$1,000,000	79	$2,636,484
63	1,100,000	80	2,636,484
64	1,210,000	81	2,622,608
65	1,331,000	82	2,590,194
66	1,464,100	83	2,540,856
67	1,610,510	84	2,473,314
68	1,771,562	85	2,386,414
69	1,948,718	86	2,279,198
70	2,143,588	87	2,156,472
71	2,357,948	88	2,018,600
72	2,304,482	89	1,866,320
73	2,377,090	90	1,700,816
74	2,443,786	91	1,530,734
75	2,503,028	92	1,358,120
76	2,553,090	93	1,185,268
77	2,593,852	94	1,014,704
78	2,621,644	95	855,994

Assume that the executive in this example retires at age 62 with an initial account balance of $1 million and elects to defer payments until age 70½, earning investment income of 10 percent a year. When payments commence at age 70½, they are made on the basis of the executive's then life expectancy and are recalculated each year as the executive's life expectancy changes.[4]

Annual payments to the executive are shown in Table 18–1. The initial annual payment at age 70½ is approximately $134,000. The payment increases each year until it reaches a projected level of $354,000 when the executive is age 88. It drops thereafter, but even at age 95 it is nearly double the initial amount.

Table 18–2 shows how the executive's account balance grows during this same period. From age 62 to age 70½ when payments begin, the initial

$1 million more than doubles. The account balance continues to grow, even though payments are being made, until it reaches a projected maximum of more than $2,600,000 at age 80, and does not drop below its original level until age 95.

The advantages of continuing capital accumulation are significant, but they must be balanced against the fact that any death benefits paid will be includable in the executive's gross estate for estate tax purposes. Payments to a spouse will qualify for the marital deduction, but distributions to other beneficiaries could attract an estate tax rate as high as 55 percent. These payments will also be taxable as income to the beneficiary.[5]

Retiring executives also need to consider whether the 15 percent excess distribution tax could offset the advantages of accumulating funds under the plan. This tax applies in addition to regular income tax to qualified plan distributions that exceed a dollar threshhold each year (e.g., $148,500 in 1994). If an executive expects to withdraw funds from the plan in a relatively short period of time, the additional 15 percent tax could produce undesirable results; the executive might be better off taking money out of the plan and investing it elsewhere. If the executive can leave funds in the plan for a reasonable period of time at a reasonable rate of return, however, the compounding effect of before-tax investment returns could produce attractive results, even taking the 15 percent additional tax into account.

This effect is illustrated in Table 18–3. Column A of this table shows the after-tax value of a $1,000 plan distribution invested at 8 percent per year. Column B shows the after-tax value this same $1,000 would generate if it were left in the plan earning 8 percent, with the gross accumulation being taxed in the year of distribution. The values in Column B are lower than those of Column A until the 10th year. Thereafter, the values of Column B become higher, even taking the 15 percent additional tax into account.

The results in an actual situation will obviously depend on the executive's tax bracket and investment returns. Nonetheless, possible imposition of the additional 15 percent tax does not necessarily mean that accumulating funds under the plan is an unwise course of action.

Installment Distributions

The taxation of installment distributions depends upon whether the executive has any cost basis, typically as a result of making after-tax contributions to the plan.[6] If the executive has no cost basis, all installment

TABLE 18–3
After-Tax Value of a $1,000 Accumulation

Year	A Outside of Plan*	B Within Plan**
1	$ 604	$ 490
2	633	530
3	664	572
4	696	618
5	729	667
6	765	720
7	840	778
8	881	840
9	924	908
10	968	980
11	1,015	1,059
12	1,064	1,143
13	1,115	1,235
14	1,169	1,333
15	1,226	1,440
20	1,552	2,116
25	1,965	3,109
30	2,488	4,568

*Taxed at distribution in year one with investment income taxed as earned; marginal tax rate of 39.6 percent.

**Tax applied at time of distribution in the year shown; marginal tax rate of 39.6 percent plus 15 percent excess distribution tax.

distributions will be taxable as received. If there is a cost basis, the general rule is that each payment will be considered to include a prorata tax-free return of this basis.[7]

Lump Sum Distributions

In general, a lump sum distribution will be taxed as ordinary income to the extent it exceeds the executive's cost basis. Under certain circumstances, however, lump sum distributions may qualify for favorable tax treatment.

To be eligible for such treatment, a distribution generally must be made after the executive reaches age 59½. In addition, the distribution must represent the full amount then credited to the executive's account and must be received by the executive within one taxable year.

To determine whether there has been a distribution of the full amount credited to the executive's account, all employer plans within a given category (pension, profit-sharing and stock bonus) must be aggregated and treated as a single plan. Thus, for example, if an employer maintains two profit-sharing plans—a conventional 401(k) plan and a tax credit employee stock ownership plan that was qualified as a profit-sharing plan—the executive must receive a full distribution of his or her entire account balance under *both* plans in the *same* taxable year. Otherwise, favorable tax treatment will be available only to the distribution made from the second plan in a subsequent year; the first distribution will be taxed as ordinary income.

A lump sum distribution made after retirement may also qualify for favorable tax treatment, provided the executive has not received a partial distribution or withdrawal at or after the time of retirement and in a year prior to the year of the lump sum payment.[8] Thus, an executive who wants to defer distributions after retiring and preserve the option of taking a lump sum distribution that will qualify for favorable tax treatment must refrain from taking partial payments after retiring.

Because withdrawals prior to retirement will not affect eligibility for the favorable tax treatment of later lump sum payments, preretirement withdrawals (if permitted by the plan) may be a useful financial planning technique for executives who foresee the need to withdraw money near retirement but want to preserve the possibility of favorable tax treatment.

If a distribution meets the above requirements, an executive who has participated in the plan for at least five years before the year of distribution can elect five-year averaging tax treatment. This election can be made only once and only after age 59½.[9]

Under five-year averaging, the executive's cost basis, if any, is subtracted from the gross distribution to determine an initial taxable amount. If this amount is less than $70,000, a minimum distribution allowance is determined and is subtracted from the initial taxable amount to arrive at a net taxable amount,[10] which is then divided by five. The tax that would be due on one-fifth of the net taxable amount (assuming a single taxpayer, no other income, and no exemptions or deductions) is then calculated. The result is multiplied by five to determine the total tax due.

A special grandfathering clause applies to executives who were age 50 or older on January 1, 1986. These individuals can elect special tax treatment even before they are age 59½ (although the option is still available only once). They also have several choices:

- They can treat the entire distribution under the five-year averaging rules.
- They can treat the entire distribution under the former 10-year averaging rules using 1986 tax rates in effect prior to the Tax Reform Act of 1986. (Ten-year averaging works like five-year averaging, with the initial tax calculated on one-tenth of the net taxable distribution and multiplied by 10.)
- If they participated in the plan before 1974, they can treat the portion of the distribution attributable to this participation as a long-term capital gain, with either 10-year or 5-year averaging on the balance. (For this purpose, the old long-term capital gains tax rate of 20 percent applies.)

Long-term capital gains treatment can produce very favorable results where it is available. In general, 10-year averaging will produce lower taxes for smaller distributions; it is apt to produce higher taxes for larger distributions because the marginal tax rate in the calculation can reach 50 percent. This pattern is illustrated in Table 18–4, which compares the after-tax proceeds under 5- and 10-year averaging for net taxable distributions ranging from $25,000 to $1,500,000.

If a distribution includes an annuity contract some part of the distribution may not be currently taxable. The value of an annuity contract as such is not taxable when distributed; the executive will be taxed only on annuity payments when actually received. The fact that this part of the distribution is not taxable will not preclude special averaging. This treatment will still be available for the balance of the distribution if it otherwise qualifies. Values not currently taxable will be taken into account in determining the marginal tax rate on the amount being taxed, however.

Employer Stock Distributions

Executives have additional choices to make if employer stock is distributed from a qualified plan. The law permits the executive to treat the net unrealized appreciation on this stock (the difference between its market value at the time of distribution and its cost when purchased by the plan) as taxable income at the time of the distribution or when the stock is subsequently sold.

TABLE 18–4

Comparison of 5- and 10-Year Averaging

Taxable Distribution	After-Tax Proceeds	
	5-Year Averaging*	10-Year Averaging**
$ 25,000	$ 22,600	$ 23,199
50,000	43,100	44 126
75,000	63,750	64 695
100,000	85,000	85,529
150,000	122,365	125,430
200,000	158,365	163,078
300,000	229,390	233,670
400,000	298,390	297,398
500,000	367,390	356,318
750,000	531,140	490,632
1,000,000	691,140	617,790
1,500,000	1,002,140	867,790

*Based on 1993 tax rates
**Based on 1986 tax rates

An executive who chooses to defer taxation will be taxed in the year of distribution only on the cost basis of the stock (plus any other assets distributed).[11] Upon a subsequent sale of the stock, the executive will be taxed on the unrealized appreciation at the time of distribution plus any gains between the date of distribution and subsequent sale. Moreover, these gains will be taxed at favorable long-term capital gains rates. If the stock is held until the executive's death, the executive's heirs will have a cost basis in the stock equal to its market value at the time of death (i.e., the appreciation in value unrealized at the time of death will not be taxed as income). The full value will be included in the executive's gross estate for estate tax purposes, however, subject to marital deduction credits and the like.

The amount of net unrealized appreciation that receives this special tax treatment will depend on whether the stock is part of a qualifying lump sum distribution. If the distribution qualifies (but without regard to the requirement that there be five years of participation), all net unrealized appreciation may be excluded from current year taxation. If the distribution does not qualify, only the net unrealized appreciation attributable to after-tax employee contributions can be excluded.

Early Distribution Tax

If an executive receives a distribution from any qualified plan before age 59½, the distribution may be subject to a penalty tax of 10 percent. This tax, if applicable, is levied in addition to any tax otherwise due on the distribution.

The following are not subject to the early distribution tax:

- Distributions that are part of a series of substantially equal periodic payments for the life (or life expectancy) of an executive (or the joint lives of the executive and his or her beneficiary).
- Distributions on account of death.
- Distributions on account of disability (as defined for Social Security purposes).
- Distributions to an executive who separated from service after reaching age 55.
- Hardship distributions from a defined contribution plan for deductible medical expenses that exceed 7½ percent of adjusted gross income.
- Distributions to an alternate payee under a qualified domestic relations order.
- Dividends on ESOP stock that are paid in cash.

An early distribution tax will not be imposed on any amounts rolled over into an Individual Retirement Account (IRA). Subsequent distributions from the IRA could be subject to this tax unless they are made at a time or for a reason that qualifies for an exemption that applies to IRA distributions. (Not all of these exemptions apply to IRA distributions.)

Excess Distribution Tax

Distributions that exceed certain stipulated dollar amounts are subject to a 15 percent excess distribution tax. Distributions from *all* tax-sheltered arrangements are aggregated for purpose of this tax. Thus, for example, taxable distributions from tax-sheltered annuities, IRAs, and all qualified plans of all employers are taken into account. Distributions that are *not* subject to this tax include payments to an alternate payee under a qualified domestic relations order if included in the alternate payee's income, amounts rolled over to an IRA on a timely basis, and the value of annuity contracts distributed that are not currently taxable. It should also be noted that this tax does not apply to benefit payments made to an executive under a nonqualified SERP.

In general, the excess distribution tax is imposed on distributions (not including qualified lump sum distributions) received during the executive's calendar year to the extent they exceed the greater of: (1) $150,000 or (2) an amount that changes each year to reflect inflation. (In 1994, this amount was $148,500.) A separate 15 percent tax applies to a lump sum distribution that qualifies for income-averaging treatment to the extent the lump sum distribution exceeds the greater of: (1) $750,000 or (2) an amount indexed to inflation. (In 1994, this amount was $742,500.)[12] This higher threshold *only* applies to amounts that qualify for special income-averaging treatment. Thus, a lump sum that is withdrawn from an IRA will not qualify for treatment under the higher threshold amount.

Net unrealized appreciation on employer stock, though not necessarily taxable in the year of distribution, will be subject to the excess distribution tax.

The excess distribution tax does not apply to amounts payable upon the death of an employee; an equivalent 15 percent tax is imposed as an additional form of estate tax. Items such as the unified credit, the marital deduction, and charitable contributions will not operate to reduce this tax. Thus, the 15 percent tax could be levied in situations where no other estate tax is payable.

When an executive is subject to the 10 percent early distribution tax on the same distribution, the 10 percent tax may be offset against the 15 percent excess distribution tax.

Rollovers

Any distributions from a qualified plan (other than certain specified items such as after-tax employee contributions, minimum required distributions, distributions over the life expectancy of the executive or the joint life expectancies of the executive and his or her beneficiary, or distributions for a specified period of at least 10 years) can be rolled over to an IRA or to another qualified plan that accepts rollovers. A spouse can also make a rollover in the case of a death benefit distribution.

Any rolled-over amounts will not be taxed in the year of distribution, and any early or excess distribution taxes will not be applied to these amounts. Distributions from the IRA will, of course, be taxable and will also be subject to early and excess distribution taxes where applicable. Note that distributions from an IRA will not qualify for special income-averaging treatment.

A rollover must take place within 60 days after receipt of the distribution. If the distribution is noncash property, all of the property must be transferred; the property can also be sold, with all or any part of the sales proceeds transferred to the IRA. Any amounts transferred to an IRA can subsequently be transferred to another qualified plan, provided the only funds contributed to the IRA were part of a total distribution from a qualified plan; this transfer privilege will not apply if the original rollover is made to an existing IRA that includes conventional IRA contributions. Further, a direct transfer may be made to an IRA or another qualified plan. In fact, qualified plans must offer this direct rollover opportunity for any distributions that could otherwise be rolled over.

DEFINED CONTRIBUTION BENEFITS

Many executives will be entitled to a distribution from a broad-based savings plan, ESOP or profit-sharing plan. Some will also have supplemental defined contribution benefits under a restoration plan. While restoration plan benefits are usually payable in cash, the distribution from the broad-based plan may be available in cash and/or in company stock. As noted, the broad-based plan must permit the executive to defer payment of benefits until normal retirement age, but it may permit deferral until age 70½. The broad-based plan may require that distributions be made in the form of a lump sum payment, or it may offer the option of installment payments over a short period of time such as 10 years. Many plans also permit distributions to be made to the executive over his or her lifetime (or over the joint lifetimes of the executive and his or her beneficiary). Thus, a retiring executive could have several choices as to when and how to receive benefits under the broad-based defined contribution plan.

While the federal tax treatment of plan assets and distributions will obviously affect an executive's choices, other factors also warrant consideration. For example:

- An executive's immediate and projected cash flow needs will have a major impact on decisions as to when and how funds should be disbursed from the plan.

- State taxation of benefits (discussed in this chapter) can also be important, particularly if the executive contemplates moving to another jurisdiction after retirement. An executive who lived and worked in Pennsylvania will not pay state tax on a lump sum distribution, for example; if the executive moves to New York, he or she will pay state taxes on any lump sum payment received after the move. Note that some states will even attempt to tax nonresidents on benefits payments if benefits were earned while the individual was domiciled in the taxing state.

- The executive may not like the investment options available to retirees under the employer plan. Some plans require that all assets held for retirees be invested in a fixed income fund; others require that some assets be invested in employer stock. In such situations, the executive can control the investment of his or her funds only by withdrawing them from the plan.

- If the market is down at the time of retirement, an executive may want to leave assets in the plan to avoid taking a loss. If the market is up, however, a distribution might be in order.

- Large lump sum payments may encourage unwise spending, even among executives. Leaving funds in the plan for as long as possible or taking installment payments may be the more prudent course for executives interested in estate building and conservation.

- Some executives may not be interested in assuming the responsibility of investing and managing a large cash distribution and may prefer to continue with the options selected and supervised by the company. Executives who do decide to withdraw funds and seek investment advice should exercise care in the choice of advisor and have a clear understanding of how the advisor is to be compensated—both through direct fees and indirect payments such as commissions.

- Investment choices made by the executive after funds have come into his or her possession will often involve some investment management expenses and/or sales fees that the executive must absorb. This represents a cost to the executive that could be avoided to the extent that it would be assumed by the employer (as is often the case) if funds were left in the plan.

RETIREMENT BENEFITS

An executive's retirement benefits will usually consist of two elements—a benefit from the employer's tax-qualified plan plus a benefit from some type of SERP. It is important to recognize that the two benefits may be payable under different provisions and that the same choices or options may not be available for both. Further, if lump sum distributions are involved, the tax treatment of the two types of benefits can be different.

Tax-Qualified Plan

The design of broad-based plans reflects employer objectives that relate to the workforce as a whole and not necessarily to executives. Further, these plans must be nondiscriminatory and cannot give executives better or more choices than are available to all employees. Thus, the options available to executives under these plans are often limited to those which the employer feels are appropriate for its entire employee population.

Many broad-based defined benefit plans limit a retiring executive's choices to receiving benefits payable: (1) for his or her remaining lifetime or (2) on a 50 percent joint and survivor basis to the executive and his or her spouse. This latter provision is mandated by law as the automatic form of payment where there is a qualified spouse, and it cannot be revoked or changed without the spouse's written consent. These plans typically offer an additional joint and survivor arrangement where 100 percent of the amount payable to the executive is continued to the beneficiary. Again, spousal consent is necessary if the beneficiary is to be anyone other than the spouse.

A choice between a straight life income and a joint and survivor benefit (J&S) should take into account the extent to which the cost of the J&S benefit is subsidized by the employer. The law does not require the employer to pay for any part of the value of this spousal protection. Thus, a plan could require the retiree to pay for spousal protection in full through an actuarial reduction in the initial amount of pension payable, and many plans do.

Other plans subsidize spousal protection by not reducing the retiree's pension or by reducing it by an amount less than the full actuarial value of the benefit. Thus, an executive who chooses a life annuity in lieu of a subsidized joint and survivor benefit will be giving up something of value.

The health and life expectancy of the executive and his or her spouse are also relevant to the form-of-payment decision. If the spouse is in poor health and is not expected to survive the executive, for example, the joint and survivor option might not be an appropriate choice.

Some broad-based defined benefit plans offer an additional payment option—taking the actuarial value of the pension in a single lump sum payment. Spousal consent is needed for this election, which revokes the joint and survivor benefit mandated by law. Factors to be considered in weighing this option include the following:

- The tax treatment of lump sum payments.
- The ease or difficulty of obtaining spousal consent; in some cases, alternative financial arrangements might be necessary in return for spousal acquiescence.
- The income needs of a spouse who survives the executive. The joint and survivor provision assures some level of spousal protection for life. This protection is forfeited when the executive elects a lump sum payment.
- The health and life expectancy of the executive and his or her spouse. Some individuals will not live as long as average life expectancy, while others will live longer. Since the lump sum value of the executive's pension is determined on a basis that reflects average length of survivorship, an earlier-than-average death could create an actuarial gain to the estate, while a late death could create a loss.
- The discount rate used to calculate the lump sum. The amount of the lump sum will reflect an assumption as to future investment income (i.e., the expected stream of future payments will be discounted at some assumed rate of return to arrive at a present value). If this rate of return is lower than what the executive expects to earn on his or her own investments, taking a lump sum payment could prove to be financially attractive; if it is higher, the reverse would be true. In essence, the investment risk and reward associated with plan values are borne by the employer in a defined benefit plan; this investment risk and reward are transferred to the individual who takes a lump sum payment.
- The employer's policy on ad hoc increases for pensioners to reflect changes in the CPI. Employers typically provide such increases only to retirees who are receiving income payments, not to those who have taken lump sums.
- An employer subsidy for joint and survivor protection. If the value of any employer subsidy for joint and survivor benefits is not

reflected in determining lump sum equivalents, the executive who elects a lump sum will lose this value, which can be significant. If an executive is entitled (at age 65) to an annual pension of $100,000, the full actuarial reduction in his pension to provide a 50 percent survivor benefit to his spouse (age 62), under typical actuarial assumptions, would be $12,300. If this benefit were subsidized by 50 percent, the executive, in effect, is given an additional annual pension of one half of this reduction, or $6,150. This additional pension would have a lump sum equivalent value of approximately $54,950, which would be lost if the executive elects a lump sum payment.

SERP Benefits

Executives need to take a number of factors into account in deciding how SERP benefits should be paid. Taxation is one such factor. The overall tax treatment of SERPs is covered in Chapters 3 and 10; some key tax considerations are summarized in the paragraphs that follow.

SERPs must be carefully designed and administered to ensure that an executive will not be considered to be in constructive receipt of the full value of his or her SERP benefit in a given year. This could happen if the SERP permitted the executive to elect at the time of retirement and without restriction to have the SERP benefit paid in a lump sum. Thus, a SERP is often designed not to provide for a lump sum payment at all, or to impose restrictions and penalties in connection with a lump sum option sufficient to prevent taxation of the full value in any one year.

It is also important to remember that lump sum distributions from a SERP do not enjoy favorable tax treatment. In general, any SERP payments, including lump sums, will be taxable as ordinary income. Further, distributions from a SERP may not be rolled over to delay tax. On the plus side, SERP payments are not subject to the 10 percent early distribution tax or the 15 percent excess distribution tax.

The distribution options available to a retiring executive under a SERP will depend on plan design. Some SERPs will require that all benefits be paid the way benefits are paid under the broad-based plan (with the possible exception of lump sum payments). This is apt to be the case in restoration plans. Other SERPs provide more flexibility, though issues of constructive receipt impose some limits.

The joint and survivor form of payment is generally not required for SERP benefits.[13] While a SERP may make a joint and survivor option available, it may not be automatic (i.e., the executive must elect this option, and no spousal consent is necessary for a different form of payment). In such cases, the executive must make a conscious election to protect his or her spouse and must take whatever steps are necessary under the plan to make any election (or nonelection) operative.

Any decision not to elect spousal protection could become an issue in divorce or separation proceedings, of course, and could be altered as a result of those proceedings.

A joint and survivor election can be an attractive estate planning tool. Benefits payable to the spouse will qualify for the marital deduction, and the value of these benefits will not be included in the executive's gross estate for estate tax purposes. In addition, because benefit payments generally terminate at the spouse's death, no values would remain for inclusion in his or her estate.

Many SERPs do not provide a lump sum option. For one thing, paying a large lump sum from an unfunded SERP can create cash flow problems for the employer. For another, such a payment would undermine any noncompete or forfeiture provisions in the SERP.

As noted, those SERPs that do permit lump sum payments usually impose restrictions to prevent application of the doctrine of constructive receipt. One such restriction may be a requirement that the payment option be elected well in advance of the executive's retirement date, for example, in the preceding calendar year. Such conditions obviously need to be factored into the financial planning process.

With the notable exception of tax treatment, lump sums from a SERP raise the same issues previously discussed in connection with lump sums from broad-based plans—and one additional issue. Unless the SERP is funded (which is not usually the case), the SERP benefit consists of an unsecured promise to pay benefits over an extended period following the executive's retirement, perhaps as much as 25 or 30 years. This promise is potentially vulnerable to bankruptcy or even a hostile change of control. A lump sum payment at retirement fully secures and discharges the employer's obligation and creates benefit security for the executive.

GROUP LIFE INSURANCE

In the absence of a group universal life plan (GULP) or special executive group life insurance benefits, an executive may face termination or a substantial reduction of group term life insurance coverage at retirement.

In fact, reductions in this coverage may begin even before the executive retires.

The cost of this coverage for active employees is relatively low, since few of them die during employment. Retiree coverage, by contrast, is quite expensive. Thus, most employers either terminate or sharply reduce coverage when an employee retires. The reduction may be full and immediate or, as is sometimes the case, graded over a period of 5 or 10 years.

Life insurance can be a very important asset for executives with estate planning needs. Coverage is generally very tax-efficient; the proceeds are not taxable income to beneficiaries and, in many states, escape inheritance taxes. Because life insurance is usually not part of the executive's probate estate, probate costs are not an issue. With careful planning, the proceeds may even escape federal estate taxation.

Thus, the loss of significant amounts of group life insurance can create estate planning problems; in addition to the loss of the actual dollars involved, there may also be liquidity problems for the estate. The retiring executive should be aware of the potential loss of insurance and, if necessary, make alternative arrangements. As noted in Chapter 7, some employers do provide additional group term life insurance for executives. These plans may not continue full coverage throughout retirement, however, so most executives need to consider whether and how much coverage they may lose, and how, if at all, to replace it.

If the executive is in good health, it might be possible to obtain individual life insurance coverage, including term insurance, at reasonable rates. The executive must take care in obtaining replacement coverage to avoid inclusion of the new insurance proceeds for estate tax purposes if this is an objective.

If the executive is not insurable, the only way to maintain coverage is to exercise the conversion privilege associated with the group term life insurance. This privilege allows a terminating individual to convert his or her group term life insurance without evidence of insurability to a permanent form of individual coverage. Because term insurance coverage is not available under this privilege, the cost of continuing coverage will be higher than would be the case if the executive were in good health.

An executive who has been covered under a GULP arrangement is more fortunate in that his or her group term life insurance under such an arrangement is portable: the executive can continue the full amount of coverage in force by paying premiums directly to the insurance company. In most cases, the premium for this continued life insurance protection is quite favorable because it is based on the mortality experience of the entire group of employees covered under the employer's plan.

The executive who has created a cash value or savings account by making additional contributions for GULP coverage has several options to consider in the context of overall estate planning needs. He or she can:

- Continue paying premiums for both the term insurance and the savings element directly to the insurance company.
- Continue contributions only for the term insurance.
- Make no further contributions (until necessary or desirable), with future term insurance premiums being paid from the cash value previously created.
- Withdraw the cash value from the policy.[14]
- Use the cash value to purchase paid-up insurance.

HEALTH CARE PROTECTION

Maintaining adequate health care coverage during retirement is a major concern for all retirees. Most large employers provide some type of coverage for their retirees, but this is not always the case.

An executive who faces the loss of employer-provided benefits at retirement should act immediately to obtain replacement coverage. Individual coverage is available from many insurance companies, Blue Cross/Blue Shield organizations, local health maintenance organizations (HMOs) and preferred provider organizations (PPOs), and through organizations such as the American Association of Retired Persons (AARP). It is important to evaluate available coverage in terms of both cost and benefits provided. It is equally important to understand coverage limits and exclusions.

Retiring executives who do have employer-provided medical benefits also need to understand how their coverage operates, since retiree benefits may differ from active benefits. For example:

- Will the basic nature of the coverage change, particularly after age 65? Some plans cease full coverage at that point and only pay some expenses not covered by Medicare, such as the initial deductible and copayments.
- How will benefits be coordinated with those payable by Medicare?
- Will retiree contributions change?
- Will dental coverage be continued? Some plans continue basic health care coverage for retirees, but terminate dental benefits.

- Will the lifetime maximum for the executive and his or her spouse change? Some plans set a relatively low maximum (e.g. $100,000 for retirees, especially after age 65).
- Is there a provision to restore any part of the lifetime maximum used? Will there be automatic restoration of some amount (e.g., $2,000) each year regardless of health, or will it be necessary to submit evidence of good health before any part of the maximum will be reinstated?
- If the executive remarries after retirement, will the new spouse be covered? If so, will there be any exclusion for preexisting conditions?
- Will annual physical examinations be covered?

Retirement is a good time to rethink other health care coverage issues. If the employer provides for a choice between two or more health care plans, for example, the choice that was appropriate during active employment may not be the right choice for a retiree. Health care coverage available through the spouse's employer should also be considered. It may make sense to cover the executive as a dependent under the spouse's plan, or vice versa, or it may make sense for each of them to retain coverage under their respective plans.

Regardless of the decision as to employer-provided coverage, an executive should apply for Medicare three to six months before his or her 65th birthday to avoid any delay in coverage and any premium surcharge for late enrollment. Further, the executive might want to ascertain whether his or her physician is willing to accept Medicare assignments.

SOCIAL SECURITY

Three aspects of Social Security are of interest to retired executives. The first is the income that is subject to FICA taxes (or SECA taxes in the case of self-employed income). The second is eligibility for retirement benefits, the potential loss of these benefits by reason of the earnings test, and the way benefits are treated for income tax purposes. The third is Medicare eligibility and benefits.

FICA/SECA Taxes

The FICA tax applies to income or wages earned as an employee. The employee's share of the Old Age, Survivors, and Disability (OASDI) portion of the tax (excluding Medicare) is currently 6.2 percent on all earnings up to a dollar maximum known as the Social Security wage base This dollar maximum increases each year to reflect changes in U.S. aver-age annual wages and is $60,600 for 1994. The employee's Medicare tax rate, which now applies to all income without limitation, is currently 1.45 percent. The FICA tax does not apply to investment income, nor to distri-butions from qualified pension, profit-sharing, and stock bonus plans.

Many retired executives will have self-employment income—directors' fees and income from consulting, for example—and will thus have to pay SECA taxes. The SECA tax (excluding Medicare) on self-employed net income is currently 12.4 percent, subject to the FICA maximum. The Medicare tax rate for self-employeds is currently 2.9 percent and applies to all net income without limitation. A self-employed individual can deduct 50 percent of the SECA tax paid when determining adjusted gross income for income tax purposes, however. The SECA tax, like the FICA tax, does not apply to items such as investment income or qualified plan distributions.

For FICA purposes, the basic rule is that SERP and deferred compensa-tion amounts will be treated as income for the year in which the amounts are earned, or vested if later, and not for the year in which the amounts are paid.[15]

In the past, this rarely resulted in additional taxes for executives, since most of them earned cash compensation in excess of the wage base at the time these benefits were accruing or became vested. Now that the Medicare tax rate applies to all income, executives will owe additional Medicare taxes during their employment years when benefits are earned or vested. If a SERP does not provide for full vesting until the year of eli-gibility for retirement (in order to create golden handcuffs, for example) the full FICA tax would be levied in the year of eligibility for retirement. While the OASDI portion of the tax would be capped at the wage base and thus might not be payable on the value of the SERP, depending on other income, the Medicare tax would apply to the full value of the SERP that became vested in the year of retirement eligibility.

Retirement Benefits

Eligibility for full Social Security retirement benefits occurs when the individual reaches Social Security full benefit retirement age—age 65 for individuals born before 1938, gradually increasing until it becomes age 67 for individuals born in 1960 or later. While Social Security retirement benefits are payable as early as age 62, benefits are reduced for each month between the time payments start and the individual's full benefit retirement age. If benefits do not commence until after the individual's full benefit retirement age, they will be increased for each year of delay up until age 70.

The maximum retirement benefit payable to an individual is a dollar amount that reflects the taxable wage bases of prior years. For retirements in 1994, this maximum dollar amount was $1,147 per month. If the retiree has a spouse who has attained his or her full benefit retirement age, the spouse may receive a benefit of 50 percent of the retiree's benefit (unless the spouse is entitled to a greater benefit on his or her own); a reduced benefit is available to the spouse if he or she is at least age 62.[16]

Earnings Test

Social Security retirement benefits can be reduced or lost for years prior to age 70 if the retiree has earned income that exceeds stipulated dollar amounts.[17] These amounts change each year; for 1994, the dollar amount for ages prior to 65 was $8,040; for ages 65 through 69, it was $11,160. If earned income exceeds these amounts, Social Security benefits will be reduced by $1 for each $2 of excess earned income for ages prior to 65, and by $1 for each $3 of excess earned income for ages 65 through 69.[18] Thus, after age 65 and through age 69, when excess earned income is more than three times the retiree's Social Security benefit, the entire benefit for that year will be lost.

It should be noted that the retiree's earned income will reduce the total benefit, including that payable with respect to a spouse. A spouse's earned income in excess of the allowable amount will reduce the spouse's benefit but will not affect the retiree's basic benefit.

Earned income for purposes of this test includes salary, wages, and net self-employment income. Amounts paid at or after termination of employment (such as severance pay and accrued vacation) are considered earned in the last month of employment. Retirement benefits and investment income are not considered to be earned income for purposes of this test. For services performed in 1988 and after, directors' fees are considered income in the year earned, regardless of when paid, even though they are subject to SECA tax only in the year of payment.

Medicare

Eligibility for Medicare coverage begins at age 65, regardless of whether the retiree has earned income; the earnings test does not apply to this coverage.

Medicare consists of two parts, Parts A and B. Part A coverage (hospital insurance benefits) is automatic for individuals who are 65 and who are entitled to a retirement benefit. Part B (supplementary medical insurance benefits) is voluntary and requires that the retiree make application and pay the necessary premiums.

As noted earlier, a retiring executive should apply for Medicare coverage as early as possible, preferably three to six months before turning age 65. Failure to apply in timely fashion could cause a delay in the effective date of Part B coverage and could even result in a surcharge on the regular premium rate. If the employer's health care plan is coordinated with Medicare and will not pay for benefits that could have been paid under Part B, a delay in the effective date of Part B coverage could mean that the executive would have to pay for expenses incurred during the delay.

Taxation of Social Security Retirement Benefits

Many individuals will receive all or part of their Social Security benefits on an income tax-free basis because their other income will be less than the thresholds set forth in the law. Most executives will have income in excess of these thresholds, however, and 85 percent of their Social Security benefits will be taxable. The low-level threshold is set at $25,000 for single taxpayers and $32,000 for married taxpayers. When income exceeds these amounts, 50 percent of the Social Security retirement benefit will be taxable. The high-level threshold is $34,000 for single taxpayers and $44,000 for married taxpayers; when income exceeds these amounts, 85 percent of the Social Security benefit will be taxable. For purposes of determining whether these thresholds have been reached, tax-exempt income and one-half of the Social Security benefit itself are taken into account.

OTHER ISSUES

Stock Options

Many stock option plans provide for accelerated vesting at retirement and allow the executive to exercise options immediately upon retiring.

Further, such plans often terminate the option within a short period after retirement.

If an executive is holding an option under an incentive stock option plan, he or she will have to decide whether to exercise the option within three months after termination of employment or at some later time (within the limits allowed by the plan). Exercise of the option within a three-month period permits the transaction to take place without any immediate tax effect (i.e., any gain will not be taxable at the time of exercise).[19] If the exercise takes place after three months, the gain will be treated as it would under a nonqualified option (i.e., as ordinary income at the time of exercise).

Insider Trading Issues

While an executive ceases to be an insider at retirement, any six-month trading restriction period on transactions made as an insider will extend *into* retirement.[20]

In this regard, note that a distribution of company stock from a tax-qualified plan at retirement will not be considered a transaction triggering short-swing profit liability. By the same token, the sale of company stock held by the plan in order to make a cash payment to the executive at retirement generally will not be considered a transaction. Under proposed amendments to the insider trading rules, each allocation of company stock to the executive's account before retirement will not be considered a purchase that will not start a six-month trading restriction period.

An in-service distribution made to an insider of all or a portion of the value of his employer stock fund in cash would be considered a sale. Such an in-service distribution would nonetheless be exempt if made pursuant to a six-month irrevocable election by the insider to take the distribution. Alternatively, the insider must refrain from selling the withdrawn stock for the following six months.

Switching investments under the plan while actively employed is also a transaction. An exemption applies if the insider elects the investment change at least six months in advance or during one of the 10-day window periods following the company's quarterly release of financial information to the public, as discussed in Chapter 13.

State Taxation of Retirement Benefits

Retiring executives need to know how benefits will be taxed at the state level, particularly if they are contemplating a change in domicile. The taxation of retirement benefits differs from state to state, and a detailed treatment of the subject is beyond the scope of this text. The discussion that follows is intended only to identify some of the issues and problems that must be considered.

While some states (e.g., Pennsylvania) do not tax retirement benefits at all, most states do tax such benefits, at least for residents. There may be exclusions, however. New York, for example, permits the exclusion of $20,000 of pension and annuity-type payments per year for individuals who are over age 59½. Where benefits are taxable, lump sum distributions may or may not be accorded favorable tax treatment (e.g., California provides such treatment).

In recent years, a few states (e.g., California) have imposed a source tax, taxing pension benefits payable to nonresidents to the extent such benefits were earned while the taxpayer was a resident of the taxing state. Some of these states (e.g., Ohio) tax only nonqualified or SERP benefits. Reciprocal agreements exist between some states (e.g., Illinois and Indiana), with the state of residence imposing the tax rather than the state where the income was earned.[21]

It is important to recognize for income tax and estate planning purposes that residency is generally determined by domicile and that a change in domicile will be evidenced by domiciliary intent (i.e., the intent to make a new place the taxpayer's home following the abandonment of an old residence). These are meaningful considerations, particularly for executives who intend to own homes in more than one location. In this regard, it should also be noted that an individual can be considered a part-time resident in some states for tax purposes.

Miscellaneous

Some other financial matters an executive needs to think about to prepare for retirement are summarized in the paragraphs that follow.

Cash flow and budgeting. The average executive may well experience a sharp reduction in cash flow in moving from full salary and bonus to retirement income. Further, a large part of the executive's assets may be relatively illiquid, including real estate holdings, stock with depressed values, and so forth. Remember, too, that withdrawals of amounts accumulated in employer pension and savings plans may be subject to the additional 15 percent excess distribution tax. In short, a review and restructuring of the executive's budget and cash expenditures is very much in order to prepare for retirement.

Financial and estate planning.   Retirement is a good time to assess total net worth, investment and asset allocation strategies, estate planning, and the like. For this purpose, the executive is well advised to work with highly competent advisors—recognizing that the legal, tax, insurance, and investment issues involved may require more than one advisor.

Perquisites.   During employment, an executive may have the benefit of many perquisites, including club memberships and perhaps a company car. Most such perquisites will be lost at or shortly after retirement, raising the issue of whether they should be continued or replaced, and at what cost.

Diversification.   It is not uncommon for a substantial part of an executive's assets to consist of employer stock, acquired through the exercise of stock options, through the savings plan, or because the company requires executives to own stock. The business rationale for requiring stock ownership during employment may no longer apply after retirement. Further, most investment counselors would not recommend that any investor put most of his or her assets in any one investment. Thus, an executive should consider whether to sell some employer stock and reinvest the proceeds in order to diversify. Again, competent financial advice is important.

Tax sheltered retirement plans.   Retired executives with self-employment income (directors' fees, consulting income, and the like) can establish self-employed pension and/or profit-sharing plans, often called H.R.10 or Keogh plans.

With both a pension and a profit-sharing plan in effect, the executive will be able to contribute as much as 20 percent of his or her gross income and deduct this amount in calculating adjusted gross income for the year.[22] Contributions can continue for as long as the executive has earned income, even beyond age 70½. The minimum distribution rules described earlier in this chapter apply to these plans, however, and distributions must commence at 70½, even if the executive is still making contributions. There are a few key limitations: (1) only earned income from self-employment may form the basis of the contribution; (2) the maximum amount of earned income that can be taken into account is $150,000 (indexed for inflation after 1994); and (3) the overall annual dollar limit on contributions to a defined contribution plan is $30,000 (which will also be increased for inflation when the defined benefit limit reaches $120,000).[23]

These plans are tax-qualified and must meet nondiscrimination requirements. If the retired executive employs other individuals in the course of doing business, for example, these employees must be included in the plan after meeting minimum age and/or service requirements.[24] In most situations, this will not be a problem.

These plans are relatively easy to establish. Many mutual funds, banks, insurance companies, and investment managers have established master plans that have been approved by the Internal Revenue Service. Any self-employed individual who wants to establish a plan executes a simple joinder agreement and contributes funds to the organization, filing simple financial information with the Internal Revenue Service on an annual basis.

A retired executive with earned income also has the option of establishing a simplified employee pension plan (SEP), which operates much like a Keough plan, or an individual IRA. The IRA, of course, has lower deduction limits ($2,000 each year) and is only available to age 70½.

NOTES

1. The taxation of nonqualified retirement arrangements is discussed in Chapters 3 and 10.
2. Or until age 62 if this age is later than the plan's normal retirement age.
3. This is not a relevant consideration for defined benefit plans where the deferral of payments generally will not increase their value to the executive but will, in most cases, operate to reduce employer costs.
4. It would be permissible to use the joint life expectancy of the executive and his or her spouse for this purpose. In most situations, this would extend the period involved, which in turn would lower the annual installments required. Under this type of payment arrangement, greater amounts would remain in the plan for accumulation.

5. The beneficiary, however, will be allowed a deduction against the amount of the distribution equal to the amount of the estate tax applicable to this amount, except to the extent the additional 15 percent tax applies to excess accumulations.

6. An executive's before-tax, or elective, contributions are considered to be employer contributions under the tax law and will be taxable to the executive when distributed from the plan.

7. Special grandfathering rules may apply to the recovery of any cost basis created under a defined contribution plan prior to 1987. For a detailed discussion of these rules, see Towers Perrin, *The Handbook of 401(k) Plan Management,* (Homewood, IL: Business One, 1992), pp. 107–108.

8. If the partial payment and the lump sum distribution occur within the same taxable year, however, the total of the two distributions will be considered as a lump sum distribution in that year for purposes of the tax law, and favorable tax treatment will be available.

9. Legislation to repeal 5-year averaging has been introduced; see Footnote 6 in Chapter 1.

10. If the initial taxable distribution is less than $20,000, the minimum distribution allowance is 50 percent of this amount; if it exceeds $20,000, the minimum distribution allowance is $10,000 minus 20 percent of the amount by which the distribution exceeds $20,000.

11. The fact that the executive defers taxation on the unrealized appreciation will not defeat income averaging on the balance of the distribution, if otherwise available, although the amount of net unrealized appreciation will be taken into account in determining the applicable marginal tax rate.

12. A special grandfathering provision applies to individuals who had account balances in excess of $562,500 as of August 1, 1986. If any such individual elected grandfathering protection by the time his or her tax return was filed for 1988, amounts accrued through August 1, 1986, can be paid without imposition of this tax.

13. If a SERP is funded or is not limited to a select group of management or highly compensated employees, it will be subject to the provisions of Title I of ERISA. Among other things, this requires spousal protection by way of joint and survivor provisions. Most SERPs, however, are exempted from Title I compliance.

14. Withdrawal of the cash value could result in the imposition of income taxes to the extent this cash value exceeds the executive's prior contributions, both for the group term life insurance and for the savings element.

15. For SECA purposes, these items are generally treated as wages only when paid. However, directors' deferred compensation earned between 1988 and 1990 was treated as wages when earned.

16. A spouse can receive this benefit regardless of age if caring for a child under 16 or a child who became disabled before age 22.

17. There is no loss of Social Security benefits for any amounts earned after age 70.

18. This test is applied on annual basis; however, a monthly test can be applied for the year of retirement so that, in effect, earned income prior to the time of retirement is not taken into account.

19. The gain, of course, would be recognized for purposes of the alternative minimum tax.

20. See Chapter 13 for a discussion of insider trading restrictions.

21. Many states also have a credit for residents who pay taxes to another state.

22. The allowable contribution is expressed as 25 percent of adjusted gross income after taking the deduction into account. Mathematically, this is equivalent to 20 percent of gross income before taking the deduction. Actually, the deduction limit for a defined benefit plan may exceed 20 percent in some cases.

23. A different limit applies to a defined benefit plan.

24. A complete discussion of all of the rules and requirements pertaining to these plans is beyond the scope of this text. For such a discussion, see Allen, Melone, et al., *Pension Planning,* Chapter 24.

Index